ISLAMIC
FINANCE
WHY IT
MAKES
SENSE

Cover art by OpalWorks Co. Ltd
Project editor: Lee Mei Lin / Designer: Rachel Chen

Image on pages 263 and 273 courtesy of Haji Noor Deen
All content information in this book is correct at press time

Published by
Marshall Cavendish Business
An imprint of Marshall Cavendish International
1 New Industrial Road, Singapore 536196

Other Marshall Cavendish Offices
Marshall Cavendish International. PO Box 65829, London EC1P 1NY • Marshall
Cavendish Corporation. 99 White Plains Road, Tarrytown NY 10591-9001, USA •
Marshall Cavendish International (Thailand) Co Ltd. 253 Asoke, 12th Flr, Sukhumvit
21 Road, Klongtoey Nua, Wattana, Bangkok 10110, Thailand • Marshall Cavendish
(Malaysia) Sdn Bhd, Times Subang, Lot 46, Subang Hi-Tech Industrial Park, Batu
Tiga, 40000 Shah Alam, Selangor Darul Ehsan, Malaysia

Marshall Cavendish is a trademark of Times Publishing Limited

National Library Board Singapore Cataloguing in Publication Data
Vicary Abdullah, Daud, 1951-
Islamic finance : why it makes sense / Daud Vicary Abdullah & Keon Chee. –
Singapore : Marshall Cavendish Business, c2010.
p. cm.
Includes index.
ISBN-13 : 978-981-261-599-2

1. Finance – Religious aspects – Islam. 2. Finance – Islamic countries. I. Chee, Keon.
II. Title.
HG187.4
332.088297 – dc22   OCN467596799

Printed in Singapore by Craft Print International Ltd

ISLAMIC FINANCE
WHY IT MAKES SENSE

DAUD VICARY ABDULLAH
AND KEON CHEE

Marshall Cavendish
Business

To my wife, Sabariah, and our four sons,
Raslan, Rastam, Adam and Azrai,
for their support and patience
in allowing me to follow a dream.
— Daud

To Amir Mikhchi (Iran), Ali Asadi (Iran)
and Mohammad Nor (Pakistan)
who showed me the gentleness of Islam.
— Keon

CONTENTS

PREFACE

AS WE WERE BOTH not born into Muslim families, getting an initial grasp of Islamic finance was rather challenging to us.

One positive outcome of this early experience is that we have obtained an excellent insight into how a person—whether new to finance, to Islam, or to both—can go about understanding Islamic finance. Our first objective is thus to attempt to shed a little light on the subject of Islamic finance and to provide a good basis for your better understanding in the future.

In helping you learn how Islamic finance works, we took the perspective of the consumer who may not know much about finance or Islam, but who, like everyone else, has to make very important financial decisions throughout his or her life.

We thus made the effort to first explain financial transactions that we often take for granted and which many of us may not actually understand, such as mortgages, investing, insurance and trade finance. We then described their Islamic versions.

Our second and equally important objective is to help you appreciate the very quintessential principle of Islamic finance. It is that of fairness—in all interactions with people, family, business partners, non-Muslims and the community. For this, we sincerely hope to have lived up to achieving this objective.

This has been an enjoyable journey for us. We hope we have helped you begin your own journey with Islamic finance.

Daud Vicary Abdullah and Keon Chee
December 2009

ACKNOWLEDGEMENTS

from Daud Vicary Abdullah

I would like to thank my co-author Keon Chee for getting me involved in this project. It was not something that I had thought of doing. However, his persistence, vision and hard work have been an inspiration to me throughout. I do not have the words to thank my mentor, Mustapha Hamat (Pak Mus) enough for his guidance and contribution throughout my career in Islamic finance. His quiet, understated manner belies a fervent passion for the truth and a desire for the world to have a clearer understanding of this topic. This really has been a case of "when the student is ready, the teacher appears".

from Keon Chee

I would like to thank my co-author Daud Vicary Abdullah for believing in me at a time when I was completely new to Islamic finance. My deep thanks and respect to Pak Mus, whom I am much awed by, for his inspirational guidance and passion.

from both of us

We would like to thank Lee Mei Lin, senior editor at Marshall Cavendish, whose enthusiasm and foresight for this project made the hard work all worthwhile. And finally, we would like to thank See Phui Yee who is a most masterful and clever editor.

FOREWORD

I AM VERY PLEASED to be writing this foreword for Daud Vicary Abdullah and Keon Chee.

When they first told me that they wanted to write a book on Islamic finance that would appeal to non-Muslims as well as Muslims, I felt immediately encouraged. I had been involved in Islamic finance for over two decades and it is a subject that is very close to my heart. In fact, I was involved with Islamic finance right from the very start when the first Islamic commercial bank, Bank Islam Malaysia Berhad, was set up here in Malaysia. It is my ongoing aspiration and commitment to help spread the message that Islamic finance is for everyone, and that it is founded on sound business, social and ethical principles that apply to both Muslims and non-Muslims. So when Daud and Keon sought my help for guidance, I gladly said yes.

Daud's professional experience in banking and finance gave me great confidence that the book will be able to provide the general public, particularly non-Muslims, with a good and comprehensive exposure on Islamic finance. Daud was a senior banker with one of the big UK-based banks, CEO of a newly established full-fledged Islamic bank in Kuala Lumpur, and a senior consultant with the well-known consulting and audit firm Deloitte for most of his career. He has acquired substantial knowledge and experience in banking and finance, conventional as well as Islamic.

I met Daud for the first time in June 2002 when he was a partner in Deloitte Consulting with responsibility for the financial services industry in Korea. As CEO of the Islamic Banking and Finance Institute (IBFIM) then, I had sought Deloitte's assistance in one of IBFIM's assignments to introduce Islamic finance products to an investment bank in Kuala Lumpur, and Daud was assigned by the firm to work with IBFIM on this project. Daud came with such fire in his eyes I became very confident that the project was going to be successfully completed, and it was.

One thing I do take credit for is that I must have inspired him to learn about Islamic finance. Because from there on, he started to study at the IBFIM, attended many other courses in Islamic finance and obtained several Islamic finance credentials. Soon after, he was appointed as a board member of the Accounting and Auditing Organization for Islamic Financial Institutions (AAOIFI), the global accounting standards-setting body for Islamic finance, which is located in Bahrain. Daud Vicary is now back with Deloitte as the Global Leader of its Global Islamic Finance Group. He is today a very well-respected Islamic banker in Malaysia as well as in other parts of the world.

I met Keon in February 2008 when Daud set up a breakfast meeting in Kuala Lumpur. Daud had been in several discussions with him earlier and was convinced that Keon would be a good writing partner for the book. I trust Daud's judgement and agreed right away to provide guidance even though Keon knew very little about Islamic finance then.

But something about Keon made me believe that it was the right thing to do. He too had an unmistakable fire about him. It also struck me that Keon, being non-Muslim, can be an excellent choice for this purpose. His perspectives could help thousands of non-Muslims learn about Islamic finance. Up till now, many who are interested in the subject, including Muslims, have found it difficult because the writing done by academics and experts in the field is too advanced for the general public. Along with the Islamic expertise that Daud brings to the table, I thought they would make quite a diverse and formidable partnership.

There will no doubt be mistakes or even inaccuracies in their writing. The Koran says, "for Allah is with those who patiently persevere" (2:153). I believe that the book they have written will move things forward and I applaud them for their efforts.

Mustapha Hamat
Distinguished Academic Fellow of IIUM Institute of Islamic Banking and Finance (IIiBF), International Islamic University, Malaysia (IIUM); and former General Manager of Bank Islam Malaysia Berhad and CEO of IBFIM

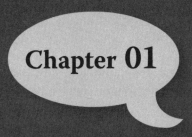

Chapter 01

WHY ISLAMIC FINANCE?

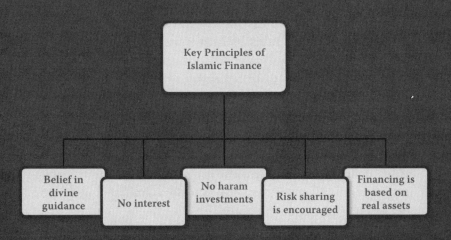

IMAGINE—A MODEL of finance that rejects interest payments has been firmly registering double-digit growth, even in the face of recent worldwide economic crises.

Islamic finance, though small in comparison to its conventional counterpart, is at the threshold of serious expansion. It is growing at a rate of 15 to 20 per cent a year, and according to *The Economist*, Islamic assets under management should rise to US$1 trillion in 2010, from US$700 billion in 2008. It is really hard for anyone not to have noticed the recent rise of Islamic finance.

But there is another reason that you might want to consider for learning about Islamic finance, besides its increasing importance in the world economy. In the Oscar-winning documentary *An Inconvenient Truth*, Al Gore calls the fight against global warming a "moral imperative". We believe that there too is a similar moral imperative about Islamic finance. It is not about finding billion-dollar petroleum projects or becoming the next Islamic finance multi-millionaire. Rather, it is to do with alleviating poverty and wealth gaps around the world.

According to the United Nations Development Project, 2.7 billion people in the world struggle to survive because of poverty. The Islamic world has over 1.4 billion people[1], and except for a handful of Muslim-majority countries in the Middle East and South-East Asia, there are high and rising poverty levels in other parts of the Islamic world. A study undertaken by the Islamic Development Bank (IDB) reveals that just five of its 56-member countries—Indonesia, Bangladesh, Pakistan, Nigeria and Egypt— account for over half a billion of the world's poor, with incomes below US$2 a day or below their national poverty lines.[2]

So when Bangladeshi economist and banker Professor Muhammad Yunus won the 2006 Nobel Peace prize for his work in microfinance in his home country, many of us were clapping enthusiastically. Through Grameen Bank, which Professor Yunus founded, microfinance provides low-income customers with small but significant loans that most others would consider a paltry sum.

In 1976 during his visits to the poorest households, Professor Yunus discovered that very small loans made a disproportionate difference to poor people. In Jobra village, for example, he noticed that women who made bamboo furniture for a living had to take out loans with very high interest rates from moneylenders, just for buying bamboo. He then put into place a microfinance scheme, through which he later made his first loan of US$27 to 42 women in Jobra.[3]

One of the major reasons for the success of microfinance has been the efforts of such finance providers to educate the destitute groups they serve about the basic workings of banking and financial services. People looking to borrow are first required to take a simple course in money management. Lessons focus on the understanding of how banks work, and how to develop savings as well as manage debt, budget and cash flow. Millions in Bangladesh, where nearly 85 per cent of the population are Muslim and 45 per cent live below the poverty line, are now able to help themselves out of poverty through the process of microfinance.

> "2.7 billion people in the world struggle to survive because of poverty."

We are not saying that Islamic finance is a cure-all for any modern-day financial crisis, but the application of its principles is undoubtedly a silver lining that could help alleviate poverty and stabilise economies at the same time.

Grameen Bank is not an Islamic financial institution, but its actions are steeped in the Islamic principles of care for the community and the unfortunate, and of mutual trust and respect. Its objective is to "bring financial services to the poor, particularly women, and the poorest—to help them fight poverty, stay profitable and financially sound. It is a composite objective, coming out of social and economic visions."[4]

WHAT IS ISLAMIC FINANCE?

Islamic finance is a form of finance that is based on Shariah, or the body of Islamic law. Shariah, which means "the path to the water source", is filled with moral purpose and lessons on the truth, and is hence more than just a set of legal rules. At its core, Shariah represents the idea that all human beings and governments are subject to justice under the law. It is a term that summarises a way of life prescribed by Allah (swt)[5] for his servants, and it extends to everything from business contracts and marriage to punishment and worshipping. It is common to use the term "Shariah-compliant" to describe anything that is permissible under Islamic law.

Halal versus Haram

In Arabic, the word *halal* refers to anything that is Shariah-compliant—that is, permissible under Islam. This includes aspects of human behaviour, speech, clothing and diet. It is the opposite of *haram*, which is anything that is forbidden. A more detailed discussion of halal and haram is found in Chapter 2.

How is Islamic finance different from conventional finance? Unlike conventional finance, which is familiar to most of us, Islamic finance has one overarching requirement—every financial transaction must be Shariah-compliant. In ensuring Shariah compliance, five key principles are strictly followed (see Figure 1.1):

1. **Belief in divine guidance.** The universe was created by Allah (swt) and He created man on earth to fulfil certain objectives through obeying His commands. These commands are not restricted to worship and religious rituals but cover a substantial area of almost every aspect of life, including economic and financial transactions. Man needs such divine guidance because he does not have the power to reach the truth on his own. Not only is man imperfect, but also his 'reasons' are often confused with 'desires.' It is the firm belief

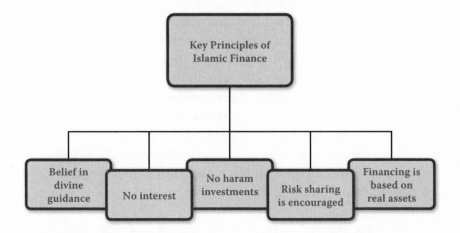

Figure 1.1 Key principles of Islamic finance

of every Muslim that the commands given by Allah (swt), and through His divine revelations to the last Messenger Muhammad (pbuh)[6], are to be followed in letter and spirit.[7]

 ◈ In a conventional financial system, religion and government are kept separate and independent of each other. This is to uphold religious freedom and secularity in government (such that it is not overly influenced by any particular religion).

2. **No interest.** That is, you cannot earn interest on a loan, or be required to pay interest on a loan.

 ◈ Compared with conventional financing, this is like borrowing money from the bank and not having to pay a cent of interest. Islamic banks of course do not loan you money for free. If you were to obtain an Islamic loan for a project, instead of being charged interest for the loan, you could be paying fees or sharing a portion of your profits from the project with the bank.

3. **No haram investments.** Money is to be invested in worthy causes, while companies that manufacture haram products like alcohol, tobacco, arms or pornography are avoided.
   * This is similar in some ways to the conventional concept of socially responsible investing (SRI), which seeks to maximise both financial return and social good. In general, SRI favours corporate practices that promote environmental stewardship, consumer protection, human rights, and diversity. Some practitioners of SRI abstain from businesses similar to those that Islamic ventures would avoid.

4. **Risk sharing is encouraged.** The idea of risk sharing is conscientiously promoted and regularly practised between business partners, such as between a customer and a financial institution:
   * For an Islamic institution, risk sharing is favoured in business dealings with its customers. This fosters the equitable distribution of risk, profits and losses. It also means that the due diligence an Islamic bank performs covers not only the creditworthiness of the customer but also the financial viability of the project. All in all, risk sharing is meant to enhance transparency, and very importantly, to promote mutual trust and fairness in dealings among business partners, institutions and consumers.

5. **Financing is based on real assets.** Financing extended through Islamic products can only expand in step with the rise of the real economy, thereby helping to curb excessive speculation and credit expansion.
   * In contrast, conventional financing is typically based on the promise to pay where real assets are not tied to the transaction. This means that conventional financing activity can grow several steps ahead of the real economy,

thereby causing speculation and unjustifiable asset price inflation.

Islamic finance offers similar services as does conventional finance. This includes taking deposits, giving loans, providing trade finance, investing in financial assets and distributing insurance. The difference is that Islamic financial transactions must be Shariah-compliant.

DEVELOPMENT OF A MODERN ISLAMIC FINANCE FRAMEWORK

Islamic finance is not new. At the time Islam began in the 7th century, Arabia stood at the economic crossroads of an active market in spices and precious metals. Prophet Muhammad (pbuh) himself was a merchant and a caravan trader before he became a Messenger of Allah (swt).

The Holy Koran, the sacred book of Islam, encourages Muslims to engage in trade and invest in their efforts for God to ensure abundant returns:

> **"Islamic finance is based on Shariah, or the body of Islamic law; Shariah means 'the path to the water source.'"**

Who is he that will loan to Allah a beautiful loan, which Allah will double unto his credit and multiply many times? It is Allah that giveth (you) want or plenty and to Him shall be your return. (2:245)

In another verse, the Holy Koran warns Muslims to "eat not your property" but to let there be trade by mutual goodwill:

O ye who believe! Eat not up your property among yourselves in vanities: but let there be amongst you traffic and trade by mutual good-will: nor kill (or destroy) yourselves: for verily Allah hath been to you Most Merciful. (4:29)

During the 18th, 19th and first half of the 20th centuries, nearly the entire Islamic world was colonised by European nations which managed the economies and finances of Muslim countries. Then as movements for independence started to bear fruit following World War II, a desire to manage their affairs in accordance with their own values and traditions emerged from the colonies.

It was only in 1963 that the first modern Islamic financial institution—called Mit Ghamr (a savings bank)—was set up in Egypt. The first Islamic bank in Asia was Malaysia's Muslim Pilgrims Savings Corporation (Tabung Haji) founded also in 1963, to help people save for performing the Hajj, the pilgrimage to Mecca and Medina.

In 1975, the IDB was established in Jeddah, Saudi Arabia. This was a significant milestone for modern Islamic finance because of the level of co-operation that took place among Islamic developing countries in its setting up. As an international banking institution, the IDB is "entrusted with the functions of promoting foreign trade and economic co-operation among Muslim countries, as well as undertaking research to enable the economic, financial and banking activities in Muslim countries to conform to Shariah."[8] Perhaps inspired by the successful launch of the IDB, modern Islamic commercial banking (accepting deposits and offering loans) came about also in 1975, when Dubai Islamic Bank opened its doors.

The World's Oldest Conventional Banks

The honour of oldest existing bank in the world goes to Italy's Banca Monte dei Paschi di Siena, which was founded in 1472. It was originally formed to make loans to the poor out of charity. *Monte*, meaning "heap", referred to the collection of money used for charitable distribution. At the time, citizens of Siena put up income from the land as guarantees against loans for farming and city infrastructure. Today, it has branches throughout Italy.

The next four oldest conventional banks are:

- Berenberg Bank, Hamburg, founded 1590;
- C. Hoare & Co., London, founded 1672;

- The Bank of Scotland (now Halifax Bank of Scotland), Edinburgh, founded 1695; and
- Bank of New York (now Bank of New York Mellon), New York, founded 1784.

Of course, a smattering of banks around the world does not make a financial system. As we will see in later chapters, a financial system consists of much more. It is made up of banks, insurance firms, fund management companies and stock exchanges, and these organisations deal with businesses, individuals and governments to carry out financial transactions—to deposit, borrow, invest and distribute money through various financial instruments including stocks, bonds, derivatives, unit trusts and insurance.

Figure 1.2 traces two generations of development of the Islamic finance industry in terms of product offerings. We do not need to examine the figure in detail, except to recognise that many of the key components of a financial system are in place.

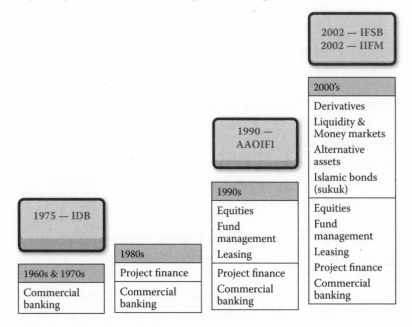

Figure 1.2 Maturing Islamic finance industry

Strengthening of International Infrastructure

Shariah is open to interpretation, and Islamic scholars are not always in complete agreement regarding what constitutes Shariah-compliant financing. Islamic finance laws and regulatory practices vary across countries. This makes it difficult to standardise Islamic financing activity. That is where international standards come in.

International standards in various disciplines—including accounting, documentation, governance and product structures—help to harmonise practices across countries as well as increase the marketability and acceptance of Islamic products around the world. For example:

- The Accounting and Auditing Organization for Islamic Financial Institutions (AAOIFI) issues international standards on accounting, auditing and corporate governance.
- The Islamic Financial Services Board (IFSB) puts forth standards for supervision and regulation. Its members include over 30 central banks.
- The organisation of International Islamic Financial Market (IIFM) focuses on standardising Islamic financial instruments.

The modern Islamic financial system is in no way mature or complete. It is about 50 years old, compared with the 500 years that the conventional system has been around for. Many important pieces are nevertheless in place, and in many respects, Islamic finance is already creating products that are as competitive as conventional products.

Growth as a Result of Three Global Economic Crises

Three recent major global economic crises in the conventional system—the 1973 oil shock, 9/11 and the 2008 subprime crisis—contributed to the growth of Islamic finance. Each economic jolt brought about a wider search by both Muslims and non-Muslims for alternatives to conventional banking and finance.

```
  •                        •                        •
──────────────────────────────────────────────────────────
Oil Crisis (1973)          9/11 (2001)        Subprime Crisis (2008)
```

The 1973 Oil Crisis

On October 15, 1973, members of OAPEC[9] (Organization of Arab Petroleum Exporting Countries) proclaimed an oil embargo "in response to the US decision to re-supply the Israeli military during the Yom Kippur war".[10] The OAPEC declared it would no longer ship oil to the US and to other countries if they supported Israel in the conflict. This brought on tremendous inflation caused by high oil prices. The 1973 oil crisis was followed by the 1973–74 stock market crash when the Dow Jones Industrial Average lost 45 per cent of its value. The market crash has been regarded as the first event since the Great Depression to have a persistent economic effect.

There was a second oil crisis in the same decade—in 1979—when the Shah of Iran fled his country, allowing Ayatollah Khomeini to gain control. The ensuing protests shattered the Iranian oil sector. While the new regime resumed oil exports, it was inconsistent and exports were at a lower volume, forcing prices to go up. Things would get worse. In 1980, following the Iraqi invasion of Iran, oil production in Iran nearly stopped, and Iraq's oil production was severely cut as well.

US Reaction to 9/11

The American reaction to the terrorist attacks of September 11, 2001 (9/11) played a significant part in the growth of Islamic finance. Many Middle East investors and financial institutions felt that the US had attempted to stigmatise the Middle East in its response to the attacks. For example, the George W. Bush administration designated numerous Middle East financial institutions and financiers as "abettors of terrorism"—and thus to be avoided. In 2006, Congress blocked the efforts by Dubai Ports World (DP World), a Dubai-based operator of port facilities, to purchase the management of shipping terminals in the US after a public outcry against Arab investments.

Activities such as these created a religious backlash among Middle East financiers. Many Middle East banks came under scrutiny, and some accounts were frozen. That became part of a religious wake-up call, which caused a rise in the number of people turning to Islamic alternatives. Middle East clients have, over recent years, transferred billions of dollars out of conventional Western banks. Many feared being caught up in strict new financial regulations being passed in the wake of the 9/11 attacks.

After 9/11, the backlash continued to extract its toll, even as other events created new conflicts, events such as the US military operation in Afghanistan and Iraq, recurring clashes between Israel and Palestine, and the arrest of individuals allegedly involved in terrorism in South-East Asia.

The 2008 Subprime Crisis

The subprime mortgage crisis was triggered by a dramatic rise in mortgage defaults and home foreclosures in the US, with major adverse consequences for banks and financial markets around the globe. Many US mortgages issued starting in 2001 were made to subprime borrowers, defined as those with lesser ability to repay the loan based on various criteria such as creditworthiness and income.

Subprime borrowers managed to buy homes for three main reasons. The early 2000s, when George Bush was US president, was a period of economic recovery. It was cheap to borrow (interest rates were at historically low levels), and home prices were low (prices were just starting on a five-year rally). For a period, it seemed as if each time a home was bought, it could be resold for a higher price and at a cheap rate of interest.

When US home prices began to decline in 2006 and 2007, mortgage defaults soared, and securities backed with subprime mortgages, widely held by financial firms, lost most of their value. The result has been a large decline in the capital of many banks and a tightening of credit around the world.

ISLAMIC FINANCE
AFTER THE SUBPRIME CRISIS

When conventional finance roars back, will Islamic finance continue its strong growth? There are several reasons we think it will.

In the Mainstream

From only providing savings accounts in the 1960s, Islamic finance today has a maturing array of products and services. The adoption of international standards has increased the use and acceptance of Islamic finance around the world. Islamic finance is now serving non-Muslim communities who find the products competitive to their conventional versions (see Table 1.1).

Table 1.1 Islamic finance reaches the mainstream

From	To
Retail financing.	A wide array of financial products and services including private equity, project finance and wealth management products.
Focused on the Muslim community.	Also serving non-Muslim community.
Offered by Muslim countries.	Also offered by non-Muslim countries with large conventional centres like Singapore, Tokyo, UK and Hong Kong.
Provided by full-fledged Islamic financial institutions.	Also provided by large international conventional banks.
Reliance on domestic conventional regulatory and accounting standards.	Development of international standards.

Some Islamic practitioners hope for the day when Islamic products can stop "imitating conventional products". To them, Shariah-compliant instruments should be built from the roots up rather than be "Islamified" or adapted from conventional products for scholarly approval. This may take some time.

Meanwhile, we have a transition and an opportunity to forge closer ties with the conventional system because both systems need one another. The main reason for the tendency to Islamify conventional products is that there is a need to encourage conventional international banks to offer Shariah-compliant products, in order to grow the market. International banks are understandably more comfortable with products they recognise, and which have similar risk profiles to conventional products.

Significant Oil Money from Middle East

More than two-thirds of Islamic funds are from the Middle East.[11] Most oil-rich countries are also in the Middle East (they have 56 per cent of world reserves; see Figure 1.3). Being Muslim, they have a natural desire to do business using Islamic finance.

Five of the six top oil-proved reserves are found in Middle East countries (see Table 1.2). Their financial clout is significant and will be a continuing influence on Islamic finance for a long time.

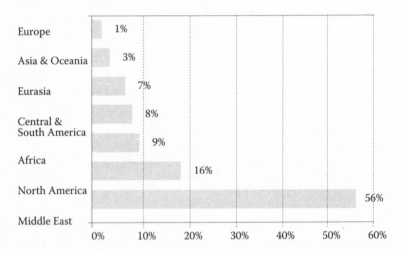

Figure 1.3 World oil reserves by region

Source: U.S. Energy Information Administration from Oil and Gas Journal (2007) (Oil includes crude oil and condensate)

Table 1.2 *Top 10 countries with highest oil-proved reserves*

Rank	Country	Billion Barrels
1	Saudi Arabia	267
2	Canada	179
3	Iran	138
4	Iraq	115
5	Kuwait	104
6	UAE	98
7	Venezuela	87
8	Russia	60
9	Libya	41
10	Nigeria	36

Source: US Energy Information Administration (2008)

Muslims Underserved and Want to Be Served

Global fund assets under management reached about US$110 trillion at end-2007.[12] That is more than 100 times the US$1 trillion in Islamic assets that *The Economist* forecasts will exist by the year 2010. This means that Islamic fund assets are currently no more than 1 per cent of global fund assets.

Yet there are 1.4 billion Muslims representing over 21 per cent of the world population of 6.8 billion, according to the CIA *World Factbook*. Many Muslims who have had to rely on conventional products would surely like to consider Islamic versions. So would non-Muslims wishing to diversify their choices and fulfil their ethical values.

Islamic finance will further develop with the impending rise in the Muslim population, which is currently in a period of rapid growth. Christianity, the largest religion in the world, is followed by 33 per cent of all people—a percentage that has remained stable for decades. If current trends continue, Islam could become the most popular world religion sometime in the mid-21st century.

Non-Muslims Find Resonance

Islamic finance is widely appealing because it is based on ethical principles that are appreciated by everyone. As we look around, we find many examples:

- ◆ From purchasing Islamic mortgages to Islamic funds, more and more non-Muslims today are participating in Islamic finance to satisfy their sense of social responsibility.

- ◆ Non-Muslims find the co-operative nature of Islamic finance very much aligned to that of conventional co-operative societies. Such societies consist of persons united voluntarily to meet their common economic, social and cultural needs through a jointly-owned enterprise. In the UK, members of building co-operatives pool resources to build housing, normally using a high proportion of their own labour. In the US, insurance began through a mutual (or co-operative) structure.

- ◆ Many countries with a minority Muslim population, such as Singapore, Hong Kong, Australia and Korea, consider Islamic finance an increasingly important part of their financial systems—in terms of creating a greater variety of financial institutions and attracting a wider source of funds, especially those from the Middle East.

Double-Digit Growth Expected

Islamic Insurance (Takaful)

Many Muslim countries are under-insured, when compared with non-Muslim nations. One of the reasons is that conventional insurance products are generally in conflict with Shariah. Another reason is that Islamic insurance (*takaful*), like Islamic finance overall, was not available until the late 1970s; it was only in 1979 that the African nation of Sudan introduced the world's first takaful product.

Table 1.3 shows insurance penetration of selected countries, which is an indication of the amount spent on insurance per person (against GDP, gross domestic product, per capita). It reveals an optimistic picture of future growth because the low-spending Muslim countries (marked with *) are some of the world's wealthiest countries. Ernst & Young, in its *The World Takaful Report 2008* publication, stated that double-digit takaful growth can be expected in many years to come.

Table 1.3 Insurance penetration of selected countries

	Insurance Penetration	GDP per capita (US$)
UK	15.7%	36,600
Taiwan	15.7%	31,900
South Africa	15.3%	10,000
South Korea	11.8%	26,000
Hong Kong	11.8%	45,300
Japan	9.6%	35,300
US	8.9%	47,000
Singapore	7.6%	52,000
Australia	6.8%	38,100
India	4.7%	2,900
Malaysia	4.6%	15,700
*UAE	1.9%	40,400
Indonesia	1.6%	3,900
*Oman	1.1%	20,400
*Qatar	0.9%	101,000
Pakistan	0.7%	2,600
Bangladesh	0.7%	1,500
*Kuwait	0.6%	60,800
*Saudi Arabia	0.6%	21,300

Source: SwissRe Sigma No. 3/2008; CIA *World Factbook* (2008 estimated GDP per capita)

Assets under Management

When it comes to the annual rate at which the Islamic fund assets industry is growing, 15 per cent is quite an often-quoted number.

Is 15 per cent too optimistic perhaps? Not according to the listing of the Top 500 Islamic Financial Institutions by *The Banker*. Published in November 2008, the report stated that Shariah-compliant assets under management of the Top 500 grew by 27.6 per cent from 2007 to reach US$639 billion in 2008. The growth in 2006 was 29.7 per cent.[13]

CONCLUSION

This chapter gave you a quick look at the key ideas behind the fast-growing Islamic finance sector:

1. the belief in divine guidance;
2. the no-interest rule;
3. socially responsible investing;
4. the sharing of risk; and
5. the using of real assets to finance deals.

We will devote the rest of the book to expanding on these ideas. Before we leave the chapter, we must mention that many people find Islamic finance difficult to understand. The reasons that are commonly cited include:

*   You need to know finance.

*   You need to know Islam.

*   You need to combine your understanding of both.

*   It is sometimes hard to tell Islamic finance apart from conventional finance.

*   Islamic scholars are not all in agreement about certain issues.

We have taken efforts to write this book with these points in mind, and to do so in accessible English. For example, we explain basic conventional financial concepts and instruments before introducing their Islamic versions.

We do expect that this strategy would not sit well with some readers, such as those who are experts in Islamic finance and philosophy. The presumption is that making comparisons and drawing analogies with conventional finance could dilute one's understanding of the true essence of Islamic finance.

We nevertheless chose this strategy of making comparisons with the conventional system because many of us grew up with it, and were exposed to Islamic finance only in the past few years. We also planned to cater to the many readers who want to understand Islamic finance but who do not have a good grounding in conventional finance in the first place.

English author Samuel Johnson (1709–1784) once said, "What is written without effort is in general read without pleasure." We hope you will enjoy the rest of the book.

---

1   *The World Factbook.* www.cia.gov.

2   "Fighting against Poverty in Islamic Societies," Dr Muhammed Obaidullah, senior economist of the Islamic Development Bank. www.islamicvoice.com

3   "Yunus makes nation proud," the *Daily Star* (Bangladeshi English daily newspaper), 14 October 2006.

4   www.grameen-info.org

5   According to the Holy Koran, Allah is the Creator of the Universe, known as "God the Father" to Christians and "*Yahweh*" to Jews. The set of initials 'swt' stands for *subhanahu wa ta'ala*, and means "Glorified and Exalted is He". It is considered more pleasing to Allah to praise Him as such, whenever He is mentioned.

6   Muslims praise the name of the Prophet Muhammad as the last messenger of Allah (swt). To show their devotion to the Prophet, Muslims put the set of initials 'pbuh' after his name; 'pbuh' stands for "peace be upon him".

7   Adapted from *An Introduction to Islamic Finance* by Mufti
     Muhammad Taqi Usmani, June 1998. www.muftitaqiusmani.com. He
     is an eminent Hanafi Islamic scholar from Pakistan. Note: A mufti is
     an Islamic scholar who has been qualified to issue religious opinions
     concerning Islamic law.

8   *The Islamic Development Bank—A Case Study of Islamic
     Co-operation* by Dr S.A. Meenai. Taylor and Francis, 1989. He was the
     first vice president of IDB.

9   OAPEC consists of the Arab members of OPEC plus Egypt and Syria.

10   "1973 Oil Crisis." www.wikipedia.com thebanker.com

11   "Understanding Liquidity Issues in Islamic Finance," presented
     at Islamic Finance Asia 2007 Singapore by the organisation of
     International Islamic Financial Market (IIFM).

12   International Financial Services London (IFSL) Research, October 2008.
     www.ifsl.org.uk

13   www.thebanker.com

Chapter 02

UNDERSTANDING ISLAM AND MUSLIMS

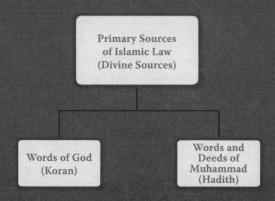

MORE THAN HALF the world is either Christian or Muslim. Considering that they are part of a diverse collection of 19 major world religions which are further divided into 270 large religious groups[1], the followers of Christianity and Islam have a large say in everyday life including politics, business, education and marriage.

But as you know, none of the major religions is homogeneous in its beliefs. While Catholics and Protestants are the biggest Christian denominations, 34,000 separate Christian groups have been identified in the world, according to the *World Christian Encyclopedia*. You can imagine that dialogue and debate can be very challenging among Christians, sometimes even more challenging than between Christians and the followers of other religions. And while there are far fewer denominations of Muslims, we see too that Muslim groups can hold divergent views that cause friction and warfare among themselves.

Fortunately, the very large majority of people who follow religion of any sort are peace-loving, tolerant and law-abiding. Muslims are no different. They follow a religion of peace, mercy and forgiveness, and most of them have nothing to do with some of the grave events which have come to be associated with their faith.

In this chapter, we focus on the most important and generally-accepted principles of Islam, such as the beliefs and practices of Muslims, and how Islam and daily life are deeply intertwined. Then, by looking at Islam's legal framework, we obtain a good overall view of the types of financial transactions that we will discuss in later chapters. From savings and spending to financing, and from insurance to investing and trade financing, the rules by which these financial transactions function are derived from the Holy Koran and other Islamic sources.

Before we delve into the principles of Islam, you might be surprised to learn that we owe a great many of our modern day conveniences to Islamic innovations. Here are some examples that changed the world.

Inventions by Muslims That Changed the World

Coffee, cheques and the crank-shaft—these are some of the Muslim innovations that we take for granted in daily life. Here is a sample list[2]:

1. Coffee—The first record of the drink is of beans exported from Ethopia to Yemen where Sufi Muslims brew the beans. They would drink coffee to stay awake all night to pray on special occasions.
2. Pin-hole camera—Tenth-century Muslim mathematician Ibn al-Haitham invented the first pin-hole camera after noticing the way light came through a hole in window shutters.
3. Chess—While a version of chess was played in ancient India, the game was developed into the form we know today, in Persia. From there it spread westward to Europe where it was introduced by the Moors in Spain in the 10th century.
4. Soap—Washing and bathing are religious requirements for Muslims. It is no wonder they perfected the recipe for soap.
5. Distillation—The means of separating liquids through differences in their boiling points was invented around the year 800 by alchemist Jabir ibn Hayyan.
6. Crank-shaft—The device that is central to much of the machinery in the modern world, such as the internal combustion engine, was created by engineer Al-Jazari to raise water for irrigation.
7. Fountain pen—This writing instrument was invented for the Sultan of Egypt in 953, after he demanded a pen which would not stain his hands or clothes.
8. The modern cheque—This comes from the Arabic saqq, a written vow to pay for goods when they were delivered, to avoid having to transport money across dangerous terrain.
9. Windmill—This was invented in 634 for a Persian caliph, and was used to grind maize and draw up water for irrigation.

WHAT IS ISLAM?

Islam is an Arabic word which means "peace and submission to Allah (swt)". A follower of Islam is called a Muslim. A Muslim strives to live in peace and harmony with the Creator, oneself, other people and the environment. Table 2.1 presents a few basic facts about Islam.

Table 2.1 Islam at a glance

Meaning of Islam	Submission to the will of Allah (swt)
Name of a believer	Muslim
Date of founding	622 CE
Percentage of world's population	>20%
Main holy book	Holy Koran
Original language	Arabic
Status of the holy book	Word and final revelation of Allah (swt), dictated by archangel Gabriel
Additional guidance	The Hadith—sayings and deeds of Prophet Muhammad (pbuh)
Name of worship centre	Mosque
Main day of worship	Friday

Islam is not only a religion but also a way of life. We saw in Chapter 1 that "Belief in Divine Guidance" is the overriding principle that governs all of man's activities. Despite man's capabilities, man does not "have unlimited power to reach the truth".[3]

Islam—Etymology and Divine Guidance

There are many Koranic verses that define Islam and allude to its divine guidance:

- The Holy Koran states that all Muslims must believe in Allah (swt), his revelations, his angels, his messengers, and in the "Day of Judgement".

And who believe in the Revelation sent to thee, and sent before thy time, and (in their hearts) have the assurance of the Hereafter. (2:4)

The Messenger believeth in what hath been revealed to him from his Lord, as do the men of faith. Each one (of them) believeth in Allah, His angels, His books, and His Messengers. "We make no distinction (they say) between one and another of His Messengers." And they say: "We hear and we obey; (We seek) Thy forgiveness, Our Lord, and to Thee is the end of all journeys." (2:285)

"Islam means 'peace and submission to Allah (swt).'"

O ye who believe! Believe in Allah and his Messenger, and the scripture which He hath sent to His Messenger and the scripture which He sent to those before (him). And who denieth Allah, His angels, His Books, His Messengers, and the Day of Judgment, hath gone far, far astray. (4:136)

- Muslims believe that Allah (swt) revealed his final message to humanity to Prophet Muhammad (pbuh) through the archangel Gabriel. For them, Muhammad was the final prophet of Allah (swt), and the Holy Koran contains the revelations he received over more than two decades.[4]

- In Islam, prophets are men selected by Allah (swt) to be his messengers. Prophets are human and not divine. The Holy Koran mentions Adam, Noah, Abraham, Moses and Jesus as prophets. All of the messengers of Allah (swt) since Adam preached the ultimate message of Islam—submission to the will of Allah (swt).

- Islam's fundamental theological concept is *tawhid*—the belief that there is only one God. The Arabic term for God is Allah. In traditional Islamic theology, Allah (swt) is beyond all comprehension. Muslims are not expected to visualise Allah (swt) but to worship and adore him as a protector.

Say: He is Allah the One and Only; Allah, the Eternal, Absolute; He begetteth, not nor is He begotten; And there is none like unto Him. (112:1–4)

Prophet Muhammad (pbuh) was born in Mecca in the year 570 (see Figure 2.1). At the age of 40, while engaged in a meditative retreat, he received his first revelation from Allah (swt) through the archangel Gabriel. This revelation, which continued for 23 years, is known as the Holy Koran.

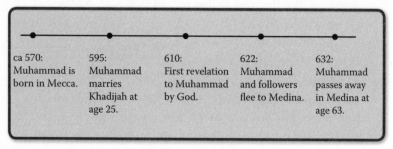

Figure 2.1 The life of Prophet Muhammad (pbuh)

The Prophet and his small group of followers suffered persecution, which grew so fierce that in the year 622, Allah (swt) gave them the command to emigrate. This migration to the city of Medina, some 260 miles to the north of Mecca, marks the beginning of the Muslim calendar.

After several years, the Prophet and his followers were able to return to Mecca where they established Islam definitively. Before the Prophet died at the age of 63, the greater part of Arabia was Muslim, and within a century of his death, Islam had spread to Spain in the West and as far east as China.

Not All Muslims Are Arab

While some may think that Muslims are found mainly in the Middle East, the religion is truly global.

In fact, the six economically-powerful countries of the Gulf Cooperation Council (GCC[5]) trade bloc has just 36 million Muslims, while India, Bangladesh, Pakistan, Indonesia and Turkey together have over 700 million, or nearly 20 times more. The number of Muslims in Indonesia alone (over 240 million[6]) exceeds the combined total in Egypt, Syria, Saudi Arabia, Iraq and Iran, the traditional heartlands of Islam. There are also substantial Muslim populations in Europe and North America, whether converts or immigrants who began arriving in large numbers in the 1950s and 1960s.

Largest Islamic Groups—Sunni and Shiite

After the death of Prophet Muhammad (pbuh), two major positions developed about the nature of authority over the Muslim community.

One group, which came to be called Sunni (meaning "tradition"), accepted the succession of the Prophet by the caliphs, who were followers elected by the Prophet himself. About 85 per cent of the world's Muslims are Sunni. Sunnis recognise four major schools of theological law—Hanafi, Maliki, Shafi'i and Hanbali. All four accept the validity of the other schools and a Muslim can choose any one that he finds agreeable. Sunnis are found in the Arab Middle East, India, Pakistan, Afghanistan, Africa and South-East Asia.

Shiite (which means "party"), the other major group, believe that any head of the community had to be a direct descendant of Prophet Muhammad (pbuh) through his daughter Fatima and her husband Ali. About 15 per cent of the world's Muslims are Shiites, with a small minority who are members of other Islamic sects.[7] Shiites form the majority in Iran, Azerbaijan, Bahrain, Lebanon and Iraq.

This historical divide between the Sunnis and the Shiites was caused more by political dispute over successors than by doctrinal differences, although differences gradually assumed theological overtones.

The Holy Koran and Sources of Islam

Sources of law are the materials and processes out of which law is developed. In modern nation states, the basic sources of law include a constitution, statutes, case law and regulations issued by government agencies.

The two primary sources of Islamic law are the Holy Koran and the *Hadith* (see Figure 2.2). The Holy Koran is the holy book of Islam, and is considered by Muslims to hold the exact words of Allah (swt) in Arabic. At the heart of the Holy Koran is the teaching of monotheism:

Allah! There is no God but He. (4:87)

The Holy Koran defines every Muslim's faith and practice. It deals with all the subjects that concern one as a human being— wisdom, doctrine, worship and law. At the same time it provides guidelines for matters other than oneself—a just society, proper human conduct and an equitable economic system. The Holy Koran is meant for all humanity, not for any exclusive group.

The Holy Koran was written down by the year 651. It is considered untranslatable because no other language carries the full range of subtle and unique meanings as conveyed by the Arabic, in which the Holy Koran was written. Muslims thus regard translations of the Holy Koran to other languages as interpretations rather than true translations.

The Hadith are the reports of the sayings and deeds of Prophet Muhammad (pbuh). Muslims believe that Prophet Muhammad (pbuh) is the very last Prophet and Messenger of Allah (swt) to

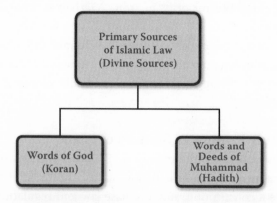

Figure 2.2 Primary sources of Islamic law

mankind. He is believed to be the summation and the culmination of all the prophets and messengers that came before him. Hence, it is the life history of Prophet Muhammad (pbuh) which provides examples of daily living for Muslims. He was entrusted with the power of explaining, interpreting and living the teachings of the Holy Koran.

The Holy Koran and the Hadith are thus regarded as absolute truths because of their divine source.

The Six Major Hadith Collections

Muslim scholars have sifted through the collections of the Hadith and scrutinised the trustworthiness of the narrators and the strength of each Hadith set. All in all, there are six major Hadith collections that are the works of some narrators who, by their own initiative, started collecting the sayings that people attributed to Prophet Muhammad (pbuh) approximately 200 years after his death. Most Sunni accept the Hadith collections *Sahih al-Bukhari* and *Sahih Muslim* as the most authentic.

- *Sahih al-Bukhari*—These prophetic traditions were collected by the Muslim scholar Muhammad ibn Ismail al-Bukhari (810–870) and published during his lifetime. It is said that notable Hadith scholars, including Ahmad Ibn Hanbal, Ibn Man and Ibn Madni, accepted the authenticity of his book.
- *Sahih Muslim*—This is the second most famous Hadith collection among Sunni Muslims, and it is considered the most authentic book of the Hadith after *Sahih al-Bukhari*. It was collected by Muslim ibn al-Hajjaj, also known as Imam Muslim. Muslims have differing views of this collection. Sunnis regard it as the second most authentic of their six major Hadith collections, while Shiite Muslims dismiss many parts of it as fabrication and untrustworthy.
- The four other collections, which are considered of lesser status, are: *Sunan an-Nasa'ii*, *Sunan Abu Dawud*, *Sunan at-Tirmidhi* and *Sunan ibn Majah*.

Other Sources of Islamic Law

There are other sources of Islamic law that have less absolute effect, including:

- *Ijma*—These are rulings on Islamic matters that are made by qualified Islamic legal scholars based on consensus.

- *Qiyas*—These are analogies drawn from the Holy Koran and *Sunnah* (sayings and deeds of the Prophet outside of the revelations of Allah (swt)) in order to make new rulings.

- Minor sources—There are four minor sources that have even less effect. These are intellectual assertions, personal opinions, considerations of public interest, and customs.

HALAL VERSUS HARAM

Haram is an Arabic term meaning "forbidden". It is used to refer to anything that is prohibited by the faith, and it can be applied to:

- Certain behaviours such as adultery, lust, hypocrisy, pornography, promiscuous behaviour, rape and abuse. The Holy Koran says:

Nor come nigh to adultery; for it is a shameful (deed) and an evil, opening the road (to other evils). (17:32)

Prophet Muhammad said in the Hadith: "If one of you were to be stabbed in the head with a piece of iron it would be better for him than if he were to touch a woman whom it is not permissible for him to touch."

- Certain foods such as alcohol and pork. Meat that is slaughtered without the name of Allah (swt) is also haram.

He hath only forbidden you dead meat, and blood and the flesh of swine, and that on which any other name hath been invoked besides that of Allah. But if one is forced by necessity without wilful disobedience, nor transgressing due limits, then is he guiltless. For Allah is Oft-Forgiving Most Merciful. (2:173)

In an incident narrated by Rafi' bin Khadij, the Prophet told Muslims who wanted to slaughter some animals using reeds, "Use whatever causes blood to flow, and eat the animals if the Name of Allah has been mentioned on slaughtering them..." (Bukhari).

⬥ Ill-gotten wealth obtained through sin, such as cheating, stealing, corruption, murder, or any means that causes harm to another human being.

⬥ Worshipping other than Allah (swt)—called *shirk*—is perhaps the most serious aspect of haram:

Say: I am forbidden to worship those other than Allah whom ye call upon. Say: "I will not follow your vain desires: if I did, I would stray from the path, and be not of the company of those who receive guidance." (6:56)

Haram also applies to the worship of wealth and other material objects, and to revering a leader beyond limits:

They take their priests and their anchorites to be their lords in derogation of Allah, and (they take as their Lord) Christ the son of Mary; Yet they were commanded to worship but one Allah: there is no god but He. Praise and glory to him: (far is He) from having the parents they associate (with him). (9:31)

Halal is an Arabic term designating any object or action that is permissible according to Islamic law and custom. It is the opposite of haram, and like haram, it covers human behaviour, speech communication, clothing, conduct, manner and dietary laws. What may be halal cannot be deduced merely by observing what is haram. For example, while divorce is not haram, it is certainly discouraged and not halal.

ISLAM AND MUSLIM LIFE ARE DEEPLY INTERTWINED

Islam may seem exotic or even extreme to many. One reason may be that religion does not dominate everyday life for probably most non-Muslims, whereas Muslims have religion always uppermost in their minds. They make no division between secular and sacred, and the Islamic religion is taken very seriously in their daily lives.

Islam is a religion of laws. The Holy Koran is a legal code that establishes right from wrong practices, lawful from unlawful acts and proper from improper behaviour. It contains laws and rules on how to regulate political, legal, economic, social and moral matters in society. There are three foundations of Islamic law that provide guidance to beliefs, duties and morals (see Figure 2.3).

Beliefs (Aqidah)

Beliefs (*aqidah*) are those matters over which Muslims have conviction. There are six aspects of belief. These beliefs are clearly articulated in the Holy Koran as required of a Muslim:

1. Belief in Allah (swt).
2. Belief in the Prophets and Messengers sent by Allah (swt), including Jesus, Moses and Abraham.
3. Belief in the Angels. The Angels maintain a record of the actions and thoughts of each human.
4. Belief in the Scriptures sent by Allah (swt), including the Holy Koran and the Hadith.
5. Belief in the Day of Judgement. On this day, all the people throughout the history of mankind will be brought forth for accounting, reward and punishment.
6. Belief in Fate. A man's fate is established by his own actions and thoughts.

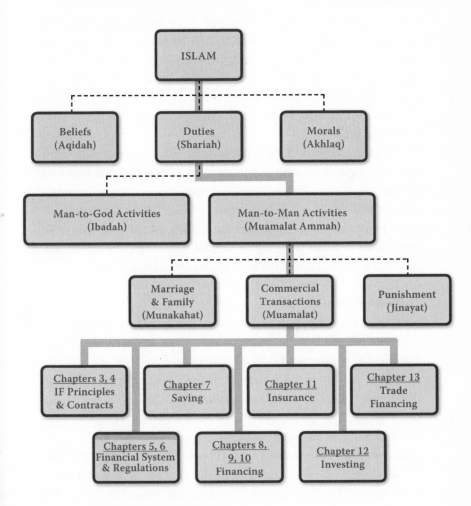

Figure 2.3 The laws and rules of Islam

Morals (Akhlaq)

Muslims believe that the level of human perfection is determined by discipline and effort. Man stands between two extremes: the lowest is below beasts and the highest surpasses even the angels. The movement between these extremes is based on man's pursuit of morals. Muslim philosophers believed that without morals, mastery over other sciences is not only devoid of value, but would obstruct insight.

Akhlaq is the practice of virtue and morality. To attain perfection and happiness, it is necessary to struggle against lust and immoral tendencies. Moral virtues bring eternal happiness, while moral corruption leads to everlasting wretchedness. Man must purge bad traits before he can integrate moral virtues. Attempts to obey the commands of Allah (swt) are successful only when one is purified; then the soul can receive the unlimited grace of Allah (swt).

Duties (Shariah)

Shariah defines the duties that man should adopt on a righteous path towards Allah (swt). It covers faith, social behaviour, legal and commercial transactions—all geared towards a total way of life. There are two main categories of duties under Shariah, covering man-to-God activities and man-to-man activities.

Man-to-God Activities (Ibadah)

Ibadah means "submission to Allah (swt) as one's Master and one as His slave to heed in obedience". The concept of ibadah is very wide. If you free your speech from filth and speak the truth, that constitutes ibadah. If you obey the Holy Koran in letter and spirit in your commercial affairs and dealings with your parents and friends, all these activities constitute ibadah as well. In short, your entire life is ibadah if it is in harmony with the laws of Allah (swt).

The Five Pillars

Ibadah is for the entire life of a human being. In Islam, belief in Allah (swt) and good works go together. A mere utterance of one's belief in Allah (swt) is not enough for one to be considered a good Muslim. The Five Pillars describe the good works that each Muslim is expected to carry out in order to achieve ibadah. These Five Pillars revolve around faith, prayer, concern for the needy, self-purification and the pilgrimage to Mecca.

1. Faith (shahadah)—"There is no god worthy of worship except Allah (swt) and Prophet Muhammad (pbuh) is His Messenger." This declaration of faith is the most important of the five pillars.

2. Prayer (salat)—Prayers are performed five times a day, at dawn, noon, mid-afternoon, sunset and nightfall, and thus determine the rhythm of the entire day. They provide a direct link between the worshipper and Allah (swt). Islamic prayers contain verses from the Holy Koran, and are said in Arabic.

3. Concern for the needy (zakat)—All things belong to Allah (swt), and wealth is held by human beings in trust. Charity is thus a requirement for every Muslim. The word zakat means both "purification" and "growth". Muslims believe that their possessions are purified by setting aside a portion for those in need, and, like the pruning of a plant, this cutting back encourages new growth. Each Muslim calculates his own zakat, which typically amounts to 2.5 per cent of earnings.

4. Fasting (sawm)—Every year in the month of Ramadan, Muslims fast from first light until sundown, abstaining from food, drink and sexual relations. Fasting is considered not only beneficial to health, but it is also regarded as a method of self-purification. By cutting oneself off from worldly comforts, even for a short time, a fasting person gains true empathy with those who go hungry as well as experiences growth in one's spiritual life.

5. Pilgrimage (The Hajj)—The annual pilgrimage to Mecca is an obligation only for those who are physically and financially able to perform it. It was here that Abraham built the first house of worship (the Kaabah), towards which all Muslims stand in unity in their daily prayers.

Man-to-Man Activities (Muamalat Ammah)

Muamalat Ammah governs man-to-man activities including marriage and family life (*munakahat*), commercial transactions (*muamalat*) and punishment (*jinayat*). Our focus in this book is on commercial transactions.

There are five categories of human action that are relevant to commercial transactions, broadly described as obligatory, recommended, permitted, discouraged and forbidden (see Figure 2.4).

Punishment is incurred for neglecting obligatory actions, such as for not having faith in Allah (swt), and for performing forbidden actions, such as gambling. The three middle categories allow for a great deal of interpretive latitude in reward and punishment.

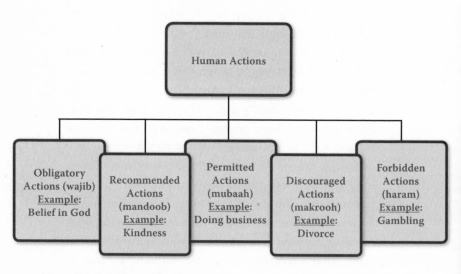

Figure 2.4 Categories of human action

SHARIAH—REGULATING EVERYDAY LIFE AND ACTIVITIES

When Prophet Muhammad (pbuh) relocated to Medina in AD 622, after 12 years of revelation in Mecca, he quickly found himself with a large community of believers. At this point, the nature of Koranic revelation changed dramatically. It became less concerned with the nature of Allah (swt) and the human relationship to Allah (swt), and more concerned with social, individual and other man-to-man duties.

The combined set of individual and social duties prescribed on every believer by the Islamic faith is Shariah, or the sacred law. This sacred law gives to the Muslim world a unity and coherence to society not found in any other major world religion. In this sense, Shariah is another word for Islam.

As mentioned above, the principle source of Shariah is the Holy Koran. The very core of the Shariah are the five pillars, which prescribe all the rituals necessary of a believer. There are, however, many social and ethical matters not covered in the Holy Koran.

For these, the Shariah bases its principles on the Sunnah of Prophet Muhammad (pbuh). The Sunnah are the collected histories of the sayings and deeds of Prophet Muhammad (pbuh), spoken and observed outside of the revelation of Allah (swt).

Still, there are other social and ethical matters not addressed by both the Holy Koran and the Sunnah. For these, the Shariah turns to sources such as ijma (scholarly consensus) and qiyas (analogical reasoning).

> **"The Holy Koran is a legal code that establishes right from wrong practices, lawful from unlawful acts, and proper from improper behaviour."**

Like other sacred laws, the Shariah consists of commandments and prohibitions covering almost every aspect of life, from marriage to criminality to the economic life of the community. There are 350 legal verses in the Holy Koran of which:

◆ 140 verses concern ibadah (worship);

◆ 70 verses concern munakahat (marriage and family); and

◆ 70 verses concern muamalat (commercial transactions).

Unlike other legal systems, however, the Shariah is not only concerned with the here and now; its primary focus is on salvation, on the life after this life. The Shariah is not simply a set of rules for living; it encompasses guidelines for gaining salvation by performing proper actions in this life.

CONCLUSION

Islam is a religion that offers guidance on beliefs (aqidah), duties (Shariah) and morals (akhlaq). This book focuses on commercial transactions (muamalat) which are man-to-man activities, as opposed to worship (ibadah) which are man-to-God.

Muamalat defines the activities related to commercial transactions that are concluded through contracts. Such activities must be Shariah-compliant in that:

◆ prohibited activities must be avoided; and

◆ commercial contracts contain elements that uphold Shariah and none that violate it.

Figure 2.3 on page 33 shows how these two broad areas will be expanded to the rest of the book:

◆ Chapter 3 examines the most important Islamic finance principles, and how Islamic ethics must come first before any commercial objectives.

◆ Chapter 4 discusses how commercial transactions must be free of forbidden elements and activities, and describes the features of a valid Islamic contract. Contracts are needed for all commercial transactions, from opening a deposit account to buying a life insurance policy.

◆ Chapter 5 considers the critical role that regulators and international bodies play in building an Islamic finance structure and making sure that the Islamic financial system works smoothly and fairly.

◆ Chapter 6 explores how a financial system provides the framework for commercial transactions to take place. A bank, for example, which is a component of the financial system, accepts deposits from consumers and makes loans to borrowers. The chapter also provides insight into how financial markets work.

◆ Chapters 7 to 13 are written mainly from the viewpoint of a consumer who needs to save, finance, get insurance, invest and use trade finance to run a business. We look into how these commonplace consumer transactions work in the conventional financial system before analysing Islamic versions. Of course, underlying each type of Islamic transaction is a requirement that the contract is Shariah-complaint.

1   *World Christian Encyclopedia: A Comparative Survey of Churches and Religions—AD 30 to 2200* by David Barrett. Oxford University Press, 2001. David Barrett is an Anglican priest from the UK.

2   www.1001inventions.com

3   *An Introduction to Islamic Finance* by Mufti Muhammad Taqi Usmani. Idara Isha'at-e-Dinayat (P) Ltd, June 1998. See also www.muftitaqiusmani.com.

4   *Islam: The Straight Path* by John Esposito. Oxford University Press, 3rd edition, 2004. Professor Esposito is the director of Prince Alwaleed Bin Talal Center for Muslim-Christian Understanding at Georgetown University.

5   The GCC comprises the Persian Gulf states of Bahrain, Kuwait, Oman, Qatar, Saudi Arabia and the United Arab Emirates.

6   *The World Factbook.* www.cia.gov

7   *US Library of Congress Country Studies.* http://countrystudies.us

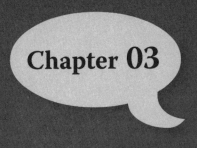

Chapter 03

BASIC ISLAMIC FINANCE PRINCIPLES

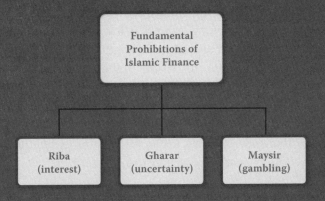

```
            Fundamental
            Prohibitions of
            Islamic Finance

     Riba           Gharar          Maysir
   (interest)    (uncertainty)    (gambling)
```

A WELL-FUNCTIONING financial system is efficient. Buyers and sellers are able to find one another easily through organised marketplaces like stock and bond exchanges. Both sides have equal access to information, and the price at which goods and services are transacted is determined naturally by market forces.

In an Islamic financial system, efficiency is also critical, but conformity to Islamic ethics is even more important. In fact, this principle dominates all other concerns. So if you were to approach an Islamic businessman with, say, a joint-venture idea to turn salt water into fresh, drinking water at a low price, his main concern would always be, "Is it Shariah-compliant?"

Because conformity to Islamic ethics dominates all other concerns in business as well as in daily life, it is essential that we have a good understanding of the goals of an Islamic economic system and the most basic Islamic principles prevalent in such a system. This understanding will in turn put us in a better position to appreciate the nature of Islamic finance contracts.

WHAT ARE THE GOALS OF AN ISLAMIC ECONOMIC SYSTEM?

Islamic scholar Ibrahim al-Tahawi[1] defined the goals of an Islamic economic system as sufficiency and peace, which can come about by eradicating hunger and fear from society, and by ensuring that every individual's basic needs are fulfilled. His list of such needs includes food, shelter, medical services, education and "all that is regarded necessary according to the custom of the society". This is a point that finds universal support among other scholars.[2]

In an Islamic economic system, non-economic goals have to be considered too, such as the fulfilment of spiritual needs. To quote Pakistani theologian Mawdudi Syed Abul A'la[3]:

> For establishing economic justice, Islam does not rely on law alone. Great importance is attached for this purpose to reforming the inner man through faith, prayers, education and moral training, to changing his preferences and ways of thinking, and inculcating in him

a strong moral sense that keeps him just. If and when these means fail, Muslim society should be strong enough to exert pressure to make individuals adhere to the 'limits'. When even this does not deliver the goods, Islam is for the use of the coercive powers of law to establish justice by force.

There is thus a difference between what is obligatory and what is desirable of an individual. What is obligatory is legally enforced, and what is desirable is ensured through education. Any deficiency in the attainment of goals is then made up by the state in enforcing what is desirable as well as taking other necessary measures. It is in this manner that the desired allocation of resources and distribution of incomes is effected.

"In an Islamic financial system, conformity to Islamic ethics dominates all other concerns."

In comparison, there are similar economic and non-economic goals in non-Islamic economic systems, such as capitalism. But according to Muslim critics, they have failed to live up to their ideals. For example, Pakistani author Sheikh Mahmud Ahmad[4] rejects the claim that capitalism is a self-adjusting process leading to the maximum satisfaction of human wants, by pointing to the chaos to which it has led. Economic crises are sufficient to refute such a claim.

Mawdudi finds that there is an undue emphasis on the rights of individual ownership and the freedom of enterprise, and these played havoc during the Industrial Revolution (late 18th to early 19th century), causing widespread suffering.

Mufti Muhammad Taqi Usmani[5] said:

The basic difference between capitalist and Islamic economy is that in secular capitalism, the profit motive or private ownership is given unbridled power to make economic decisions. Their liberty is not controlled by any divine injunctions. If there are some restrictions, they are imposed by human beings and are always subject to change through democratic legislation, which accepts no authority of any super-human power ... This is exactly what Islam does. After recognising private ownership, profit motive and market forces, Islam has put certain divine restrictions on the economic activities. These restrictions being imposed by Allah Almighty, Whose knowledge has no limits, cannot be removed by any human authority. The prohibition of riba (usury or interest), gambling, hoarding, dealing in unlawful goods or services, short sales and speculative transactions are some examples of these divine restrictions. All these prohibitions combined together have a cumulative effect of maintaining balance, distributive justice and equality of opportunities.

FUNDAMENTAL PROHIBITIONS OF ISLAMIC FINANCE

In Chapter 1, we briefly introduced five key principles that define Islamic finance—the belief in divine guidance, interest cannot be charged in any transaction, money is to be invested only in worthy causes, risk sharing is encouraged between business partners, and financing must be based on real assets. These principles can be viewed as activities that are prohibited and those that are encouraged.

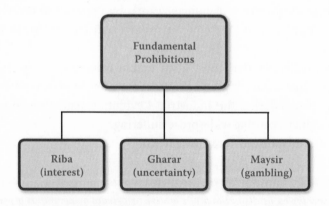

Figure 3.1 Fundamental prohibitions of Islamic finance

In this chapter, we discuss three fundamental prohibitions, beginning with the following overview (see Figure 3.1):

1. *Riba* (or interest) is prohibited. Riba covers any return of money on money, whether the interest is fixed or floating, simple or compounded, and at whatever the rate. Riba is strictly prohibited and must not be present in any form of contract or transaction. The presence of riba in any contract would void the contract. Riba has been tackled in a great amount of writing and research, and there is general agreement about the meaning and implications of riba.

2. *Gharar* (or uncertainty) is prohibited. Contracts and transactions must be free of uncertainty that is major and excessive. Uncertainty that is slight or minor, which exists in most transactions, is permitted.

3. *Maysir* (or gambling) is prohibited. Gambling includes games of chance, such as betting money in a slot machine, or borrowing money to speculate on currency movements. Maysir is often used as grounds for rejecting conventional insurance and derivatives.

In addition to these fundamental prohibitions, there are other practices that are either forbidden or encouraged:

1. **Price manipulation is prohibited.** The price of goods and services should be determined by market demand and supply factors, with no interference even by regulators. However, some Islamic scholars have declared that fixing prices is sometimes necessary to combat cases of market manipulation. For example, if demand is being artificially propped up to raise prices to benefit speculators, the regulator can come in to stabilise prices.

2. **Adequate information disclosure is encouraged.** When two parties come together to contract, both must have fair and equal access to information. If one party is denied such access, he has the right to cancel the contract. This feature

is meant to protect the weak from being exploited and to preserve the sanctity of contracts.

3. **Mutual co-operation and benefit is encouraged.** Many verses in the Holy Koran and the sayings of Prophet Muhammad (pbuh) refer to this. For example:

Help ye one another in righteousness and piety, but help ye not one another in sin and rancour: fear Allah: for Allah is strict in punishment. (5:2)

In practice, Islamic suppliers of funds become investors rather than mere creditors. Additionally, in the spirit of community welfare, every Muslim gives a portion of his wealth to the needy and the community in terms of *zakat*.

There are other norms of Islamic ethics, but of them all the prohibitions against riba, gharar and maysir are the most significant. Where there is evidence of riba and excessive gharar, those activities would clearly violate Islamic ethics.

Conventional finance, in comparison, encourage many similar norms, including information transparency and risk taking. The difference, however, is that under an Islamic system such encouraged norms are much more aggressively pursued. Let us now examine the three major prohibitions in greater detail.

PROHIBITION AGAINST INTEREST (RIBA)

The question of why riba is prohibited is often uppermost in the minds of people who are used to the conventional financial system; they wonder how something that is so prevalent in the world's economy is not allowed in Islam.

Riba Was Originally Forbidden in Other Religions[6]

Ironically, riba was also prohibited by Judaism and Christianity, both of which came about long before Islam.

The Torah (the most holy book of Judaism) states that the practice of riba is forbidden among Jews, but Jews are allowed to practise riba when dealing with non-Jews. Riba was strictly forbidden in Christianity too. Certain Christian traders who were influenced by the Jews tried to convince the church that certain kinds of riba represent a charge for administrative services. To them, a service charge is not riba. Consequently, many adopted this principle. It even influenced some Muslim scholars who argued that a low rate of interest could be considered a service charge, and therefore it should be permissible.

> **"Islamic suppliers of funds become investors rather than mere creditors."**

Philosophers such as Aristotle (384–322 BCE), who preceded Christ, considered interest an unnatural income because the lender gains without performing any work. Money cannot beget money. According to Aristotle, there are three ways of seeking profit in business:

1. Through natural trade, that is, through the exchange of essential commodities in daily transactions, such as the exchange of clothing with food.
2. Through the exchange of essential commodities for money, such as the exchange of dollars for food. This form of trading is practised in modern society.
3. Through unnatural trade where money is treated as a commodity that can be traded (rather than as a means of exchange). The profit realised from such a trade is classified as riba.

Philosophy and religion were thus unanimous in prohibiting riba. With these prohibitions, why then is the practice of riba so widespread today? There could be several reasons:

- The spirit of materialism dominated the minds of early Christian traders as they separated religion from economic activities. To them, what is forbidden in religion need not be unlawful in business.

- Some influential economists such as Adam Smith (1723–1790) supported a low rate of interest as sufficient inducement to encourage lenders to loan out their savings.
- The Jews who dominated the economy held firm that riba was unlawful among themselves but permissible if practised on others.

The combination of these and other reasons caused the practice of riba to become so widespread that today all non-Islamic banks practise it.

To appreciate the overwhelming power of riba, consider the words of former Nigerian president Olusegun Obasanjo when he spoke in 2000 about Nigeria's mounting debt-burden to international creditors:

> *All that we had borrowed up to 1985 was around US$5 billion, and we have paid about US$16 billion. Yet we are still being told that we owe about US$28 billion. That US$28 billion came about because of the injustice in the foreign creditors' interest rates. If you ask me what the worst thing in the world is, I will say it is compound interest!* [7]

Why Is Riba Prohibited?

Islamic ethics view lending with interest payments as a relationship that favours the lender, who charges interest at the expense of the borrower. Because Islamic law views money as a measuring tool for value and not an "asset" in itself, no one should be able to earn an income from money alone. The religious perspective on riba is very clear. The Holy Koran says:

> *Those who devour usury will not stand except as stands one whom the Evil One by his touch hath driven to madness. That is because they say: "Trade is like usury, but Allah hath permitted trade and forbidden usury. Those who after receiving direction from their Lord, desist, shall be pardoned for the past; their case is for Allah (to judge);*

but those who repeat (the offence) are companions of the Fire: they
will abide therein (for ever). (2:275)

Islam encourages businesses to increase their wealth through
trade, and not from lending and borrowing. The amount of interest
charged is immaterial as there is general consensus that any amount
of riba, no matter how small, is prohibited.

Besides its religious restriction, riba is considered unfair and
exploitative. For instance:

- The earning of interest from a borrower means that
  the borrower's money is being taken without providing
  anything in return. Not only does this make the borrower
  worse off, it does not bring about mutual co-operation
  and goodwill between lender and borrower.

- The lender, on the other
  hand, is earning money
  without working for
  it or bearing any risk.
  This is unjust. A party
  to a financial contract is
  entitled to returns only if
  it will bear risk.

> **"Riba is
> considered
> unfair and
> exploitative."**

- Interest-based financing tends to increase the wealth
  gap between rich and poor. Conventional banks usually
  require collateral, in the form of assets, for business loans.
  This leads them to focus their lending to established
  businesses and borrowers who can offer collateral.
  Smaller businesses with no or few assets to pledge as
  collateral are either charged high interest or denied
  financing. In the long run, large businesses get larger
  while small businesses, often owned by families, are
  disadvantaged and likely to suffer closure as a result.

Riba destroys the spirit of brotherhood amongst men. The Holy Koran says:

> *The Believers are but a single Brotherhood: So make peace and reconciliation between your two (contending) brothers: And fear Allah that ye may receive Mercy. (49:10)*

The Two Main Sources of Riba

Riba can be classified based on its source, which is whether it arises from debt or from sales transactions (see Figure 3.2).

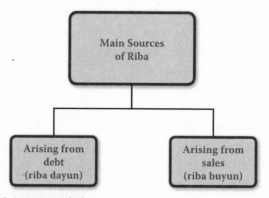

Figure 3.2 Main sources of riba

Riba Arising from Debt

Riba arising from debt (*riba dayun*) can occur in two ways. It can happen when interest is charged in relation to the duration of a loan. For example, if you were to take out a one-year $1,000 loan from a bank at a 5 per cent rate of interest, you would have to pay a total of $1,050 after one year. The amount of interest of $50 represents riba (this is called *riba qardh*).

Interest after one year	= 5% × $1,000 = $50
Total to be paid to bank	= $1,000 + $50
	= $1,050

Riba arising from debt can also occur when you default on your payment, and a penalty is imposed. Using the same example, suppose you are unable to repay the $1,000 loan a year later but finally do so after two months, and the bank charges you a penalty of $200—the penalty of $200 is considered riba (this is called *riba jahaliyyah*).

Riba Arising from Sales

Riba also arises from sales transactions (*riba buyun*). For example, if you exchanged on the spot (same day and time) 1 kg of barley for 3 kg of barley, this excess of 2 kg of barley is considered riba (this is called *riba fadhl*).

There is another more subtle aspect of riba, and it stems from the deferment of time. For example, if you exchanged 1 kg of barley on 1 April for 1 kg of barley to be received on 15 April, this barter exchange of the same commodity in equal amounts but at different times causes riba (this is called *riba nasiah*). What is prohibited is the artificial delay, which is not considered a natural aspect of a business transaction.

Sales Transactions in a Riba-Compliant Way

Prophet Muhammad (pbuh) offered clear direction on sales transactions that do not cause riba when he said:

> *"Sell gold for gold, silver for silver, wheat for wheat, barley for barley, date for date, salt for salt, in same quantities on the spot; and when the commodities are different, sell as it suits you, but on the spot."*

This saying of Prophet Muhammad (pbuh) illustrates riba with the six commodities[8] identified. The scope of riba subsequently covered other commodities through analogical reasoning (*qiyas*). These commodities can be classified into two main "categories", with various "types" contained within each category (see Table 3.1 overleaf).

Table 3.1 Categories of commodities

Category of Commodity	Types of Commodity (within the Category)
Medium of exchange	gold, silver, cash (any currency)
Food stuff	grains, meats, vegetables, fruits and spices

The following eight examples of transactions show how exchanges of these commodities can be made in ways that comply with, or violate, riba restrictions.

Transaction 1: no riba

1 kg of carrots is exchanged on the spot for 1 kg of carrots	No riba

In this transaction, an exchange is made on the spot within the same category (food stuff) and between the same types (carrots). The same amount of carrots is exchanged.

Transaction 2: riba fadhl

1 kg of carrots is exchanged on the spot for 3 kg of carrots	Riba fadhl

This is a slight but important variation where an unequal amount of carrots is exchanged. Riba fadhl results. It applies to the exchange of similar commodities that are "like for like" but are exchanged in different amounts. This would be beneficial for one party but unjust for the other.

Transaction 3: no riba

RM1,000 is exchanged on the spot for RM1,000	No riba

This transaction is similar to Transaction 1 but using a different category. An exchange is made on the spot within the same category (medium of exchange) and between the same types (RM).

Transaction 4: no riba

1 kg of carrots is exchanged on the spot for 500 gm of onions	No riba

Here, an exchange is made on the spot within the same category (food stuff) and between different types (carrots and onions). Differences in weight, measurement or number of units are allowed so long as the exchange is done on the spot and not deferred.

Transaction 5: riba nasiah

1 kg of carrots is exchanged in 30 days' time for 500 gm of onions	Riba nasiah

This transaction is identical to Transaction 4 except that the exchange is deferred for 30 days. The deferment brings about riba nasiah.

Transaction 6: no riba

US$1,000 is exchanged on the spot for 1 ounce of gold	No riba

This transaction is similar to Transaction 4. An exchange is made on the spot within the same category (medium of exchange) and between different types (US$ and gold).

Transactions 7 and 8: no riba

S$10 is exchanged on the spot for 5 kg of salt	No riba
S$10 is exchanged in one week for 5 kg of salt	No riba

In Transactions 7 and 8, exchanges are made between different categories (medium of exchange and food stuff) and different types (S$ and salt). In such exchanges, there are no restrictions on weight, measurement, number of units or time of exchange. Both do not bring about riba.

These explicit rules are meant to state with certainty the exchanges that are allowed, and those that violate riba or are unjust. In the end, trade should be conducted between people in a transparent, mutually-beneficial manner so that no party is ever unjustly rewarded or unjustly penalised.

PROHIBITION AGAINST UNCERTAINTY (GHARAR)

When an investment is made in an asset, such as a business or a stock, investment returns coming from the future can be either positive or negative. Such uncertainty always exists.

Uncertainty in Arabic is called gharar. Gharar also means "risk" and "hazard". Unlike riba, gharar is not precisely defined.

Gharar is considered to be of lesser significance to riba in that while the prohibition of riba is absolute, some degree of gharar is acceptable. Only *excessive* gharar, where uncontrollable risk leads to speculation and gambling, must be avoided.

Gharar also implies deceit, and this can be seen in business transactions that cause injustice of any form to any of the parties. For example, if the seller of a home intentionally conceals a termite problem, the buyer would be exposed to unfair risk or gharar.

The concept of gharar thus broadly implies uncertainty and deceit.

> "If the seller of a home intentionally conceals a termite problem, the buyer would be exposed to unfair risk or gharar."

Major Gharar (Gharar Fahish) Is Prohibited

As mentioned, not all forms of uncertainty are forbidden. Only major gharar (*gharar fahish*) is absolutely prohibited and must be avoided.

Many examples of major gharar are provided by Prophet Muhammad (pbuh) in the *Hadith*, the sayings and deeds of the Prophet (see Table 3.2).

Table 3.2 Examples of major gharar

Example of major gharar	Why it is prohibited
Sale of fish in the sea	The fish may never be caught.
Sale of birds in the sky	The birds may never be caught.
Sale of an unborn calf in its mother's womb	The calf may not be born alive.
Sale of unripened fruit on a tree	The fruit may not ripen.

In each of these examples, it is in the best interest of both buyer and seller to be very clear and specific about what is being bought, sold and at what price. To remove gharar from the first transaction, for example, you may pay a fisherman a fixed price, such as $500, to catch fish for you for five hours. The object of the transaction would be clear—to pay a fisherman for five hours of work.

Some of the main concepts in which major gharar can occur are summarised as follows:

1. **Uncertainty of ownership or possession.** A good example is the sale of fish in the sea where delivery is doubtful.
2. **Inadequacy of information.** Selling a house without disclosing its termite problem to the buyer is a case of major gharar. The lack of knowledge can be related to price, characteristics of the item, or the date of future performance. Furthermore, Islam emphasises the need to protect the weaker party who may have limited access to, or understanding of, relevant information.
3. **Interdependent and conditional contracts.** Contracts must not be combined or linked. If the sale price is dependent on a specific event which may or may not take place, then major gharar exists. For example, in a car hire-purchase agreement where you first hire the car for a few years before purchasing it at a stated price, the hire and purchase agreements must be separate and independent from one another.

4. **Games of chance (or maysir).** Gharar is also used in the context of gambling and games of chance.

Major Gharar in Conventional Finance

There are two conventional finance areas in particular where major gharar occurs—insurance and financial derivatives.

- ❖ With insurance, there could exist major uncertainty and unfairness to a policyholder who pays premiums for many years and not collect any payouts because the insured event never occurs. Or there may be unfairness for the insurer when a policyholder who pays for just one month is given a large payout when the insured event occurs the following month.

- ❖ With derivatives, such as futures and options for the future delivery of a bushel of corn, the object of the sale (the corn) may not exist at the time the trade is executed.

Some readers may have a hard time understanding the general prohibition against conventional insurance and derivatives. After all, insurance works to reduce risk, and derivatives are generally used to offer certainty to many users. However, as you have seen, there are many ways that these conventional instruments can be abused, and with devastating effect. The fact that these conventional products can be excessively and unfairly abused makes them forbidden as a result.

We will further discuss the Islamic versions of conventional insurance and derivatives in later chapters.

Minor Gharar (Gharar Yasir) Is Permitted

We often sign contracts for large purchases, like cars and homes, when we do not fully understand all the legal and technical terms. This would be considered minor gharar, since our lack of understanding over an aspect of the contract would not obstruct completion and delivery. When the purpose of the transaction is fulfilled, the sale is considered valid. Minor gharar (or *gharar yasir*) is permitted where:

- ❖ the uncertainty is slight;
- ❖ the contract is charitable, such as a future inheritance; or
- ❖ there is a public need for the transaction.

Here are some examples of transactions that would be considered valid:

- ❖ buying an unopened durian without first tasting the fruit;
- ❖ paying $10 to watch a movie even if you have to leave midway in case of an emergency; and
- ❖ willing your home to a charity now, when its value upon your death in the future is uncertain today.

Investing in the Stock Market—Major or Minor Gharar?

One question you may have is whether investing in the stock market is major or minor gharar. When you buy stocks, you buy them at a certain price, and in return you receive a share of ownership in a company. Each of the elements in this transaction is clear and unambiguous. There is no major gharar in this instance.

But when people think of the stock market, they always think of prices rising and falling, and of individuals making and losing huge fortunes. Buying a stock is sharing risk and reward with other shareholders. It is in fact an activity that is encouraged because effort, skill and resources are used to generate a profit.

Prices in the stock market can be expected to fluctuate like in any other market, such as the home market. If you bought a $500,000 home today, as long as the terms and conditions are transparent, straightforward and without ambiguity, the contract would be valid. When you sell the home 10 years later, the market price would have changed according to market conditions. Yet the underlying contract would still be valid.

The way the stock is traded, however, does matter. Short selling, for example, is *haram* (forbidden) as there is major gharar. In a short sale, you sell a stock that you do not own at say, $10, in the hope that its price would fall to $6 or even less, so that you can buy it at that lower price. Not only does this create money from money, the deal is unjust and could trigger a flood of short sales that can cause a company to lose its value very quickly. Day trading—where you make buy-and-sell transactions of often the same securities throughout the day—is considered speculation, and is thus haram.

In the end, market participants are certainly allowed to profit, but this should add value to the entire economic system.

Prohibition Against Gambling (Maysir)

If you put a dollar into a slot machine and pulled the handle, the result is either you win or you lose. That is the simple definition of gambling, where every transaction is based on one side winning and the other side losing.

Or take the example of you and your friend putting down $50 each in a bet, where if the stock market goes up on a particular day, you win, or if it goes down, your friend wins. Paying for fish in the sea is also a form of gambling because one's gain is very uncertain, and there is not enough information for both sides to make a mutually-beneficial agreement.

What makes gambling even worse is when it takes place in a casino, where the odds of winning are strongly stacked against you. Islam does not tolerate this unjust seizure of another person's wealth, something that cripples the poor, and widens the wealth gap between rich and poor.

The Social Costs of Gambling

Gambling represents an unproductive exchange of property. Because of its volatile and highly uncertain outcomes, gambling often leads to arguments, violence and other crises.

Despite injunctions against gambling even before the time of Prophet Muhammad (pbuh), gambling still took place at all levels of society during his lifetime. Common games of chance in those days were cards, dice, backgammon and guessing games where bets are usually placed.

The word "maysir" is actually a word that refers to a betting game using arrows. In one version, 10 people would purchase an arrow each, where seven of the arrows had notches representing a certain proportion of a camel and three were blank. All 10 arrows would be placed in a container and each person would draw an arrow. The unlucky three who drew out arrows with no notches would have to provide a camel for slaughter, and divide its meat among the group of 10.

> "**That is the simple definition of gambling, where every transaction is based on one side winning and the other side losing.**"

CONCLUSION

Muslim and non-Muslim communities both have the same economic and financial needs. They seek to fulfil those needs in a manner that is fair, stable and progressive.

Islamic finance, which derives its principles from the Holy Koran, the Hadith, the *Sunnah* (sayings and deeds of the Prophet outside of the revelations of Allah (swt)) and other religious sources, differs from conventional finance in that its business practices must all be based on Islamic principles without exception.

These principles have higher priority over efficiency, effectiveness, even profitability, and they rule on activities where:

- ◆ truthfulness and fairness are encouraged;
- ◆ interest on money (riba) is prohibited;
- ◆ excessive uncertainty is prohibited (major gharar); and
- ◆ gambling is prohibited (maysir).

The principles discussed in this chapter are not exhaustive. The most important takeaway is to understand the sources of Islamic finance principles, and the ways by which those principles dominate all manner of business transactions and daily living. With this basic understanding in place, one can then go on to appreciate the benefits as well as the challenges posed and faced by Islamic finance today.

Producing financial products that are Islamic, and are viable versions of their conventional counterparts, is still an ongoing work-in-progress. Fortunately, this challenge is being given more attention today as a critical mass of Islamic institutions and professional bodies now exists. This is a subject we will take up in Chapter 5 where we discuss the Islamic financial industry.

In the next chapter, we examine the critical importance of contracts in any business situation, but with the additional requirement that contracts must observe Islamic finance principles.

---

1 *Islamic Economics—A School of Thought and a System;*
   A Comparative Study by Ibrahim al-Tahawi. Majma' Al-Buhuth al-
   Islamiyah, 1974.

2 *Muslim Economic Thinking: A Survey of Contemporary Literature*
   by Muhammad Nejatullah Siddiqi. Islamic Foundation, 2007. He is a
   distinguished Islamic scholar from India.

3 *Economics of Islam* by Mawdudi Sayyid Abul A'la. Islamic Publications,
   Lahore, 1969. Mawdudi was a Sunni Pakistani journalist, theologian and
   a prominent political figure in his home country, Pakistan.

4 *Economics of Islam: A Comparative Study* by Sheikh Mahmud
   Ahmad, Lahore (1972). He was a Pakistani author and one of the first to
   state clearly the Islamic principles necessary in the field of economics.

5 *An Introduction to Islamic Finance* byMufti Muhammad Taqi
   Usmani. June 1998. www.muftitaqiusmani.com.

6 The feature "Riba Was Originally Forbidden in Other Religions" was
   adapted from *"Penubuhan Bank Islam"* (*The History and Background
   of Bank Islam*), 1982.

7 *The Modern Universal Paradigm* by Rodney Shakespeare. Universitas
   Trisakti, Lembaga Penerbit Fakultas Ekonomi, 2007. He is a qualified
   UK barrister and visiting professor at Trisakti University in Indonesia.

8 The term *ribawi* is used to describe commodities that are prone to
   attracting riba.

Chapter 04

AN OVERVIEW OF ISLAMIC FINANCE CONTRACTS

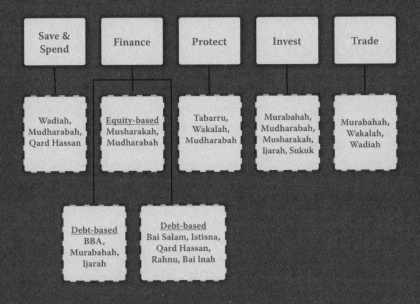

Save & Spend	Finance	Protect	Invest	Trade
Wadiah, Mudharabah, Qard Hassan	Equity-based Musharakah, Mudharabah	Tabarru, Wakalah, Mudharabah	Murabahah, Mudharabah, Musharakah, Ijarah, Sukuk	Murabahah, Wakalah, Wadiah

Debt-based
BBA,
Murabahah,
Ijarah

Debt-based
Bai Salam, Istisna,
Qard Hassan,
Rahnu, Bai Inah

IF YOU OWN a home or have a new 42-inch LCD television set that you financed with a loan, you have no doubt dealt directly with business contracts before.

The whole idea of having a contract to satisfy the consent of parties involved is universal in both Islamic and non-Islamic systems. Having one is the best means to reflect the intentions and obligations of the parties.

An old adage goes, "Better fences make better neighbours." It is easier to draw up the boundaries before a mishap than afterwards. In business, it can be perilous without contracts.

A CONTRACT IS
LEGALLY ENFORCEABLE

A contract is an agreement between two or more parties that creates an obligation to do or not do particular things. For example, if you were to sign a 15-year home mortgage contract, it means the bank agrees to give you a loan to pay for your chosen home, and for you to pay the bank back in fixed monthly instalments over the next 15 years. At its most basic level, a contract is an agreement that is legally enforceable.

Laws That Govern Contracts

Contracts are usually governed and enforced by the laws where the agreement was made. Depending on the subject matter of the agreement (such as the sale of goods or a property lease), the majority of contracts is controlled by common law. This is a tradition-based but constantly evolving set of laws that is mostly judge-made from court decisions over time.

Creation of a Contract

In the eyes of the law, a legally-enforceable contract arises with the fulfilment of certain conditions. Let us suppose, for example, that A and B enter into a sales and purchase agreement, where A sells B a couch for $1,000.

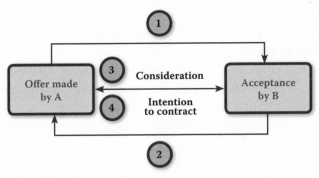

Figure 4.1 Conditions of a contract

As illustrated in Figure 4.1:

❶ There is an offer made by A to sell a couch for $1,000.

❷ There is an unconditional acceptance of that offer by B.

❸ There is a promised exchange of benefits between A and B (also called a consideration).

❹ A and B have an intention to create a legal relationship.

The terms of an offer by A must be definite and certain. An acceptance by B is a clear expression of B's agreement to the terms of the offer. A consideration is something of value passed between A and B. In our example, A promises B a couch while B promises $1,000 for the couch. Each party to the contract will gain some benefit on fulfilment of the conditions of the contract, and will incur some obligation in exchange for that benefit.

Recognising Contracts

Contracts can be recognised in several ways. They can be bilateral or unilateral, and they can be express or implied.

A bilateral contract is a mutual exchange of promises between two parties. For example, a loan agreement between you and the bank is a bilateral agreement. A unilateral contract is one in which the offeror requests performance, rather than a promise, from the person accepting the offer. A classic example is a reward advertisement where money is offered in exchange for the return of a lost pet. The person who returns the animal has satisfied the performance requirement; there was no need for him to promise to return the animal.

An express contract is an agreement made in words, either in oral or written form. Here are two examples of such contracts, one illustrating the oral form and the other, the written.

    ◇ I offer to sell you my stamp collection, and after some
       negotiations you agree to purchase it on the terms
       we have worked out, for $10,000. This is an express
       oral contract.

    ◇ Your landlord presents you with a pre-printed lease on
       the apartment you want. You agree to the terms and sign
       it. This is an express written contract.

An implied contract is formed by the behaviour of the parties such that it clearly shows an intent to enter into an agreement, even if no obvious offer or acceptance was clearly stated in words or writing. Here is an example of an implied contract:

    ◇ You go into a convenience store, pick up a 20 oz. bottle of
       Coke, take it to the cashier, pay for it and walk out of the
       store without a word being said.

Breach of Contract

When a dispute arises over a contract between two parties, one party may accuse the other of failing to perform under the terms of the agreement. Under the law, a party's failure to fulfil his or her end of the bargain under a contract is known as breaching the contract.

When a breach of contract happens (or when a breach is alleged), and informal attempts at resolution fail, the party suffering the breach may wish to have the contract enforced on its terms through a lawsuit and the court system, and try to recover any financial harm caused by the breach. For example:

    ◇ You hire a contractor to lay copper pipes for your new
       kitchen sink. If, instead, the contractor uses rust-prone

iron pipes, you can recover the cost of correcting the breach—taking out the iron pipes and replacing them with copper pipes.

Or the parties can agree to have a mediator review the dispute, which is usually far less costly than sending the case to court.

> **"A contract is an agreement between two or more parties that creates an obligation to do or not do particular things."**

KEY FEATURES OF ISLAMIC FINANCE CONTRACTS

The Holy Koran provides for a basic freedom to enter into contracts and transactions for mutual benefit. The Arabic word for contract is *aqd*, which means "to bind" or "to strengthen". For a contract to be Shariah-compliant, it must have the following four features, some of which are different from those of conventional contracts:

1. **There are at least two parties in an Islamic contract.**
2. **There is offer and acceptance by both parties on the purpose and terms of the contract.** An offer can be made by either seller or buyer. Similarly, the acceptance can also come from either of them. So if seller A offers to sell his car for $50,000 and buyer B accepts it, this forms a valid contract.

Likewise, if the buyer B states that he is ready to buy the car at $50,000 and the seller A expresses his acceptance, this will constitute a contract.

Offer and acceptance can be written or verbal.

3. **The purpose of the contract must not be *haram* (forbidden) or offensive to Shariah.** A conventional mortgage that charges the borrower 5 per cent interest would be considered a haram contract because the practice of lending money on interest is prohibited. A contract to buy and sell liquor would also be haram.

4. **The subject of the contract must change hands upon completion of the contract.** For example, if the contract is for the sale of a scooter by David to Alice, ownership of the scooter must be transferred to Alice when the contract period ends. Or if the scooter is leased to Alice, the possession of the scooter must be transferred to Alice in order to achieve the purpose of the lease contract.

There are other attributes that must be observed:

1. **The terms of the contract should be achievable.** Selling a car for $50,000 is achievable and reasonable in a normal business environment. But what if someone tried to sell you the Statue of Liberty, or a seat in a rocket to planet Mars, for $50,000? Shariah would render such a contract invalid because the terms are not achievable.

2. **The contracting parties must be aware of the exact quality, quantity and specifications of the object of the contract in order to eliminate *gharar* (uncertainty) that could lead to a dispute.** This can be achieved by the inspection of goods conducted by the buyer before entering into the contract, or through detailed description if the inspection is not possible due to the object being far away from the contracting place.

3. **The contracting parties should be above 15 years of age and possess a sound mind.** This is meant to protect minors, insane persons and the terminally ill, among others.

Although the above major ingredients may be found in all types of contracts, Islamic jurists have taken great pains in examining every one of these contracts, and in defining their nature as well as the parties involved in respect of their roles, rights and responsibilities. For example, a sales contract is different in nature from a car rental agreement despite the inclusion of common contract elements, such as the presence of two parties, offer and acceptance, and Shariah compliance. The subject of the rental contract, the car, will continue to be the property of the owner whereas in the sales contract, ownership of the car is transferred to the buyer.

There is no doubt that these contracting attributes, if adopted completely, can drastically reduce the number of commercial disputes among people.

"The Holy Koran provides for a basic freedom to enter into contracts and transactions for mutual benefit."

COMMONLY-USED ISLAMIC FINANCE CONTRACTS

Let us next briefly examine the most commonly-used Islamic finance contracts from the standpoint of a typical consumer. Each contract will be discussed in greater detail in later chapters.

As consumers, we need to make financial transactions, some of which are shown in Figure 4.2 overleaf. For any of these financial transactions to be completed, contracts have to be drawn up and signed, and obligations, fulfilled.

Observing legal formalities with Islamic finance contracts is no different. In fact, Islamic finance contracts are often more strict in their requirements. Figure 4.3 overleaf shows some of the main

Islamic finance contracts—in their Arabic terms—that are available based on various consumer transactions, and it is followed by brief descriptions of how these contracts work.

The terms used are understandably challenging if you are seeing them for the first time. We have therefore provided simplified descriptions for now. One comforting observation is that several of the contracts, such as *mudharabah* (profit-sharing), can be used for different types of financial transactions.

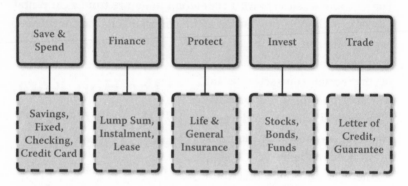

Figure 4.2 Common financial transactions that consumers make

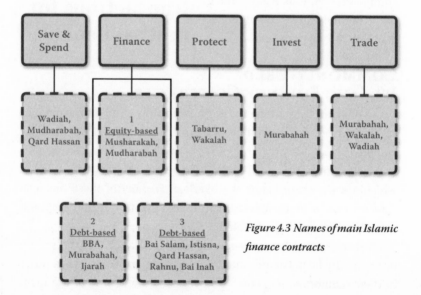

Figure 4.3 Names of main Islamic finance contracts

Saving and Spending

When you open a deposit or checking account at a commercial bank, you have three main choices.

◆ A *wadiah* savings account means that the deposit is for safekeeping only. The bank is *not obligated* to offer you a return although it is allowed to provide gifts, as long as those gifts are not officially required.

◆ A mudharabah savings account is a profit-sharing account. Before you open such an account, you and the bank would have to agree on a profit-sharing ratio. When the account is in place, based on that pre-agreed profit-sharing ratio, the bank would invest your deposit and share the profits with you accordingly.

◆ A *qard hassan* savings account provides no returns at all. This would be equivalent to an interest-free loan in conventional finance.

Financing

Despite the variety of contracts that are available for financing, the very large majority of contracts used are defined in box 2 of Figure 4.3 containing BBA (or *bai bithaman ajil*), *murabahah* and *ijarah*, all of which are debt-based.

◆ A BBA (cost plus profit margin) financing contract would be suitable if you were to buy a house, and you need a long-term mortgage loan which you would like to repay by instalments for the next 20 years.

◆ A murabahah financing contract is similar to a BBA contract but for shorter-term needs. It would be suitable if, say, you have a retail toy business and you need to purchase a container shipment of toys for the Christmas season, but you need some financing to do so.

◆ An ijarah financing contract is used for leasing assets for which ownership of the asset is not taken. Leasing is like renting except that the duration of using the asset is typically a few years, and the asset is usually large in value, such as a car, a house or heavy machinery.

One reason why these three types of contracts form the very large majority of debt-based financing contracts is that Islamic scholars are in general agreement about how they should work. The other similarly-based contracts (box 3 under Finance in Figure 4.3) have less general agreement. And compared to the equity-based financing contracts, BBA, murabahah and ijarah are more popular because of their similarities to their conventional counterparts. Consumers, after all, like familiarity.

Equity-based financing methods of mudharabah and *musharakah* (box 1 under Finance in Figure 4.3) have general agreement among Islamic scholars about how they work, but are less popular because these methods are less familiar to consumers than those of debt-based, when it comes to financing.

◆ In a mudharabah financing contract, the bank only provides capital to you for a project based on a profit-sharing ratio. Note that unlike a mudharabah savings account, where the bank puts the money to productive use, a mudharabah financing contract is the exact opposite, where *you* are the entrepreneur who puts the money financed to productive use. This sort of financing requires the bank to do more due diligence on the nature of the borrower's project.

◆ In a musharakah financing contract, the bank and you become joint-venture partners. Both parties provide capital and decide on a profit-sharing agreement. As in mudharabah financing, musharakah financing requires the bank to be very careful about who it would choose as business partner.

Protecting Using Insurance (takaful)

Conventional insurance is associated with *riba* (interest) and major gharar, both of which are forbidden.

Islamic insurance, called *takaful*, is based on two main concepts, which have to do with how policyholders and the insurance operator deal with one another.

- An insurance contract based on mudharabah means that policyholders and the insurance operator share risk by agreeing to a profit-sharing arrangement.

- An insurance contract based on *wakalah* (agency) means that policyholders appoint the insurance operator as an agent to operate the insurance scheme. The insurance operator is paid a fee for doing so, and does not share in the profits.

Investing

Investing is encouraged in the Holy Koran. For example, owning shares in a listed company is a form of equity partnership, and such investing is encouraged with various *halal* (permissible) and haram rules to be observed, of course. Later in the book, we will highlight at the consumer level:

- How to invest and manage investment risk.

- How funds are constructed using various Islamic finance contracts.

- What is halal and haram in Islamic investing.

- Investing with Islamic unit trusts (or mutual funds).

We will also examine an important question:

- Do we have to sacrifice returns in order to invest based on Islamic principles?

Trade Financing

Whether you run your own business or work for a large international company, you will have to deal with trade finance if you buy and sell internationally. Trade financing in the Islamic context is mostly based on the contracts of murabahah and wakalah.

The lingo of trade finance can be quite complex. In a later chapter, we will spend some time explaining it in general before reviewing the Islamic finance contracts underlying various trade finance instruments.

CATEGORIES OF ISLAMIC CONTRACTS

Like conventional contracts, Islamic contracts can be unilateral or bilateral.

1. **Unilateral contracts.** These do not require the consent of the recipient and generally favour the recipient with, for example, gifts, and "free" benevolent loans that require only the return of principal.
2. **Bilateral contracts.** These are bound by specific rules based on agreement between the two parties. As these contracts have a larger variety, there is no set way of categorising them.

Here is a generally-accepted method where each type can be further broken into three categories (see Figure 4.4).

1. **Contracts of exchange.** These deal with the trading, buying and selling of assets, including *usufruct* (the right to use an asset that belongs to someone else). The asset can be a piece of land, a house, or both.
2. **Contracts of participation.** These include the different types of partnership like profit and loss sharing, and joint venturing.
3. **Supporting contracts.** These are all other types of contracts.

Of the three categories, the most basic is the contract of exchange, which involves the transfer of ownership and the transfer of use of a property from one party to another. A contract of exchange captures the essence of commercial activities, and all other contracts have at least a semblance of this contract.

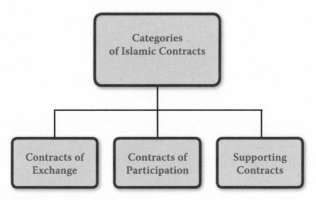

Figure 4.4 Categories of Islamic contracts

Conclusion

Without contracts, financial transactions such as opening a savings account and buying an insurance policy would be impossible. Contracts bring about legal obligations on parties so that benefits can be transferred fairly according to stated terms.

Contracts used in Islamic finance serve the same purposes as those of conventional finance—they allow the consumer to save, finance, invest and perform other financial transactions. The difference of course is that Islamic contracts adhere to Shariah principles.

In the next chapter, we discuss the types of institutions and features that make up any well-functioning financial infrastructure. These include banks, insurers, payment systems, regulations and other features with which financial transactions can be performed.

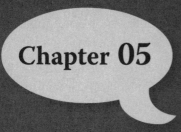

Chapter 05

Building an Islamic Finance Framework

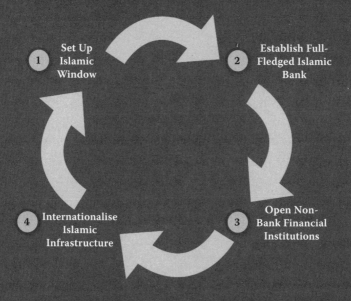

1. Set Up Islamic Window
2. Establish Full-Fledged Islamic Bank
3. Open Non-Bank Financial Institutions
4. Internationalise Islamic Infrastructure

A STABLE and efficient financial infrastructure is a critical must-have in a modern competitive economy. Think of all the daily things we take for granted, such as:

- Depositing your pay cheque into your bank account and reviewing your balance two days later through the Internet.

- Selling an antique book on eBay and someone from Kuwait whose currency is the dinar has to pay you in Euros.

- Buying travel insurance from your credit card company, losing your luggage in San Francisco and making a claim while you are overseas.

Each of these common transactions sets off a whole chain of events amongst a great number of parties. Any glitch in the chain can spell losses, sometimes even ruin reputations and cause all sorts of unexpected reactions. Here are two recent examples:

- 18 June 2008—UK supermarket chain Sainsbury took its groceries website offline after it developed a fault with online ordering. The site takes about 90,000 orders per week, and Sainsbury offered all affected customers a £10 e-voucher each when the site was restored.

- 14 July 2008—On this day, Japan Stock Exchange (JSE) failed to open for trade until nearly 3 p.m. owing to technical problems, and entailed significant losses for the stockbroking industry. The problem was not with JSE, but with the network, which stretched from London to Johannesburg, and involved many different players in between that JSE had no control over.

Islamic finance similarly demands a strong and stable infrastructure to support the needs of the economy.

An Overview of a Financial Infrastructure

Banks, insurers, financial products, payment systems, regulations, accounting standards and financial training are all part of a financial infrastructure. These components are needed for a country to be efficient and productive, and for financial transactions to be executed accurately and in a timely manner.

Figure 5.1 is a simple illustration of a financial infrastructure. The regulator plays a central role in supervising institutions and other players, with the ultimate aim of creating a financially-stable economy.

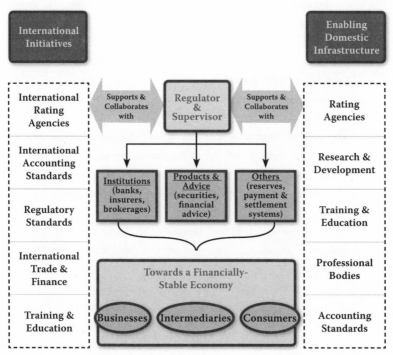

Figure 5.1 Pieces of a financial infrastructure

Role of the Regulator

Left to themselves, financial systems are prone to bouts of instability and loss of confidence. Financial regulators thus oversee a country's vital financial infrastructure resources with great care.

Regulators also play a developmental role by working in partnership with the government and private sector to identify and fill gaps in the infrastructure. If a strategic goal is to develop Islamic finance, for example, then the industry can expect to be offered motivating ideas like attractive tax schemes, training grants and subsidised research.

Regulators additionally work closely with the governments of other countries, and with international organisations, to integrate the local economy with that of the world. Ultimately, the main beneficiaries of regulation are the economy and its consumers, businesses and intermediaries.

The Role of the State

The state, generally through the regulator, has four responsibilities in an Islamic economic system[1]:

1. To ensure compliance with the Islamic code of conduct by individuals through education and, when necessary, through coercion.

2. To maintain healthy conditions in the market to enable its proper functioning.

3. To oversee the efficient allocation of resources through guidance as well as intervention and participation in the process.

4. To take positive steps in the field of production and capital formation to accelerate growth and assert social justice.

Iraqi Islamic scholar Muhammad Baqir al-Sadr said that besides enforcing relevant laws, the state guarantees social security, thus ensuring the fulfilment of needs of each individual and maintaining a balance in the standards of living in the society. He shows that the creation of a "public sector" is the means to discharge such responsibilities.[2]

In addition, the state has the function of undertaking fresh legislation to regulate and guide affairs that are not covered by Shariah. Such legislation mainly deal with the connection between man and the world of nature, as distinct from the ties between man and man. These relationships evolve with changing knowledge and the discovery of new resources, among other developments. They have to be properly regulated in order to uphold justice and protect the interests of society.

Renowned Islamic scholar Dr M. Umer Chapra regards an active economic role by the state as being an inalienable feature of an Islamic economic system. Besides organising social security, the state maintains stability in the value of money, harmonises international economic relations, and creates the conditions favourable for full employment and a high rate of growth.[3]

Beginnings of a Modern Infrastructure

Money was invented as a convenient alternative to barter. Without the invention of money, our highly-developed civilisation could not exist. Imagine trying to pay your utility bill with a box of chocolates or the taxi driver with a bag of groceries.

As societies grew more complex and social roles more specialised, money provided an indispensable means to exchange and distribute goods and services.

The Bank of St. George, which was founded in Italy in 1406, is said to be the world's first modern bank. In that role, the bank dealt with money, accepted deposits and gave out loans. It lent considerable sums of money to many rulers throughout Europe during the

"Islamic finance demands a strong and stable infrastructure to support the needs of the economy."

15th and 16th centuries. Ferdinand Magellan, the first person to lead an expedition across the Pacific Ocean, maintained an account at the bank. So did Christopher Columbus who founded America in 1492.

ISLAMIFYING A CONVENTIONAL INFRASTRUCTURE

The first modern experiment with Islamic banking took place in Egypt only in 1963. Called Mit Ghamr, it was a savings bank based on profit-sharing. It is no surprise then that countries wanting to build an Islamic financial infrastructure have to begin with what is existing, and that is almost always a conventional infrastructure.

Fortunately, there is a fairly beaten path to "Islamifying" an infrastructure[4] (see Figure 5.2), by:

1. setting up an Islamic window;
2. establishing a full-fledged Islamic bank;
3. opening non-bank financial institutions; and
4. internationalising the Islamic infrastructure.

Figure 5.2 "Islamifying" a conventional financial infrastructure

❶ Setting Up an Islamic Window

An Islamic window is a unit within a conventional bank through which Shariah-compliant instruments are formulated and distributed. Islamic windows are more common in South-East Asia and Western countries than in the Middle East, where the tendency has been to establish full-fledged Islamic banks. According to the Top 500 Islamic Financial Institutions report by *The Banker*, about 30 per cent of the 500 largest Islamic financial institutions are windows. At the start of an Islamic window, three operational functions must be in place:

1. ensuring Shariah compliance;
2. segregation of funds; and
3. accounting standards.

Ensuring Shariah Compliance

Islamic finance is based on the principles established by the Shariah and rulings (called *fatwa*) issued by Islamic scholars. These rulings can be complex and are sometimes subject to interpretation.

As a result, Islamic financial institutions, including windows, often appoint Shariah boards whose role typically involve:

- presiding over the Shariah compliance of all the transactions in the bank;

- supervising the development of Shariah-compliant investment, products and procedures;

- certifying Shariah compliance of the bank's product documents, contracts and agreements;

- advising on Shariah training programmes for staff; and

- preparing an annual report accompanying the financial statements on the bank's Shariah compliance.

Shariah councils instil confidence in the public that the bank's activities conform to Islamic teachings. The number of members on such councils typically ranges between three and seven. Councils do not directly get involved in the operations of the bank, but resolve issues pertaining to whether or not the activities of the bank are in line with Islamic principles. The auditors of the bank are required to make sure there is adherence to the decisions of the council.

Financial regulators may appoint their own Shariah board of experts to advise them on the products and services offered by the institutions under their jurisdiction. Such an appointment is of national interest to ensure that banks and other institutions are consistent in their application of Shariah principles.

An additional task for the regulator is to join and participate in the activities of international bodies, such as the Islamic Financial Services Board (IFSB) which issues standards for the effective supervision and regulation of Islamic financial institutions. (The IFSB is discussed in more detail later in this chapter.)

Segregation of Funds

Islamic funds should be segregated from the bank's conventional funds, which may be used in *haram* (forbidden) activities. For example, if the conventional portion of the bank has issued interest-bearing bonds for a casino, and has earned investment banking fees for doing so, these funds cannot be intermingled with Islamic funds. This requires that banks establish different capital funds, accounts and reporting systems. In this sense then, when a conventional bank opens an Islamic window, it is in fact setting up a separate entity from the rest of the bank.

Accounting Standards

At the start of the modern Islamic finance industry in the 1970s, Islamic institutions developed their own accounting solutions for their new products. This made comparisons across institutions and countries difficult. Then in 1990, the Accounting and Auditing Organization for Islamic Financial Institutions (AAOIFI) was established to disseminate accounting and auditing standards that can be applied internationally by all Islamic institutions. (The AAOIFI is discussed in more detail further into the chapter.)

❷ Establishing a Full-Fledged Islamic Bank

As the activities of the Islamic window expand, the bank may consider fully segregating the window from its main operations to form a separate subsidiary, or even converting itself into a full-fledged Islamic bank.

One advantage of opening a subsidiary over a full conversion is that, with the former, the parent bank can continue servicing its conventional customers, while the subsidiary expands its Islamic activities in clear separation from its conventional business.

At some point, a Muslim-majority country would face the decision of whether or not to completely transform its financial sector into a fully Islamic system. For some countries like Iran and Sudan that have predominantly Muslim populations, this is more likely to develop. On the other hand, countries such as Malaysia, Indonesia and Kuwait have mixed financial systems that are co-existing. The presence of a dual system for these countries has given them a natural competitive edge to establish themselves as diversified international financial hubs, appealing to both Islamic and conventional investors.

❸ Opening Non-Bank Financial Institutions

As full-fledged Islamic banks increase their operations and the population's appetite for Islamic financial products increases and broadens, there will arise other opportunities, particularly for the non-bank sector. Products such as insurance, fund management, derivative instruments and money market securities—some of the important offerings of this sector—could be distributed.

| Insurance | Fund Management | Derivative Instruments | Money Market Securities |

Insurance (Takaful)

Conventional insurance is not considered Shariah-compliant for several reasons. Firstly, it involves the policyholder paying the insurer for an event that may never take place (such as accidents or critical illness). This practice is considered gambling (*maysir*), which is forbidden by Shariah. Secondly, conventional insurance companies hold a large portion of their investment portfolios in interest-based bonds, another forbidden practice in Shariah.

Takaful, on the other hand, circumvents these two as well as other difficulties. We will discuss takaful in greater detail in Chapter 11.

Fund Management

After banking and insurance, the next important area of development typically takes place in fund management, through which Islamic finance consumers may look to invest and grow their money.

Islamic stock and bond funds will emerge alongside existing conventional funds, and the rise of these markets will require the presence of expertise and an adequate legal framework. For example, Islamic funds need more stringent due diligence to screen investments for adherence to Shariah principles. Islamic bonds (or *sukuk*) entail a legal framework for the establishment, management and accounting of special purpose vehicles (SPVs).

An SPV is a separate subsidiary company set up to contain investments. Such a plan protects the assets of the parent company even if the subsidiary goes bankrupt (the protection applies the other way as well for the SPV). SPVs are typically used to finance large projects without putting the entire firm at risk. We will discuss Islamic fund management and investing in greater detail in Chapter 12.

Derivative Instruments

Derivative instruments are widely used in the conventional system for managing risk. Derivatives, however, have the dubious reputation of being highly risky and bringing much of the global financial system to its knees during the subprime crisis. It is the abuse of derivatives that strongly violates Shariah, where a few speculators risk large sums of money to gamble and profit from great uncertainty (major *gharar*) at the expense of a much larger group of people.

Derivatives though are not totally haram. They are permissible so long as they are used to directly cover a risk. Islamic derivatives are in their early development stage and the proper use of derivatives to manage risk does offer hope that Islamic derivatives could become commonplace one day.

A major joint effort is currently being undertaken by the conventional finance-based International Swaps and Derivatives Association (ISDA) and the organisation of International Islamic Financial Market (IIFM) to develop Shariah-compliant derivatives.

Money Market Securities
Money market instruments provide short-term liquidity for institutions, governments and businesses. If any of the following two scenarios ever resemble your business situation, you would likely have had a need to tap the money market:

- You need to import $5 million worth of toys from China and you currently do not have the funds. Your business is tight on cash for 60 days because of late customer payments. You borrow $5 million from the money market.

- Your company has $10 million in its cash account that is earning low returns, and the funds will not be utilised for at least another 30 days. You call up your corporate banker to tap the money market by lending out the $10 million for 30 days.

Islamic money markets are not new. Bank Negara of Malaysia, for example, introduced the organisation of Islamic Interbank Money Market (IIMM) as early as in 1994. While there have been no serious operation issues, IIMM and other Islamic money markets face one obstacle—the inadequate amount of short-term tradable Islamic instruments.

One reason for this is that bond and money markets work hand in hand. A large portion of conventional money market instruments consist of medium- to long-term bonds, with less than one year to maturity. As Islamic bonds are not yet widespread, and the fact they are seldom traded but are held to maturity, few Islamic bonds end up as money market securities.

Efforts are being expanded to create a critical mass of Islamic finance instruments that can be traded easily in the money markets. One of these major efforts is being undertaken by IIFM.

❹ Internationalising the Islamic Infrastructure

Along with achieving a domestic diversity of Islamic financial institutions, regulators seek to promote greater integration with the global Islamic and conventional financial systems.

International trade is one of the main beneficiaries of financial integration as it facilitates the efficient exchange of capital, goods and services across geographical borders. In many countries, international trade represents a significant share of GDP (gross domestic product), and its importance has risen in recent centuries because of industrialisation, advanced transportation, globalisation, multinational corporations and outsourcing. Without international trade, nations would be limited to the goods and services produced within their own borders, and their financial infrastructure would not be adequate to attract capital inflows and direct investments important for a country's economic progress.

INTERNATIONAL ISLAMIC FINANCIAL ORGANISATIONS

Earlier in the chapter, we briefly mentioned three important international organisations—AAOIFI, IFSB and IIFM—that have provided a foundation for the growth of Islamic finance.

AAOIFI   IFSB   IIFM

The Accounting and Auditing Organization for Islamic Financial Institutions (AAOIFI)

For the Islamic finance industry—though emerging, but rapidly growing and evolving—standards are important as they give shape to the market and help to define characteristics of the industry ... and also provide the basis for continuing the development of this industry.

— Dr Mohamad Nedal Alchaar, Secretary-General of AAOIFI

The AAOIFI was established in 1990 and is located in Bahrain. It is a non-profit, independent Islamic international body that prepares accounting, auditing, governance, ethics and Shariah standards for Islamic financial institutions and the industry globally. Among its members from over 40 countries are central banks, Islamic financial organisations, and even non-Islamic institutions.

International Standards Body Needed

According to credit ratings company Standard & Poor's (S&P), the regional differences between banks in the methods used to prepare accounts—and even in the interpretation of Shariah law—confuse potential investors, and can restrict the sector's rate of growth. Banks in Britain differ in their accounting operations from banks in Bahrain, which in turn differ from banks in Malaysia and Indonesia. Internationally-accepted procedural methods relating to financial reporting will help bring about greater uniformity.

The AAOIFI claims that financial accounting should be overhauled to focus on the extent of its adherence to the principles of Shariah. The organisation wants central banks and Islamic institutions to adopt its rules, thereby bringing further harmonisation to the Islamic financial sector.

AAOIFI Standards versus IFRS

Since its formation, the AAOIFI has issued more than 60 accounting, auditing, governance and Shariah standards for Islamic institutions. Many countries have adopted its standards (such as Jordan, Lebanon and Qatar), while others have issued guidelines that are based on those standards (such as Australia, Malaysia and South Africa).

However, quite a few AAOIFI accounting standards have come into conflict with those of the International Financial Reporting Standards (IFRS), which are generally accepted by international organisations, such as the OECD (Organization for Economic Co-operation and Development), national accounting bodies, multinational companies as well as international auditors. The reason for the conflict is that Islamic financial institutions have certain unique requirements that cannot fully comply with IFRS.

Should the AAOIFI have different standards from the IFRS? Yes, because they are based on different worldviews. Islamic accounting needs to reflect Shariah-compliant business practices that conventional accounting rules do not. Also, the contracts used by the Islamic financial institutions are different from those of conventional banks. One common difference, for example, arises from the fact that Islamic banks cannot receive or pay interest.

Islamic Financial Services Board (IFSB)

Fifteen per cent of the world's population controls 80 per cent of its wealth, while 23 per cent of the people in the developing world survive on less than US$1 a day ... The assumption that the free market will be self-disciplined is erroneous. The market is managed by people whose primary aim is to make profits, for the corporations, and for the managers themselves. The welfare of society is not the concern of these people. The free market cannot therefore be left absolutely free. Governments must oversee the market closely, and in many instances must provide necessary rules and regulations.

— Excerpted from Keynote Address by former Prime Minister of Malaysia, Dr Mahathir Mohamad, at the Inauguration of the IFSB, 3 November 2002

The IDB accepts deposits and provides financing to promote foreign trade among member countries. There are also special funds to assist Muslim communities in non-member countries.

Educational and Training Institutes

Professionals excelling in Islamic finance require a well-rounded knowledge of finance combined with an understanding of Shariah law. Several notable educational institutes have made significant progress in promoting generally-accepted educational standards and qualifications:

- The Islamic Research and Training Institute (IRTI), established in 1981, is part of the IDB group. It undertakes research and provides training and information services to the member countries of the IDB and Muslim communities in non-member countries.

- The International Centre for Education in Islamic Finance (INCEIF) in Malaysia offers professional and academic qualifications up to PhD level in Islamic Finance. The INCEIF has tie-ups with institutions of higher learning in many countries, including South Korea, Indonesia, Pakistan, the UK and Sri Lanka.

- The International Islamic University Malaysia (IIUM) is a private university which opened in 1983 in Malaysia. It operates under the direction of a Board of Governors with representatives from eight sponsoring governments[6] and the OIC.

- The Bahrain Institute of Banking and Finance (BIBF) was founded in 1981. Its Center for Islamic Finance, established in 1997, was recognised as the "Best Islamic Finance Training Institute 2008" by *Islamic Business and Finance* magazine.

Islamic Rating Agencies

Credit rating agencies, such as S&P and Moodys, assign ratings to issuers of debt instruments. An issuer is a borrower, and can be any company or government agency.

A credit rating of 'A' as opposed to a 'C', for example, is a reflection of the borrower's greater ability to pay back its loans. A poor rating means that the borrower has a greater risk of defaulting on a loan, thereby causing lenders to expect a higher rate of return to compensate for the added risk.

In 2005, the Islamic International Rating Agency (IIRA) was set up to cater to the unique credit-rating needs of the Islamic finance industry. The IIRA offers several assessment plans, including sovereign ratings, credit ratings and Shariah quality ratings. Both sovereign and credit ratings evaluate the likelihood that an entity will repay its debt obligations in a timely manner. Shariah quality ratings review the level of compliance with the principles of Shariah.

CONCLUSION

The modern Islamic financial sector is less than 50 years old. There is still a long way to go to achieving sizeable critical mass before the sector can offer comprehensive alternatives to conventional banking products and financial services.

There are a number of challenges to overcome, some of which include differences in Shariah interpretation and a general lack of consistency in financial reporting. But none of these are unique to the industry as conventional finance faces similar challenges on an ongoing basis.

Perhaps the industry's more unique challenges are to create greater customer awareness and to provide a wider range of products and services at competitive prices. It is natural for consumers, both Muslim and non-Muslim, to want to understand what they are purchasing and how Islamic products are different from conventional products in terms of features and price.

In the next chapter, we go beneath the hood (that is, the framework) to see what goes on in financial markets. There are lenders and borrowers like yourself, there are financial instruments like stocks and bonds, and there are intermediaries like banks and investment companies. We will find out how these pieces fit together to form financial markets.

---

1   *Muslim Economic Thinking: A Survey of Contemporary Literature* by Muhammad Nejatullah Siddiqi. Islamic Foundation, 2007.

2   *Our Economics* by Muhammad Baqir al-Sadr, Beirut (1968).

3   *The Economic System of Islam—A Discussion of its Goal and Nature* by M. Umer Chapra. Islamic Culture Centre (London), and University of Karachi, 1970.

4   Many of the ideas in this section were adapted from a July 2007 IMF Working Paper entitled "Introducing Islamic Banks into Conventional Banking Systems," by Juan Solé, an economist for the IMF.

5   These are the Basel Committee on Banking Supervision, International Organisation of Securities Commissions (IOSCO) and the International Association of Insurance Supervisors (IAIS).

6   The eight governments are Malaysia (host country), Bangladesh, Egypt, Libya, Maldives, Pakistan, Saudi Arabia and Turkey.

Chapter 06

HOW FINANCIAL MARKETS WORK

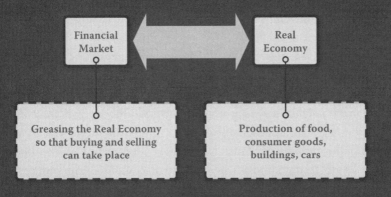

Financial Market ⟷ Real Economy

Greasing the Real Economy so that buying and selling can take place

Production of food, consumer goods, buildings, cars

WHEN FADZLEE wanted to buy a Swatch watch for his son on his 10th birthday, he logged on to eBay and found over 4,000 different pieces listed by sellers from around the world. Some were new while most were second-hand. He found one he liked, placed a bid for it, and joined a list of 30 other hopeful buyers.

What eBay and other auction sites like Yahoo and Amazon offer is a marketplace for millions of collectibles, jewellery, appliances, computers, equipment and other miscellaneous items to be listed, bought and sold daily. These auction sites act as intermediaries between buyers and sellers.

Intermediaries play an essential role in markets by bringing buyers and sellers together. Imagine that you were trying to sell an original photograph of Albert Einstein and you only had your immediate neighbours as potential buyers. One neighbour may offer you a dollar, another, $100, while others may not even have heard of the eminent Mr Einstein. When you have a tiny market like this, you will find it almost impossible to discover the true "market" price for your photograph, or even a buyer. In this situation, you are said to be in an "illiquid" market.

Now if you put the same item on eBay or Amazon, you can reach millions of potential buyers and be sure of being closer to discovering the true market value of the photograph. Such markets where there are thousands of buyers and sellers facing one another at any one time are considered "liquid".

In this chapter, we will learn that financial markets work in the same "liquid" way by allowing people to easily buy and sell financial securities (such as stocks and bonds), and perform financial transactions (such as saving and investing) through intermediaries (such as banks and brokerages). We will focus our attention on the most common types of financial securities that are used by savers and borrowers, and the main intermediaries in any financial market.

AN OVERVIEW OF A FINANCIAL MARKET

We deal with the financial market nearly every day of our lives, using it as a channel to carry out our financial activities. This market consists of banks, insurance companies, fund management firms and stock brokerages; these are the intermediary organisations that manage our money.

It is through these intermediaries that you can save your money in bank deposits, borrow to purchase cars and houses, pay monthly contributions for insurance to provide yourself with financial protection, import goods from overseas by issuing a letter of credit, or issue stocks and bonds to raise money (see Figure 6.1).

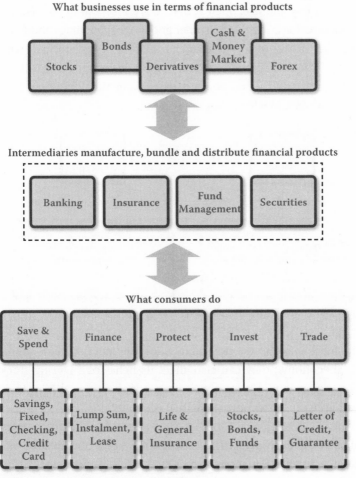

Figure 6.1 Activities in a financial market

Relationship between a
Financial Market and the Real Economy

It is important to understand the relationship between a financial market and the real economy, and how one may affect the other (see Figure 6.2).

The real economy consists of firms engaged in the production of goods and services that can either be consumed now or put to use with a view to creating more in future. The activities of the real economy employ real resources to produce something that people can buy and use. Such activities are essential to life, as they manufacture, for example, consumer goods, cars, buildings and food.

On the other hand, a financial market is concerned with "greasing" the real economy by moving funds around so that those who wish to buy can do so, and by making sure that funds are available when and where they are wanted.

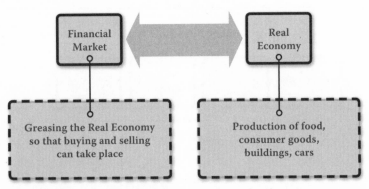

Figure 6.2 Relationship between financial market and real economy

Financial markets do not merely respond to the demands of the real economy; they can also affect its behaviour. During stock market expansions, for example, when people are wealthier, their spending can help to improve the real economy.

In the next section, we look at stocks, bonds and the complex product called derivatives. These are the most essential instruments used in a financial market to raise capital (through stocks and bonds) and to manage risk (through derivatives).

Why Businesses Create Financial Instruments

Let us imagine that you have just resigned from your job as an accountant to start a bakery shop called SuperBaker.

As a new business owner, you will need cash. You can borrow from the neighbourhood bank, which charges interest, and you might also get capital from your brother Jack, to whom you could issue stock that represents his ownership interest in your business.

Assuming Jack agrees to invest with you; the percentage of the business that he owns will depend on the amount of capital with which SuperBaker began. If there are only two stockholders—you and Jack—and you put in $70,000 while Jack puts in $30,000, then you own 70 per cent and Jack, 30 per cent, of the business.

> **"Financial markets do not merely respond to the demands of the real economy; they can also affect its behaviour."**

In formal terms, you and Jack are considered common stockholders. As a common stockholder, you are a part-owner of the company. Holders of common stock exercise control by electing the board of directors and voting on company policy. In the case of SuperBaker, you are the majority owner with 70 per cent while Jack is the minority owner, with 30 per cent. You can think of the bank and your brother as investors. When they give you money, they expect a return.

Borrowing Costs Money

When you borrow by taking a loan from the bank, you have to pay interest on a regular basis as such payments are contractual in nature.

For example, if you borrow $1,000 for three years, and the rate of interest charged is 5 per cent per year, then you will have to pay 5 per cent or $50 interest per year for three years. Then at the end of three years, you settle your last interest payment as well as return the principal of $1,000. This is what your cash flow will look like over the three years:

	Borrow $1,000	Year 1 Pay interest	Year 2 Pay interest	Year 3 Pay interest	Year 3 Repay principal
Cash flow	+1,000	-50	-50	-50	-1,000

The bank, on the other hand, experiences the exact opposite series of cash flow:

	Lend $1,000	Year 1 Receive interest	Year 2 Receive interest	Year 3 Receive interest	Year 3 Receive principal
Cash flow	-1,000	+50	+50	+50	+1,000

The lender earns interest income from you for the risk and the opportunity cost of lending you his money.

In a financial market, large companies borrow money in much the same way by issuing bonds that are bought by thousands of investors. These bonds come with similar characteristics to the loan we discussed. Investors or lenders buy bonds at, say, $1,000 apiece and receive periodic interest payments over the duration of the bond.

Ownership through Stocks

What about Jack's investment? When an investor such as your brother Jack puts money into your company, he is taking a risk with you in the hope that the sum of money he invested would become larger as time passes. Whether he receives a good return or even a negative return would depend on your performance and how you run the company. As Jack's stock rises and falls, so does the value of your ownership interest.

Issuing Stock Options (Derivatives)

Let us suppose that the bakery shop does well, and that one of the main reasons is a young baker, Maggie, you hired two years ago fresh out of school. While you cannot pay her a top-notch salary, you are afraid she might leave your business for a better-paying job. One way to entice her to stay is to give her ownership interest in the bakery of, say, 10 per cent (you and Jack would then together own 90 per cent). But giving ownership interest is a permanent move. Once she owns the shares, she will remain an owner even when she leaves the business one day. How do you manage this two-edged risk?

You want a way to retain her interest, yet ensure that she continues to perform and stays loyal to your business for at least the next two years. After seeking the advice of your university lecturer, you decide that a better way is to give her stock options. These stock options can be structured in a way that gives her the right to buy shares of the company at a very favourable, discounted price anytime after two years, and only if the business performs well and achieves certain revenue goals.

Such a stock option is called a derivative. It gives Maggie the right, but not the obligation, to buy shares of your business. If Maggie decides to exercise the option to buy shares, you will have no choice but to honour her decision by selling her the shares.

You are probably already familiar with derivatives. Let us look at the ever-popular housing option, which works just like a derivative, by supposing you are interested in buying an apartment. You and the seller agree that the price will be $200,000. You give the seller $2,000 to hold the unit and stop entertaining other prospective buyers for one week, meaning that you have one week to raise the $200,000 purchase price, or else you lose your $2,000.

In the derivatives world, this agreement is known as a call option. You paid the seller $2,000 for the right, but not the obligation, to buy the apartment for $200,000. If you change your mind because you found a better deal elsewhere, you can just walk away. You lose the $2,000, but if the price of apartments similar to the one you have an eye on rises to $300,000 during that week, you will have found yourself in a very favourable position. That is because you can exercise your option to buy the apartment for $200,000 when it is potentially worth much more—$300,000. Remember that the seller is contractually obligated to sell you the apartment for $200,000, and he cannot back out of the deal.

Technical Supplement:
The Many Types of Derivatives

A derivative is a financial product whose value is derived from an underlying asset. Such an asset can be a stock, an apartment or even a tonne of flour. And as with the housing option just described, an example of a derivative is a call option on an asset. If you buy such a call option, it is nothing more than your buying the right to own, within a specified time, the underlying asset at a stated price. There are many types of derivatives and some of them can be quite complicated. Let us look at a few common types by continuing with SuperBaker and looking at its future.

| Forwards | Futures | Swaps | Credit Derivatives |

Forward Contracts

As the owner of SuperBaker, you are worried about the volatility of the price of flour. With reports of China stockpiling the commodity and a record wheat crop in Australia, you cannot tell where flour prices are headed. You want a way to protect your business against a spell of unpredictable events that could cause flour prices to go through the roof or take a dive.

At a baking trade show, you meet John, the owner of a flour mill who is willing to enter into a forward agreement with you. You and John have opposite exposures to flour prices. Rising prices would increase your cost but boost John's profits. On the other hand, you would be happy with falling prices (lower cost) but not John (less profit).

A forward contract is the most basic of derivatives that is struck between two parties. For example:

- You, flour buyer, agree to buy 10 tonnes of flour for $200 per tonne in three months' time.
- John, flour seller, agrees to sell 10 tonnes of flour for $200 per tonne in three months' time.

In three months' time, if the market price of flour rises to $240 per tonne, John the miller is obligated to sell the flour to you for $200 per tonne. The point of the forward contract is that you and the John are able to lock in a price three months ahead of time. By doing so, both of you have removed your price risk.

Forward contracts do pose some challenges. Because they are agreements between two parties, counterparty risk can be high. This is the risk that accepted orders are not filled for some reason or another. With your case, counterparty risk could take these scenarios:

- If the market price of flour rises to $240 per tonne, John may decide to renege on the deal and sell it directly for $240 in the marketplace instead.
- It is hard to guarantee the quality of the flour; it may arrive wet or with worms.
- What if either you or John decide to get out of the contract for legitimate reasons? For example, the flour is stolen the night before delivery.

Futures Contracts

Futures contracts began as a response to the abovementioned and other challenges experienced with forward contracts.

In a futures market, there are thousands of buyers and sellers whose interests converge in one marketplace where risk may be managed. This marketplace is called a futures exchange. It acts as an intermediary between buyers and sellers in a similar way to, for example, what eBay provides for online auctions.

The trading of futures contracts is different from forward

contracts in the following ways:

- Futures contracts have standardised terms to facilitate trading. A flour futures contract, for example, would have specific details of contract size, origin of the flour, delivery times and acceptable protein levels. Forward contracts, on the other hand, usually have customised terms that are specific to a situation. For example, the forward contract may specify a special type of flour from a remote location that very few sellers can supply.
- The futures exchange (see Figure 6.3) uses a function called clearing to guarantee the trades that come through. If a buyer puts in a buy order and it is accepted, the clearing function guarantees that the order will be filled. This eliminates counterparty risk.

Figure 6.3 A futures exchange

Like a forward contract, a futures contract obligates the buyer and seller to buy and sell. But there is one difference—because the terms in a futures contract are standardised and the exchange is open to thousands of buyers and sellers, it is very easy for someone to get out of a position before the contract matures. In a forward contract, however, where terms are customised and there is no exchange to speak of, it is much less likely for parties to change their positions.

Swapping to Achieve Comparative Advantage

You decide that it is time to take SuperBaker to the next level. John wants to retire and would like to sell you his flour mill for $20 million. You have 10 bakeries, and having your own flour mill will not only help you to secure your supply but also give you a new line of business in selling flour.

You approach ABC Bank and it offers you financing based on a choice of either a fixed rate of 5% or a variable rate of EIBOR + 1.5%. The set of initials EIBOR stands for the Emirates Interbank Offered Rate, and it is the interest rate charged by banks in the United Arab Emirates for interbank transactions. It is also the benchmark reference rate commonly used by borrowers and lenders to conduct financial transactions at many Islamic banks. As a market rate, EIBOR fluctuates depending on market conditions.

You prefer a fixed rate as you do not like the idea of increased monthly payments if interest rates rise. The rate of 5% however seems a bit high, and you ask ABC Bank for more favourable terms. While it is unable to reduce its terms, ABC Bank is able to find another customer from the XYZ Bank who has the opposite requirements to yours. IceTreats is a chain of ice cream shops that wants to finance its expansion with loans. While it can obtain a loan at a fixed rate of 4%, IceTreats prefers a variable-rate loan. IceTreats considers the variable rate of EIBOR + 2.5% offered by XYZ Bank too high.

A swap is feasible in this situation because each party has a comparative advantage that the other party seeks (see Figure 6.4).

The Situation			
Company SuperBaker	Fixed can borrow at 5%	Variable can borrow at EIBOR + 1.5%	Prefers fixed
Ice Treats	can borrow at 4%	can borrow at EIBOR + 2.5%	variable

Figure 6.4 Swapping based on comparative advantage

This is an interest-rate swap, the most common type of swap in business. In this arrangement, SuperBaker obtains a $10 million loan from ABC Bank at EIBOR + 1.5%, and IceTreats obtains a loan of $10 million from XYZ Bank at a fixed rate of 4%. Then each month, SuperBaker will make an instalment payment based on a fixed rate of 4% to IceTreats, and IceTreats will in turn write an instalment amount based on EIBOR + 1.5% to SuperBaker. Each party in the end received payment terms more favourable than if they had not done the swap. SuperBaker would have paid 5% fixed and IceTreats would have paid EIBOR + 2.5% (see Figure 6.5).

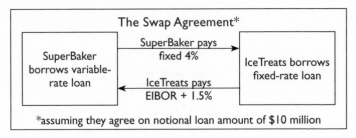

Figure 6.5 How swapping benefits both parties

Selling Debt with Credit Derivatives

The economy is doing well and ABC Bank is receiving more requests for loans. The bank, however, has limited funds to lend out and is kicking itself for not being able to take advantage of the rising interest rates in the economy.

Fortunately for ABC Bank, it can structure SuperBaker's loan into a credit derivative, and sell it to an investor called Kenny at a discount to its true value. For example, if the loan value is $9.5 million, Kenny might be offered a price of $8.5 million. If he accepts by paying ABC Bank $8.5 million, the bank is able to obtain fresh funds to create new loans and reduce its credit risk (in case SuperBaker defaults on its payments). For Kenny the investor, he stands to pocket $1 million during the next 10 years when SuperBaker is making its monthly payments.

We have devoted a few pages to a technical supplement on derivatives because they are complex instruments yet important for managing risk, even if they are controversial amongst Islamic finance scholars.

Islamic Derivatives

Those against derivatives say that they are inherently speculative, and so would contravene the prohibition on gambling (*maysir*). Others say that derivatives are permitted as long as they are used solely to hedge existing positions. In 1995, Islamic scholar Hashim Kamali wrote[1]:

> *There is nothing inherently objectionable in granting an option, exercising it over a period of time or charging a fee for it, and that options trading like other varieties of trade is permissible (mubaah) and as such it is simply an extension of the basic liberty that the Koran has granted.*

Today, many types of Islamic derivatives are available including sophisticated swaps, structured products and options. For example, in 2006, Malaysia's Bank Islam and Bank Muamalat Malaysia agreed to execute a derivative master agreement for the documentation of Islamic derivative transactions. In 2008, CIMB Islamic bank in Malaysia launched a forex-hedging tool where investors can enter into an Islamic transaction with the bank. Law firm Allen & Overy has structured sophisticated swaps that generate cash flows similar to those of conventional derivatives, but using established Shariah-compliant contracts.

Islamic derivatives are a recent innovation. Soon, we believe that they will not only match products that are available in conventional finance but also compete closely with them.

SEEKING FUNDS WITH AN IPO

Years later, your bakery business becomes even more wildly successful and you have just opened your 20th branch. You are thinking of expanding your business overseas in China and India, which means large financial resources are needed. You also expect to hire professionals to help expand into those countries.

As you are still paying off your loans, you find that it is difficult to get other loans at a good rate. What you can consider is an initial public offering or IPO. An IPO is when a company issues common stock or shares to the public for the first time. Smaller, younger companies seeking capital to expand often do so by issuing IPOs.

Technical Supplement: How an IPO Works

Financial markets allow companies and governments to raise funds by selling securities. At the same time, they allow investors to earn a return on the securities they buy. There are two parts to a financial market, and it starts with the primary market, followed by the secondary market.

The Primary Market

The primary market is where borrowers such as SuperBaker issues (sells) new securities that previously did not exist. Such securities are normally long-term instruments like stocks and bonds. If the company is selling stock for the first time, we say that the company is conducting an IPO. An IPO is part of the process of getting listed on a stock exchange, and common stock is the instrument used. An underwriter sets the IPO price, also called the issue price.

Underwriters are investment banks who are hired by the company going public. They advise the company on its valuation, the number of shares that should be issued, and the price per share. Valuation is based on the company's current as well as projected sales and earnings prospects, and a fair amount of intuitive judgement is used.

An investment bank thus acts as the middleman or intermediary between issuers and investors. An issuer sells its securities to an investment bank, who in turn assumes the risk of reselling the securities to investors. Investment banks earn the difference between what they pay the issuer for the securities and what they sell them for to the public.

IPO shares are sold during a subscription period, which typically lasts up to a few weeks. The purpose of such a period is to sell as many shares as possible. Some IPOs are so hot that they can be completely sold out in just a few days, and become oversubscribed. Sometimes, IPOs are not fully subscribed and the underwriter absorbs any unsold shares. During the subscription period, all shares are sold for the same price—both large and small buyers pay the same price regardless of quantity purchased. Moreover, during the same period, shares can only be purchased; they cannot be sold.

The Secondary Market

At the end of the IPO subscription period, the share trades in the secondary market, which is usually a formal exchange. Examples of such an exchange are the Malaysia Exchange (MYX) or the New York Stock Exchange (NYSE). Once shares start to trade, the share price is determined by investor expectations and can go up or down according to market sentiment.

When you can borrow from a market with thousands of investors, you can expect to get a much better deal because these investors are competing with one another to lend you money, and to earn from your company's performance. That is what financial markets are about. It is a meeting place between lenders and borrowers, between investors and companies.

In the next section, we briefly examine the roles of various intermediaries. Besides banking, there are insurance, securities and fund management companies.

What Financial Intermediaries Do

Financial intermediaries work by bringing many interested buyers and sellers into one centralised place called a market, thus making it easier for them to find each other. These are some of the important markets that financial intermediaries bring together:

- ◆ Capital markets consist of bond markets, which provide financing through the issuance and trading of bonds, and stock markets, where shares are issued and traded.

- Commodity markets facilitate the trading of commodities like rice, oil and gold.

- Money markets provide short-term debt financing and investment, usually lasting up to one year.

- Derivatives markets provide instruments for the management of financial risk. These include futures, forward and options markets.

- Insurance markets help to redistribute risk.

- Foreign exchange markets facilitate the trading of foreign currencies.

Without these financial markets, borrowers would have difficulty finding lenders on their own. Intermediaries such as banks help in this process. For example, banks take deposits from those who have money to save. The bank can then lend this money to those who seek to borrow in the form of loans and mortgages.

Banking

Historically, the primary purpose of a bank was to provide loans to trading companies. Banks provided funds to allow businesses to purchase inventory, and collected those funds back with interest when the goods were sold. Banking services subsequently expanded to include those that are directed at individuals.

After the first modern bank appeared in the 15th century (Bank of St. George in 1406), many other financial activities were added over time. Banks are important players in investing funds. They are primary owners of industrial corporations, and a significant influence on economies and politics. They provide almost all payment services, and a bank account is considered indispensable by most businesses, individuals and governments. Table 6.1 shows the diversity of banking services available today.

Table 6.1 Types of banking services

Type of Banking	General Focus
Retail banking	Individuals
Business banking	Small and medium enterprises
Corporate banking	Large business entities
Private banking	Wealth management services to high net worth individuals and families
Merchant banking	International finance for companies such as foreign corporate investing, letters of credit and transferring funds internationally
Investment banking	Through securities underwriting, investment banks raise funds for businesses and governments by registering and issuing debt or equity and selling it on a market.
Islamic banking	Banks that offer all of the above types of banking but adhere strictly to Islamic law
Central banking	Non-profit banks owned by governments to regulate the financial industry and manage the economy

Banks are susceptible to many forms of risk which have triggered occasional systemic crises. Risks include:

 ❖ liquidity risk—the risk that many depositors will request withdrawals beyond available funds;

 ❖ credit risk—the risk that those who owe money to the bank will not repay; and

 ❖ interest rate risk—the risk that the bank will become unprofitable if rising interest rates force it to pay relatively more on its deposits than it receives on its loans, among others.

Fund Management

Fund management is the professional management of securities (such as stocks and bonds) and assets (such as real estate and ships) to meet specified investment goals for the benefit of investors.

Such investors may be institutions (such as insurance companies, pension funds and corporations) or private investors (such as individuals via collective investment schemes).

The term "asset management" is often used to refer to the investment management of collective investment schemes, while the more generic "fund management" may refer to all forms of institutional investment as well as investment management for private investors.

Investment managers who specialise in discretionary management on behalf of wealthy private investors may refer to their services as "portfolio management", often within the context of private banking. The provision of "investment management services" includes elements of financial analysis, asset selection, stock selection, plan implementation and ongoing monitoring of investments.

Investment management is a large and important global industry. The US has by far the largest source of funds under management, followed by Japan and the UK, although the Asia-Pacific region has shown the strongest growth in recent years. Some of the largest asset managers in the world by assets under management are Barclays Global Investors (UK), State Street Global Advisers (US), Fidelity Investments (US), Legg Mason (US), Vanguard Group (US) and Allianz Global Investors (Germany).

Securities

Securities broadly consists of stocks and bonds that are traded in securities markets called primary and secondary markets. The main difference between the two markets is that in the primary market, the money for the securities is received by the issuer of those securities from investors, whereas in the secondary market, the money goes from one investor to the other.

In the primary markets, securities may be offered to the public in a public offer or privately to a limited number of qualified persons in a private placement. Often a combination of the two is used. The distinction between the two is important to securities regulation and company law. Securities that are privately placed are often not publicly tradable, and may only be bought and sold by sophisticated qualified investors. As a result, the secondary market is not as liquid.

Growth in informal electronic trading systems has challenged the traditional business of stock exchanges. Large volumes of securities are also bought and sold "over the counter" (OTC). The process of OTC dealing involves buyers and sellers trading with each other by telephone or electronically on the basis of prices that are displayed electronically. Such electronic displays are usually services of commercial information vendors such as Reuters and Bloomberg.

Insurance

The insurance industry allows individuals and businesses to pool and shift risk that they are not willing or able to bear for themselves. Policyholders can insure against a variety of risks through protection against financial losses resulting from such perils as accidents, fire and sudden death. By purchasing insurance policies, individuals and businesses can receive reimbursement for losses due to covered events.

Insurance companies are large establishments that provide insurance and assume the risks covered by the policy. Insurance agencies and brokerages sell insurance policies for the carriers. There are three basic types of insurance—life insurance, general insurance and reinsurance.

Life Insurance

Life insurance pays a sum of money upon the occurrence of the insured's death or other event, such as terminal illness or critical illness. In return, the policyholder agrees to pay premiums at regular intervals or in a lump sum.

General Insurance

General insurance is any insurance that is not life insurance. Such insurance may be for individuals (like when you wish to insure your home and car), or for commercial use (such as a construction company buying workmen's compensation insurance that pays for medical care and the physical rehabilitation of injured workers. General insurance for individuals are packaged to be sold in large quantities whereas that for commercial consumption is usually designed for relatively small, legal entities.

Reinsurance

Insurers do not take on all the risks of their policyholders on their own. They instead transfer some of their risk to reinsurers.

Reinsurance is insurance for insurers. Insurers buy reinsurance for risks they do not wish to retain. Reinsurers in turn help the industry to provide protection for a wide range of risks, including those that are the largest and most complex. Insurers also benefit from the capital relief that reinsurance provides, and from reinsurers' product development skills and risk expertise. As such, reinsurance is an indispensable part of the insurance system that makes insurance more secure and less expensive. Ultimately, policyholders benefit from more protection at a lower cost.

While insurance is often restricted to the boundaries of a country or geographic region, reinsurance is a global business that deploys capital across countries and lines of business. Reinsurers are sophisticated companies that have the legal expertise to give them access, and offer their services, to various markets. In sum, reinsurers provide three key benefits for insurers:

1. **Risk transfer.** Reinsurance allows an insurer to cover some of the risks that the insurer itself cannot manage. For example, if an insurer can only provide a maximum cover of $10 million for any given policy, it can reinsure amounts in excess of $10 million to a reinsurer.
2. **Income smoothing.** Reinsurance helps to make an insurance company's results more predictable by absorbing larger losses and reducing the amount of capital needed to provide coverage.

3. **Reinsurer's expertise.** Because of their global reach, reinsurers have specific knowledge and know-how over that of insurers. Their sought-after expertise might include dealing in a certain country or industry, or with catastrophic risks such as earthquakes and droughts.

CONSISTENT FEATURES OF ISLAMIC FINANCIAL INSTITUTIONS

Conventional and Islamic financial institutions are ultimately commercial enterprises, taking risks and seeking returns on their investments and efforts.

However, Islamic institutions have some very distinct features stemming from their strict adherence to Islamic principles. We can deduce that Islamic institutions share these three key features:

1. The abolition of interest but the promotion of profits and losses sharing. This is the principal basis for all activities which involve money, assets and labour. It aims to balance the risk and reward to all factors of production.

2. The management of the Islamic institution must be based on *Muamalah Islamiah* (Islamic acts and practices). In other words, all management activities shall not contravene Islamic principles.

3. The Islamic institution does not practise activities that are contrary to the interest of the Islamic community.

> **"Islamic financial institutions have some very distinct features stemming from their strict adherence to Islamic principles."**

These features may be relevant to some conventional institutions but not all. For Islamic institutions, they are universally relevant.

Conclusion

Through financial markets, people are able to buy and sell financial securities in order to raise and provide capital. Intermediaries play an important role in bringing many interested buyers and sellers into one place, thus making it easier for them to find each other.

By now, you should have a good basic grounding in key financial concepts and Islamic finance principles. You would be able to move smoothly through the next seven chapters, in which we will go into detail the financial transactions that concern most consumers like yourself, along with their Islamic finance versions. The transactions should all be familiar to us—saving, financing, insurance, investing and trade financing.

---

1   *Islamic Commercial Law: An Analysis of Futures and Options* by by Mohammad Hashim Kamali. Islamic Texts Society, 2000.

2   *Mubaah* is a permitted action that is neither forbidden nor recommended, and so is religiously neutral.

3   There is a difference between the insured and the policyholder. The insured is the person whose life is insured. The policyholder is the owner of the insurance policy. If I buy a life insurance policy on my own life, then I am both the policyholder and insured. If I buy a life insurance policy on my children, then I am the policyholder, and my children are the insured.

4   Adapted from "*Penubuhan Bank Islam*" (*The History and Background of Bank Islam*), 1982.

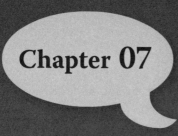

Chapter 07

SAVING AND SPENDING

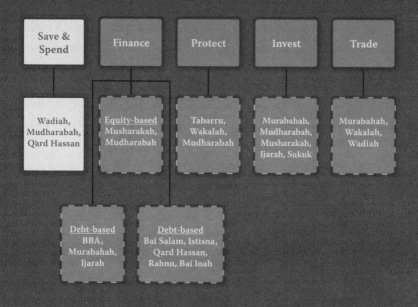

Save & Spend	Finance	Protect	Invest	Trade

| Wadiah, Mudharabah, Qard Hassan | Equity-based Musharakah, Mudharabah | Tabarru, Wakalah, Mudharabah | Murabahah, Mudharabah, Musharakah, Ijarah, Sukuk | Murabahah, Wakalah, Wadiah |

Debt-based BBA, Murabahah, Ijarah	Debt-based Bai Salam, Istisna, Qard Hassan, Rahnu, Bai Inah

COMMERCIAL BANKS play an essential role in an economy as an intermediary between those who have surplus money to deposit (that is, lending to the bank) and those who have a need for money (borrowing from the bank). By accepting deposits from customers and lending the money out in terms of a loan, the bank is able to not only earn a profit but also enable commerce to take place in the process.

Without the bank as intermediary, surplus funds could remain idle while customers who need funds to carry out business will find it difficult to do so. The economy would sputter along as a result.

In this chapter, we discuss conventional deposit accounts, which everyone should be familiar with, and why they are not Shariah-compliant. We then discuss Islamic versions of deposits and some of the issues surrounding them.

CONVENTIONAL DEPOSIT ACCOUNTS

When you open a deposit account with a bank, your money is securely kept by the bank and you can subsequently withdraw that money on demand. Banks may charge a fee for this service as well as pay you some interest on your deposited funds.

As a deposit account holder, you can withdraw your money in many ways—such as by cheque, ATM, Internet banking or wire—depending on the services provided by the bank.

For the bank, deposits are a principal source of funds that are held primarily for transaction purposes. Such deposits are paid low interest or no interest, and therefore represent a cheap supply of funds for banks to lend and invest. Banks compete for such funds by offering essential consumer banking services for free or at low cost. Such services include cheque writing, ATM cards, safe deposit boxes and immediate liquidity.

There really are just three main types of deposit accounts—checking accounts, savings accounts and fixed deposits—although there are many variations of these (see Figure 7.1).

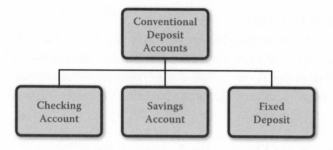

Figure 7.1 Types of deposit accounts

Checking Accounts

Checking accounts allow you to write cheques on the money you have in your account. These accounts usually earn no interest or pay the least, compared with savings accounts and fixed deposits.

The purpose of a checking account is to securely and quickly provide frequent access to funds on demand, through a variety of different channels for transactions. Checking accounts are not meant for earning interest or for savings, but for the convenience of business and personal users. Hence they usually do not bear interest.

Savings Accounts

Savings accounts pay interest but cannot be withdrawn such as by writing a cheque. These accounts let customers set aside a portion of their liquid assets while earning a monetary return. Obtaining funds held in a savings account may not be as convenient as in a checking account. For example, one may need to visit an ATM or the bank, instead of just writing a cheque.

Some savings accounts may even limit the withdrawals, payments and transfers that you can perform everyday. True savings accounts do not offer cheque-writing privileges, although some institutions may call their higher-interest, checking accounts "savings accounts."

Fixed Deposits

A fixed deposit usually pays interest but cannot be withdrawn for a certain term or period of time. When the term is over, it can be withdrawn or it can be rolled over (that is, held for another term). Generally speaking, the longer the term, the better will be the yield on your money.

ISLAMIC DEPOSIT ACCOUNTS

Like conventional banks, Islamic banks have products for savings, checking and fixed deposit. The difference is that they are structured to comply with Shariah principles.

Conventional deposits are prohibited by Shariah because of *riba*. For example, when a conventional bank raises funds through deposits, customers of such an exercise are often entitled to returns based on a fixed interest rate determined by the bank. With floating-rate deposits, on the other hand, depositors are paid interest at a rate that is linked to a benchmark, such as the Singapore Interbank Offered Rate (SIBOR). In both situations, the rate of return is never negative, and the original sum of the deposit is guaranteed to be returned with interest. Such deposits that pay and guarantee interest clearly involve riba.

"Islamic banks offer products for savings, checking and fixed deposits, structured to comply with Shariah principles."

Not all conventional products are exposed to riba and hence there are many such products offered by Islamic banks without any need for modification. Examples of such products are those for which fees are charged, including the safekeeping of securities, safe deposit boxes, the wiring of money and import-export transactions.

Shariah-compliant deposit accounts are based on three main structures: *wadiah*, *mudharabah* and *qard hassan*.

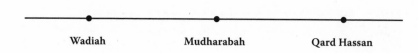

Wadiah	Mudharabah	Qard Hassan

Wadiah Deposits

In a wadiah deposit, the bank safekeeps your money and pays it back to you on demand. Unlike a conventional deposit, a wadiah account does not promise a fixed return, although the bank has the discretion to provide you with *hibah* (gift). Because the bank has discretion, you may in theory get no returns at all.

In practice, banks generally do offer some form of hibah. If Islamic banks were to refrain from such a practice, they would find it difficult to attract depositor funds. Yet at the same time, Islamic banks cannot promise that it will surely provide customers with hibah. There are two types of wadiah accounts:

◆ *wadiah yad amanah*; and
◆ *wadiah yad dhamanah.*

Wadiah Yad Amanah (WYA)

With such an account, the bank performs a pure safekeeping function for deposits. For example, if you deposited $10,000 in cash, the bank has to keep the money in its vaults. As a safekeeper, the bank:

◆ is not allowed to utilise the funds for profit generation or any other purpose; and
◆ does not charge any fees for safekeeping.

As a result, no returns in any form can be expected. You as depositor also face the risk that the bank does not guarantee the return of your money, in the event of a loss due to theft, fire or some unforeseen mishap. So if a gang of robbers stole money from the vault, among which is your deposit, the bank is not obligated to make it up to you, unless it was due to the bank's negligence or fault. Table 7.1 overleaf summarises the risk and return features of WYA.

Table 7.1 Risk and return features of wadiah yad amanah accounts

| Risk | It is possible for you to get back less than what you deposited, although unlikely. While the bank promises to protect and safekeep your money, it does not offer a 100% guarantee in pay back. |
| Return | No monetary returns are possible because the bank merely agrees to safekeep your money. |

Wadiah Yad Dhamanah (WYD)

In this case, the bank guarantees the return of the money, even if the money is stolen. In return, the bank:

◆ is allowed to utilise the funds; and

◆ enjoys all profits and absorbs all losses.

It is with this version of wadiah that the bank provides hibah. Table 7.2 summarises the risk and return features of WYD.

Table 7.2 Risk and return features of wadiah yad dhamanah accounts

| Risk | Your principal is guaranteed in that you will not get back less than what you deposited. |
| Return | Non-guaranteed returns are given at the bank's discretion. |

Mudharabah Deposits

The typical mudharabah arrangement comprises an investor (or *rabb al-mal*) who supplies the capital, and an entrepreneur (or *mudharib*) who provides the expertise on investing.

In a mudharabah deposit, you as the customer making the deposit are the investor while the bank is the entrepreneur. With your money deposited, you become a capital provider to the bank, who then assumes the role of fund manager. The bank has freehand in the management of your money for profit.

How are profits shared, in respect of your investment? At the outset of your mudharabah deposit, you and the bank would agree to a profit-sharing ratio (PSR). If the PSR was struck at, say, 60–40, any profit that the bank subsequently makes will be shared with you in that ratio.

In the event of losses, however, you as capital provider will have to bear them all. The bank, as fund manager, will suffer no losses, other than its time and effort. But by the same token, the bank is not allowed to take any form of remuneration *unless* the project is profitable.

The roles of capital provider and fund manager may also be reversed, as we will see in a later chapter on financing based on mudharabah. There, we will observe the bank in the role of capital provider or investor, and the customer as fund manager or entrepreneur. Figure 7.2 illustrates how a mudharabah deposit account works with the customer as capital provider.

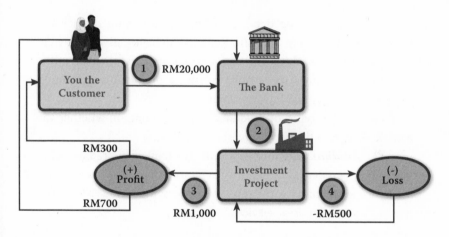

Figure 7.2 An example of how a mudharabah deposit account works

❶ Suppose you deposit RM20,000 with a bank and the PSR is 30–70 (30% to you and 70% to the bank).

❷ The bank takes the money to invest in a project. It does not guarantee that the investment will be profitable.

❸ Now suppose there is a net profit of RM1,000. The profit is shared as follows:

To you   = 30% × RM1,000
             = RM300
To the bank = 70% × RM1,000
             = RM700

Your account would then show a balance of RM10,300 (RM10,000 + 300).

❹ In the event of a loss of, say, RM500, you as depositor will be the only one to bear the loss:

To you   = 100% × -RM500
              = -RM500
To the bank   = $0 (no loss)

Your account would then show a balance of RM9,500 (RM10,000 – 500).

The actual return on deposits is known only upon maturity or the periodical payment of profit. Returns can be negative, as seen in the above example, although Islamic banks are careful to direct the investments towards those with relatively predictable outcomes, such as mortgages and business loans.

There are two types of mudharabah, depending on whether the bank is limited in the way it invests the deposits.

* *Mudharabah muqayyadah.* The bank is limited by how it can deploy the funds. Such limitations could be on the period of time, the type of business, the business location or the kinds of services.

* *Mudharabah muthalaqah.* The bank has the freedom to utilise the funds without restrictions. (Without restrictions means the restrictions of mudharabah muqayyadah are not in force, not that the bank can invest in anything it likes.)

Qard Hassan Deposits

There is another type of deposit account—based on qard hassan—which offers absolutely no returns at all, and the bank can use the money as it wishes. If you have ever lent $100 to a friend or a relative, and he paid you back $100 one year later, you would have had given out a qard hassan interest-free loan. As can be expected, such deposits are not as popular and less available because depositors do not receive returns.

ISLAMIC SAVINGS ACCOUNTS

Savings Accounts Based on WYD

The most common form of Islamic savings accounts is based on wadiah yad dhamanah (WYD), where the bank guarantees the return of money deposited on demand. Some depositors like such accounts because they offer safe custody of their money, and the possibility of some profits in the form of hibah. Since depositors are not taking part in any sort of business risk (the bank absorbs all losses), they are thus justifiably entitled to only non-guaranteed hibah.

IN THE MARKETPLACE

Maybank of Malaysia (www.maybank2u.com. my) offers a savings account based on WYD. The product has attractive terms to encourage savings from a young age, requiring a minimum deposit of only RM1 (about US$0.28) for trust and minor accounts. The bank also offers  checking facilities where a current account for individuals and joint holders could be opened with a minimum of RM1,000. As a safekeeping account, it does not guarantee any returns although gifts might be expected, if not assured.

Savings Accounts Based on WYA

Wadiah yad amanah (WYA) accounts are uncommon. Since the bank is not allowed to utilise the funds, and the depositor is not guaranteed his money back if there is a legitimate physical loss (such as from theft), it is easy to see that such accounts will not be as commercially available as WYD accounts.

ISLAMIC CHECKING ACCOUNTS

Current accounts are based on the three Islamic methods we discussed above:

1. Wadiah current accounts guarantee the paying back of money but not any returns.
2. Mudharabah current accounts are less popular than those of wadiah mainly because the customer is responsible for all losses incurred, and he may get back less than what he had put in.
3. Qard hassan current accounts allow the bank to utilise the funds without having to provide any returns.

IN THE MARKETPLACE

The Islamic Bank of Britain (www.islamic-bank) offers an Islamic checking account based on qard hassan. While the depositor is not entitled to any returns, he is provided with basic privileges like debit cards, cheque books, ATM withdrawals and online access. These privileges cost the bank money and are offered to attract depositers.

ISLAMIC GENERAL INVESTMENT ACCOUNTS

Islamic banks have general investment accounts that work like conventional fixed deposits. They are typically based on mudharabah muthalaqah, which means that the bank has the freedom to utilise the funds with few restrictions. Returns to depositors are based on pre-agreed PSR, and the actual returns are not known ahead of time.

Fixed deposits have higher profit-sharing ratios in favour of the depositor than do savings accounts. This is understandable because they cannot be withdrawn for a certain period of time and generally speaking, the longer the term, the better the yield you can expect on your money.

IN THE MARKETPLACE

Asian Finance Bank in Malaysia (www.asianfinancebank.com) offers a general investment account based on a 50–50 PSR between the customer and the bank. The minimum placement period of one month requires a minimum deposit of RM5,000 while for a two-month placement, the minimum deposit is RM500.

Case Study: Gazala Starts Work after Graduation from University

Gazala just found a job in Kuala Lumpur, her first after university. She visits an Islamic bank to open some accounts for banking, and begins with a savings account to have her monthly salary deposited directly into it. She puts RM500 into the account, which is the minimum amount required of adults. The savings account is based on wadiah yad dhamanah; she is happy to have the bank safekeep her money while receiving some hibah (gifts) whenever they might be distributed.

To pay her bills, especially those by mail, she also opens a current account. Her priority is to obtain the conveniences of a cheque book, ATM card and regular account statements at little or no cost. The bank has such a product based on qard hassan and she finds it acceptable to receive no returns for the account.

Twelve months into her job, Gazala has saved RM5,000. She does not expect to use the money in the next six months and wants to earn a higher return. She opens a general investment account based on mudharabah. She considers it fair and therefore agrees to the 50–50 PSR offered by the bank. Some of her colleagues use the same product and they were satisfied that the bank invested the money prudently. At the same time, Gazala accepts the investment risk that comes with the account.

COMPARING ISLAMIC AND CONVENTIONAL DEPOSITS

Monetary benefits are paid to depositors in both Islamic and conventional banks, but they are not the same. Payment to depositors by Islamic banks is variable while that to depositors by conventional banks tends to be fixed. Islamic banking is based on shared risk. How does this work?

Let us suppose a conventional bank accepts a deposit of $1,000 from you, and by its practice pays you, the customer, a fixed return of, say, 1 per cent per annum. Now suppose the bank then lends your $1,000 to John, and John later defaults on his loan. The conventional bank would have to pay you from its own resources. You did not share risk with the bank and yet you got paid your money back as well as interest.

Islamic banking not only prohibits interest but also regards such an arrangement as in your favour and unfair to the bank. An Islamic bank would accept your $1,000 deposit, invest it and profit-share with you, based on the bank's investment performance and a pre-agreed PSR. This is the case of a mudharabah account. With such an account, you will bear all losses, should the bank incur any. If you prefer a safer option, the bank can safekeep your money in a wadiah account and promise to return it upon maturity.

With the mudharabah account, the actual amount of returns to the depositor is not specified at the start. The fact that the depositor does not know his actual returns ahead of time, and his returns depend on the investment performance of the bank, indicates that risk is being shared. The depositor does not earn interest on a fixed rate in the Islamic banking system, but accepts some of the business risks and earns a share of the bank's profits on the investment.

The Islamic bank's financial statements reflect this difference. When the bank incurs a profit or loss, the value of the depositor's account is increased or reduced accordingly, and instantaneously reflected at its fair value. In a conventional bank, the value of its deposits is not directly linked to its investment activities. When the conventional bank makes a profit or a loss, the value of the depositor's account remains unchanged.

ISLAMIC CREDIT CARDS

Credit cards are a convenient and popular way of paying for goods and services without using cash at the time of purchase, and most working adults have at least one credit card.

Credit cards are generally opposed to desirable Islamic economic behaviour because they can encourage wasteful spending. When we consider how conventional credit cards have been misused through overspending and wrongly tapped on for emergency funds, we can understand the painful indebtedness they cause from the very high interest rates and penalties they charge.

Debit cards, on the other hand, are generally accepted in Islamic practice because they draw on the individual's own funds from the bank.

Shariah nevertheless permits the use of credit cards. Various requirements have to be observed as compared with conventional credit cards:

- Islamic credit cards cannot offer cash advances, which is a form of money-lending.
- Interest is not compounded on account balances. An additional interest charge due to any delay in payment is prohibited.
- Credit card users can carry out only *halal* (permissible) transactions. Credit card issuers will normally decline transactions on *haram* (forbidden) activities, such as buying alcohol and paying the entrance fee to a casino.

IN THE MARKETPLACE

Bank Islam in Malaysia (www.bankislam.com. my) offers a Shariah-compliant credit card that is available to both Muslims and non-Muslims. The card is free of riba as it does not charge interest. It is also free of gharar (uncertainty) as the maximum charges are declared upfront.

Some Product Issues

Islamic deposit products have several issues, especially those concerning riba. Part of the challenge for Islamic products is that they have to be competitive when compared with conventional products, and be Shariah-compliant at the same time.

Receiving Rewards without Risk

When your deposit is based on wadiah or qard hassan, you can almost always be sure that you will get your money back. The initial sum of your deposits does not decline even if the bank incurs losses from the investments it makes on your funds.

Yet Islamic banks offer gifts and other benefits to depositors in order to attract and retain their funds. The issue that arises is whether such benefits are permissible under Shariah, since depositors are not exposed to any risk. Receiving returns without any risk taking is unfair and is equivalent to riba. On the one hand, such benefits and gifts are not contractual in nature, and the bank is not obligated to offer them. Gifts thus do not bring about riba.

When such gifts become predictable and recurring, however, they start to look like riba as the customer would be receiving benefits without taking on any risk. Riba arises because the depositor is being rewarded for the use of his money.

Guaranteed Return in Mudharabah

Mudharabah deposits expose the depositor to both profits and losses. It is possible that the bank's investment experience is negative. However, instances are not uncommon where the original amount deposited in a mudharabah account is guaranteed to incur no losses. This could be due to local requirements (the regulator may require such protection for vulnerable groups of people), or to market practice (in order to attract funds). In any case, any sort of guarantee on the principal amount placed in a profit-sharing account is generally viewed as constituting riba.

CONCLUSION

You have just acquired a flavour of some of the practical product differences between conventional and Islamic finance. Islamic finance forbids riba, unjustness and earning a return without taking risk, but encourages profit and risk sharing. In the end, while the differences in actual cash flows could be the same, the underlying structures are quite distinct.

There is obvious competition for funds, especially in a dual system where both conventional and Islamic banking are available. For this reason, it is sometimes difficult to tell the difference between conventional and Islamic products unless one carefully examines their underlying structures.

For non-Muslims who have access to both conventional and Islamic deposit products, we urge you to maintain an account in each type. This direct experience will give you a practical perspective that this and other books cannot give. Besides, the amount to start a savings account is minimal.

In the next chapter, we begin the first of three chapters on financing. Islamic financing based on debt is the most popular form of financing. If you are already familiar with how conventional financing works on home mortgages and car loans, you should be able to absorb the chapter quite comfortably.

Chapter 08

FINANCING (BASED ON DEBT)

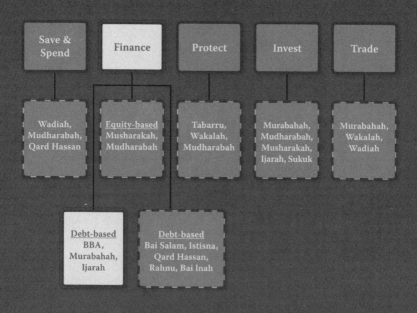

YOU HAVE A GREAT BUSINESS IDEA. You want to buy over a building, then convert it to a budget hotel but you do not have enough money to fund the whole project. This is where you might consider using the services of a financing company.

The need for financing is universal in society, whether or not it is based on conventional or Islamic finance. For most people, one of the strongest motives for financing is to increase personal wealth. For the bank that loans out the money, it too expects to increase its own wealth, by charging interest on the loan. This is the case with a conventional bank.

Loans can be made for periods as short as a few months to meet immediate cash needs, or as long as 20 or more years for buying a home or constructing a large oil rig. A rule of thumb is that loans, if arranged for similar purposes, are more costly the longer you take to pay. As seen in Figure 8.1, a one-year car loan would usually be cheaper than one that is for 10 years. This is because the bank would have to bear more risk the longer it has to wait to get its money back.

> **"The need for financing is universal in society, whether or not it is based on conventional or Islamic finance."**

This rule of thumb does not always work, of course. Sometimes a short-term car loan can be more expensive than one of a longer-term, such as when there is greater demand for shorter-term loans.

Another important factor that affects the amount you would pay for a bank loan is your creditworthiness, as perceived by the bank. If you have a clean record of always having paid back your loans on time, and you hold a good job with a stable income, the cost of your loan would be cheaper than if you have bad debt problems or a sketchy employment record.

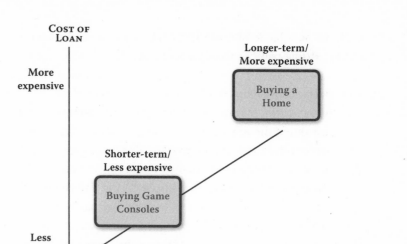

Figure 8.1 General relationship between duration and cost of loan

AN OVERVIEW OF ISLAMIC FINANCING

For those new to Islamic financing, it may seem to have the substance of conventional loans in disguise because their cash flow patterns can be very similar. When we examine Islamic financing, it is essential to always keep one foot firmly planted on the Islamic finance principles we have earlier discussed:

* Islamic financing does not deal with *riba* (interest). This is a fundamental rule—the lender cannot earn interest and the borrower cannot pay interest. Instead, the lender, such as a bank, can earn a profit by first buying and owning the asset (and thereby assuming ownership risk) and then selling the asset to you at a specified profit margin. The fact that the bank takes on ownership risk (no matter for how short a period) entitles it to a profit.

* Islamic financing cannot be for the purpose of funding a *haram* (forbidden) asset or activity. It would hence not

be possible to obtain Islamic financing to build a beer bottling plant or to buy a pig farm.

◆ Islamic financing emphasises the duty to disclose information in order to protect the weak. So rather than assuming the role of creditor, the provider of funds is encouraged to act as an investor. By taking a stake in the borrower's project, mutual co-operation and benefit are brought about. Contract transparency is also enhanced because as a partner, you will want other partners to have full information in order to have the project succeed for mutual benefit. Further, contracts and transactions are structured to be free from *gharar* (uncertainty).

How does Islamic financing work then? There are three main methods of financing that may be offered by an Islamic bank. It could:

1. become a joint-venture partner in your project and share the profits and losses with you (equity-based financing, to be discussed in Chapter 10); or
2. buy the building and lease it to you (leasing will be discussed in Chapter 9); or
3. buy the building and sell it to you at a profit (debt-based financing, discussed in this chapter).

In this chapter, we look at two of the most popular debt-based Islamic financing methods—*bai bithaman ajil* (BBA) and *murabahah*.

We will examine how these methods work by looking at two common consumer transactions of financing: a long-term loan for you to buy a home and a short-term working capital loan to pay for game consoles for your toy business. But first, let us understand the way it works with conventional loans.

HOME PURCHASE WITH A CONVENTIONAL LOAN

For many individuals, buying property is the largest financial commitment in their lifetimes. It is no wonder, since property can cost several hundreds of thousands to a few million dollars each.

And for most individuals, buying a home means having to get a loan. Since home loans are lumpy assets and you are committed to them for a long period of time, it is essential that you understand how mortgage loans work—before we even explore Islamic home-financing choices.

> **"Home loans are lumpy assets and you are committed to them for a long period of time; you should first understand how mortgage loans work."**

How a Mortgage Loan Works

Let us now suppose you buy a $500,000 apartment with a down payment of 20 per cent (that is, $100,000), and you take a 20-year $400,000 loan, which the bank is charging at a fixed rate of 6 per cent per year. Your monthly instalment would work out to be $2,865.72.

This amount is easily calculated with a standard formula that can be found in financial calculators and Excel spreadsheets, and requires as input:

- Loan amount = $400,000
- Monthly interest rate of 6%/12 months = 0.5%
- Number of monthly instalments = 20 years × 12 instalments per year = 240

Any financial adviser or bank officer should be able to explain this formula to you. The amount of $2,865.72 for this illustration is fixed throughout the duration of the loan.[1] Each monthly instalment goes towards settling some interest and principal. The total interest due is based on the loan principal remaining, which is the amount that is currently owed. Let us go through the mathematics by referring to Table 8.1, which shows the status of the loan for the first 12 months.

Table 8.1 *An example of a mortgage payment schedule*

Month	Principal [left axis*]	Monthly Instalment	Monthly Interest [right axis**]	Repayment [right axis]	Principal [end of month]
[1]	[2]	[3]	[4]	[5]	[6]
A 1	400,000.00	$2,865.72	2,000.00	$865.72	399,134.28
B 2	399,134.28	$2,865.72	1,995.67	$870.05	398,264.23
3	398,264.22	$2,865.72	1,991.32	$874.40	397,389.82
4	397,389.82	$2,865.72	1,986.95	$878.78	396,511.04
5	396,511.04	$2,865.72	1,982.56	$883.17	395,627.88
6	395,627.88	$2,865.72	1,978.14	$887.58	394,740.29
7	394,740.29	$2,865.72	1,973.70	$892.02	393,848.27
8	393,848.27	$2,865.72	1,969.24	$896.48	392,951.79
9	392,951.79	$2,865.72	1,964.76	$900.97	392,050.82
10	392,050.82	$2,865.72	1,960.25	$905.47	391,145.35
11	391,145.35	$2,865.72	1,955.73	$910.00	390,235.35
12	390,235.35	$2,865.72	1,951.18	$914.55	389,320.80

* The Principal remaining, which decreases as time passes, is depicted on the left axis in Figure 8.2 on page 140.
** The Monthly Interest, which is based on the Principal remaining and decreases as time passes, is depicted on the right axis in Figure 8.2.

Look at Month 1 (Row A)
At the start of the loan, the loan principal is $400,000 [column 2]. The interest for the first month works out to:

(6%/12) × $400,000 = $2,000 [column 4] where (6%/12) or 0.5% is the monthly interest rate.

This means that $2,000 of the $2,865.72 first monthly instalment goes towards interest, and the remainder of $865.72 [column 5] goes towards paying down the loan principal.

At the end of one month, and after the first instalment is paid, the outstanding loan principal decreases to $399,134.28 ($400,000 − $865.72) [column 6]:

Monthly instalment = $2,865.72
Interest paid   = (6%/12) × loan remaining
                     = 0.5% × $400,000.00
                     = $2,000.00
Principal repayment = $2,865.72 − 2,000.00
                     = $865.72
Loan remaining (after 1 month)
                     = $400,000 − 865.72
                     = $399,134.28

Look at Month 2 (Row B)

In the second month, the same series of steps are taken:
Monthly instalment = $2,865.72
Interest paid   = (6%/12) × loan remaining
                     = 0.5% × $399,134.28
                     = $1,995.67
Principal repayment = $2,865.72 − 1,995.67
                     = $870.05
Loan remaining (after 2 years)
                     = $399,134.28 − 870.05
                     = $398,264.23

As can be seen in Figure 8.2 overleaf, the loan principal remaining decreases over time as the principal is repaid every month—from $400,000 initially to $0 at the end of 20 years.

Since the amount of interest paid is based on the loan remaining, the amount deducted for interest from each fixed monthly instalment decreases over time as the loan remaining decreases. This decreasing interest deduction also means that the amount of principal repaid increases every month.

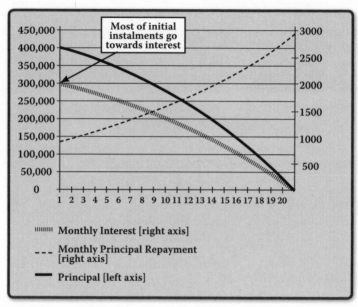

Figure 8.2 How a mortgage decreases in amount over time

IN THE MARKETPLACE

Commercial banks in Singapore typically offer loans on (a) fixed interest rates, (b) variable interest rates that they can change at their sole discretion, and (c) market-pegged interest rates that vary with market factors such as SIBOR (Singapore Interbank Offered Rate) or SOR (Swap Offer Rate).

These choices cater to the different preferences of home buyers. For example, those who want certainty in their instalment payment would opt for fixed rates. Those who want a level of transparency that is influenced by market conditions might choose market-pegged rates. It is not possible at the time of obtaining a loan to determine which will be the cheapest option for you over the loan's duration.

HOME PURCHASE WITH AN ISLAMIC LOAN (USING BBA)

Let us now go through the same transaction but with an Islamic loan. One of the most popular Islamic financing products to meet long-term financing needs is bai bithaman ajil (BBA), and its method involves a sale where payment is deferred to a future date. Figure 8.3 shows how a basic BBA transaction works.

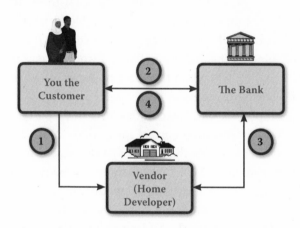

Figure 8.3 An example of a BBA transaction with three parties

❶ You identify a home you desire.
❷ You approach the bank to obtain financing.
❸ The bank buys the home from the developer and pays in full.
❹ The bank sells the unit to you at a marked-up selling price:

[Purchase Price] + [Profit Margin] = Selling price

after which, you make equal monthly instalment payments to the bank for the next 20 years.

Assuming that the monthly instalment is the same as the previous example ($2,865.72), then over 20 years, a total of $687,773.82[2] would have been paid. This would be the selling price that the Islamic bank would quote you, which means that:

[Purchase Price] + [Profit Margin] = Selling price
$400,000 + $287,773.82 = $687,773.82

A BBA transaction is thus said to work on a cost-plus contract, whereby the sale price (with profit) of the asset is paid in instalments over a long period.

In such a transaction, the cost and profit margin may or may not be known to you, as it is not a requirement for these details to be specifically mentioned. However, it is possible to work backwards to figure out exactly what is being charged. (At this point, you might be thinking that this is no different from a conventional loan with interest. We will get to this matter later. Meanwhile, let us go through a few more examples.)

The example just illustrated is that of a three-party situation—you, the vendor and the financial institution. In an even simpler situation (see Figure 8.4), the vendor and the bank can be the same entity. For example, the bank may own foreclosed property, among which is your dream apartment, and thus becomes the vendor when you approach it with plans to buy the apartment. A foreclosed property is one on which the borrower has defaulted payment and which the lender (bank) has repossessed.

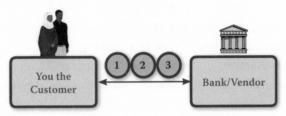

Figure 8.4 An example of a BBA transaction with two parties

❶ You identify a home you desire out of an inventory of homes owned by the bank.
❷ You approach the bank to obtain financing.
❸ The bank sells the unit to you at a marked-up selling price:
　[Purchase Price] + [Profit Margin] = Selling price

Using an Agent for a BBA Transaction

In either of the above two situations, the Islamic bank runs the risk of your changing your mind. Suppose the bank buys the asset, and you change your mind about the purchase or you are unable to go through with it, the bank would be stuck with an asset that could have fallen in value at the time of disposal.

The bank, to mitigate this risk for itself, can appoint you as an agent to deal with the vendor (see Figure 8.5 overleaf). The bank may appoint you as an agent for two main reasons:

1. **To mitigate the risk of your changing your mind.** As an agent, your job is to buy the asset and take possession of it on behalf of the bank. You also have the responsibility as a trustee to safekeep the asset on behalf of the owner (that is, the bank). If the asset is negligently damaged while you are in your agent role, you are responsible for the losses.
2. **You may have the expertise to deal with a certain type of asset, expertise that is unfamiliar to the bank.** As an agent, you would be responsible for defining the specifications, executing the order and then inspecting the goods upon delivery. This would make sense if, for example, you desire a luxury home in a foreign country, and you are better-informed than the bank about such homes, including the specific developers to approach.

Ultimately as an agent, you cannot simply reject the goods and escape contractual payment obligations, except in extraordinary circumstances.

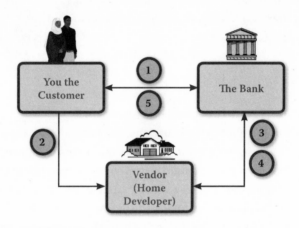

Figure 8.5 An example of a BBA transaction with customer as agent

Here is a brief explanation of a BBA transaction with customer as agent:

❶ The bank appoints you as an agent in an agreement whereby it promises to sell, and you promise to buy, a home on specified terms and conditions, and at a marked-up price.

❷ You identify a vendor and select a home on behalf of the bank (since you are acting as an agent of the bank).

❸ The vendor transfers ownership to the bank. The bank is involved at this stage to oversee the process, as there are legal issues to deal with that you would not be expected to be knowledgeable of.

❹ The bank pays the vendor.

❺ At this point, the agency contract comes to an end. The bank sells you the home at a marked-up price and transfers ownership to you, after which you pay the marked-up price in instalments.

The Importance of Proper BBA Contracting

Contracts are essential in any business transaction. Not only do they provide clarity to the roles of various parties, but they also specify the rights and obligations of each party. What may be legally correct (in a conventional sense), however, may not be Shariah-compliant.

When a customer is appointed by a bank as an agent to meet the terms of a BBA transaction, such as in a home purchase, both parties will have to fulfil the requirements of a series of legal relationships (see Figure 8.6):

1. **Between Promisor (bank) and Promisee (you).** At the start, an agreement is struck between the bank and you where the bank promises to purchase the home and you promise to subsequently buy the home from the bank.

2. **Between Principal (bank) and Agent (you).** As an agent of the bank, you act on behalf of the bank to identify a vendor and secure the asset. The bank thereafter purchases the home.

3. **Between Seller (bank) and Buyer (you).** The bank next sells the home to you.

4. **Between Creditor (bank) and Debtor (you).** You agree to defer payment of the home through monthly instalments for the duration of the loan.

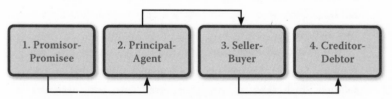

Figure 8.6 The four legal relationships in a typical BBA transaction

Each stage exacts specific rights and obligations, and for the entire BBA transaction to remain Shariah-compliant, it is critical that all of these legal relationships are put in place, executed and fulfilled.

WORKING CAPITAL WITH AN ISLAMIC LOAN (USING MURABAHAH)

Murabahah is another type of cost-plus financing. As with BBA, you identify an asset, the bank buys it and then sells it to you at cost plus a profit margin. It is a rule in murabahah that the bank must reveal the cost and profit margin. The sale price is then paid in one lump sum or in instalments. In comparison, BBA is also a cost-plus sale, but payment is always by instalment.

In South-East Asia, murabahah is commonly used in the financing of working capital whereas in the Middle East, it is used for working capital as well as for longer-term project finance.

What is Working Capital?

Working capital deals with the short-term needs of businesses. It includes a company's short-term assets (such as cash, inventory, and money that customers owe you or accounts receivable), and its short-term liabilities (such as salaries, taxes to be paid, money owed to suppliers or accounts payable, and bank loans). Short-term is generally defined to be 12 months or less.

Suppose you have an urgent need to buy a $50,000 truck for your tyre business and you only have $30,000 in cash to spare. You have $100,000 tied up in inventory and accounts receivable. In such a situation, you might want to take a short-term loan that can be paid off when your inventory is sold and your customers have paid you.

The goal of managing working capital is to ensure that the company is able to continue its operations, and that it has sufficient cash flow to pay short-term debt and upcoming operational expenses.

Murabahah is straightforward like BBA, as shown in Figure 8.7. Let us consider this scenario: you own a toy shop and a corporate customer wants to purchase 1,000 sets of the latest electronic game console for its staff as gifts; you do not have enough copies and so you scout around for a wholesaler that does.

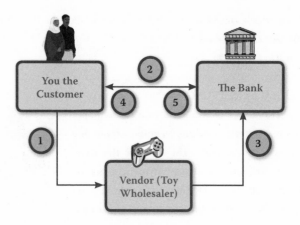

Figure 8.7 An example of a murabahah transaction

❶ You find a toy wholesaler who quotes you a price of $100 for each game console. You do not have $100,000 in cash for the purchase but you expect sufficient cash inflows from unpaid customer accounts in the next three to four weeks.

❷ You approach an Islamic bank for a loan and present your corporate customer's purchase order as proof of a ready market for the game consoles.

❸ The bank purchases the game consoles from the toy wholesaler.

❹ The bank sells the consoles to you at an agreed marked-up price of $105,000 to be paid in one lump sum in 30 days' time.

[Purchase Price] + [Profit Margin] = Selling price
$100,000 + $5,000 = $105,000

❺ Your corporate customer pays you for the consoles, and you pay the bank after 30 days as agreed.

Instead of a lump sum payment, instalment payments can also be made. For example, the murabahah contract may require you to make 10 equal monthly instalments of $10,500 each:

$10,500 × 10 installments = $105,000

You can work backwards with a spreadsheet to figure out the profit margin of the bank[3]:

Rate = 10.76%

IN THE MARKETPLACE

Bank Muamalat in Malaysia (www.muamalat. com.my) offers working capital financing based on murabahah. The cost of the asset must be revealed, and the payment schedule and amounts by the customer are agreed upon between the bank and the customer. In the case of Bank Muamalat, it appoints the customer as

an agent to purchase the assets on its behalf. Assets must have saleable value and may consist of inventory, semi-finished goods and raw materials.

Effective Rate versus Flat Rate

The rate of 10.76 per cent in the last example is called an effective rate. It is the actual rate you are paying over a year.[4]

Another rate that is often quoted is the flat rate. It is about half the effective rate, and people often confuse the two. Here is an example to explain the difference.

Susie just graduated and got her first job, and she is eyeing a yellow VW convertible. Even with some help from her dad, Susie still has to borrow $60,000. A bank has offered a flat rate loan of 3 per cent over five years.

The flat rate is not the actual rate she is paying. The flat rate is used as a convenient way to calculate the amount of interest she has to pay over the five years. In Susie's case, she would be paying total interest of $9,000:

Total interest   = Loan amount × flat rate × duration

= $60,000 × 3% × 5 years

= $9,000 over 5 years or 60 months

On a monthly basis, her interest is $150:

Monthly interest   = $9,000/60 months
                      = $150

From here, we can calculate the amount of her monthly instalment:

Monthly instalment   = ($60,000 + 9,000)/60 months
                     = $1,150

Is Susie really paying 3 per cent interest a year? Not really.

To find out what she is actually paying, let us examine Table 8.2. The table shows various flat rates (2 to 5 per cent) charged, loan durations (one to 10 years), and the resultant effective interest rates incurred:

Table 8.2 Flat rates versus effective rates

		FLAT RATES						
		2%	2.50%	3%	3.50%	4%	4.50%	5%
DURATIONS	1	4.35%	5.43%	6.50%	7.58%	8.66%	9.73%	10.80%
	2	4.13%	5.15%	6.16%	7.17%	8.17%	9.17%	10.17%
	3	4.04%	5.03%	6.02%	6.99%	7.96%	8.92%	9.87%
	4	3.99%	4.96%	5.84%	6.87%	7.81%	8.74%	9.66%
	5	3.95%	4.90%	5.78%	6.77%	7.69%	8.60%	9.49%
	6	3.91%	4.85%	5.72%	6.69%	7.58%	8.47%	9.34%
	7	3.88%	4.81%	5.66%	6.61%	7.49%	8.36%	9.21%
	8	3.86%	4.77%	5.61%	6.54%	7.40%	8.25%	9.08%
	9	3.83%	4.73%	5.61%	6.47%	7.32%	8.15%	8.97%
	10	3.80%	4.69%	5.56%	6.41%	7.24%	8.06%	8.86%

For Susie, the actual rate of interest she is paying is 5.84 per cent, or slightly less than two times the flat rate of 3 per cent.

DIFFERENCES BETWEEN BBA AND MURABAHAH

Murabahah is used for shorter-term financing and payment can be made in a lump sum or by instalment. The bank discloses the cost of the underlying asset and the profit margin that it earns.

BBA, on the other hand, is used for longer-term financing and payment can be made by instalment only. The cost of the underlying asset and the profit margin are not openly disclosed, although it is easy to calculate both figures based on the instalment amounts that have to be made.

The key differences between the Islamic principles of BBA and murabahah are shown in Figure 8.8.

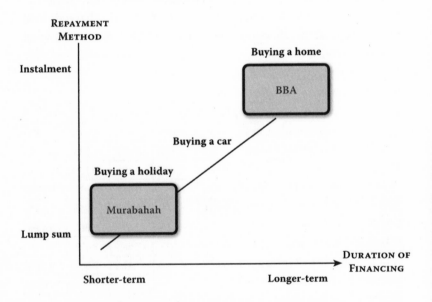

Figure 8.8 Key differences between a BBA and murabahah contract

AN INTEREST-BEARING SYSTEM IN DISGUISE?

To some, it seems that BBA and murabahah are similar to conventional, interest-based financing. If the bank purchases a home for $100,000, and turns around to sell it to you at a marked-up price of $120,000 to be paid in monthly instalments, it would appear that we have merely substituted a mark-up profit rate for the rate of interest. In fact, the difference between the two may disappear if proper care is not exercised.

Certain conditions are thus imposed to ensure that BBA and murabahah financing are both free from riba and gharar.

Legal Relationships Are Set Up and Enforced

Like most Islamic finance contracts, BBA is constructed with several, separate legal relationships, each of which must be fulfilled consecutively (not at the same time) in order that riba is avoided. For example, in a typical BBA transaction, three legal relationships are set up:

1. Promisor-Promisee;
2. Seller-Buyer; and
3. Creditor-Debtor.

Each relationship must start and end before the next one can begin. If any one of these relationships is removed, the whole transaction would likely violate Shariah rules. For example, say the bank loans you the money directly rather than buying the home from the developer and selling it to you. By doing so, you and the bank would be entering into a riba-based, creditor-debtor relationship, as a result of skipping the first two steps.

The additional steps often required in Islamic transactions point to a greater amount of administrative and legal requirements. Shariah-compliant loans can hence be more expensive to execute. Muslims who wish to deal only with Shariah-compliant products would typically have no qualms about paying more, if needed.

Risk Taking Should Be Rewarded

In order for the bank to make a return, it must bear risk. In our example, the bank and you enter into an agreement for the bank to purchase the asset (a home) and your promising to buy it subsequently. To make this happen, the bank has to take on the risk of home ownership temporarily before selling the home to you and then entering into a creditor-debtor relationship with you.

The bank taking ownership at the start faces price exposure and the risk that the asset could be destroyed even before handing it to you. In the eyes of Shariah, this risk taking by the bank even for a short time legitimises profits for the bank.

Contracts Must Be Legally Enforceable

Suppose the promise between you and the bank is not legally enforceable, and the following sequence of events occurs:

Day 1: The bank purchases the home for $400,000.

Day 2: The home drops sharply in value to $350,000.

Day 3: You renege on your promise.

Without the promise being legally enforceable even if it is Shariah-compliant, you can break your promise. And when you do, the bank suffers an unfair loss. Of course it can happen the other way, as when the home shoots up in value and the bank declines to sell you the home at $400,000. With BBA and murabahah, the promise of any party must be legally enforceable.

Profit Rate and Payment Terms Must Be Fixed

Both BBA and murabahah are debt-based contracts. For this reason, both the price and the payment terms must be known and fixed at the time of contracting. This is to prevent the occurrence of any gharar for both parties, when market interest rates change.

The fact that the deferred price is more than the spot price is acceptable, so long as payment terms are fixed at the time of contracting. And once the terms are fixed, they cannot be increased in case of late payment, or decreased in case of early payment.

Conventional loans, on the other hand, are usually floating-rate products. The cost of borrowing is adjusted up and down as interest rates change. The BBA and murabahah rates, once determined for a given contract, are not allowed to change regardless of what happens with interest rates in the economy.

BBA with "Floating Rate" Option

The practice of fixed-rate financing does bring risk to both the customer and the financial institution.

When rates are fixed during a low interest rate environment, customers are able to lock in a low cost of borrowing while banks cannot raise rates when those in the economy rise. Conversely, when rates are fixed during a high interest rate environment, banks are able to lock in a high profit margin while customers cannot benefit when rates fall.

A variable-rate financing product based on BBA was introduced in some countries, such as Malaysia, to balance out the risk that both customers and financial institutions face.

IN THE MARKETPLACE

Asian Finance Bank in Malaysia (www. asianfinancebank.com) offers a home financing scheme with two profit rate options—one that is fixed and the other that is pegged against a variable market rate but which is capped at a fixed ceiling rate.

The profit margin is computed based on a ceiling rate of 12 per cent. For a five-year, $60,000 loan, for example, this works out to $1,334.67 monthly. This is the amount that you are committed to pay every month.

If the Base Lending Rate (BLR[5]) plus margin used as a benchmark in the pricing calculation is 8 per cent per annum for a certain month, the instalment would be $1,216.58. This means that you would have overpaid for that month, and the bank would give you a rebate of $118.09 ($1,334.67 – $1,216.58). This rebate represents the difference between the ceiling profit rate of 12 per cent per annum and the rate of 8 per cent per annum for that month.

If, in the next month, the benchmark rate plus margin rises to 14 per cent, the bank would still charge at the ceiling rate of 12 per cent. This ceiling rate offers comfort to both the customer and the bank—the customer knows the maximum that he can be charged, and the bank is able to hedge against changing market rates up to the ceiling rate.

Profit Rate Benchmark Must Be Acceptable

The profit rate is often normally related to a market interest rate such as SIBOR (Singapore Interbank Offered Rate) and EIBOR (Emirates Interbank Offered Rate). This method of benchmarking is permitted in Shariah, although it is not ideal. It is allowed for practical reasons because similar market forces affect the cost of both Islamic and conventional borrowing, especially in an integrated financial market.

Dealing with Defaults, Late and Early Payments

Borrowers are in theory able to default, or wilfully delay payment, without incurring penalties because instalment payments are fixed. Wilful default by borrowers is a problem in BBA and murabahah financing.

Conventional lending, on the other hand, has a built-in disincentive against defaults—defaulters have to pay penalties and additional interest. Conventional lending also provides an incentive of a discount or rebate when the borrower repays earlier. Such penalties or rebates are due to time value of money, and are not allowed in Islamic financing.

In Case of Early Repayment

Some Islamic banks do grant rebates in case of early repayment, but only if it is an act of kindness and voluntary on the part of the bank. The rebate cannot be specified ahead of time in the contract.

Handling Late Payment and Defaults

There are several ways to provide a disincentive to handle late payments and defaults while remaining Shariah-compliant:

- The borrower is made to donate an amount to a charitable purpose. Such a payment cannot benefit the bank.
- The borrower is made to pay all remaining instalments immediately. This is not popular as it puts tremendous pressure on the borrower.
- The borrower is made to provide a security or a guarantor for the loan so that the bank has recourse, in the event of default.
- The loan instalments are rescheduled. If there are penalties, those amounts cannot benefit the bank and should be donated.

CONCLUSION

Debt-based financing using BBA and murabahah are the most popular Islamic financing methods. One reason for their popularity is that they resemble conventional loans in the way they are structured, for example, through the financing of lumpy assets like homes and cars with payment by instalment.

Beyond this similarity of outer appearance, there are very fundamental differences between conventional and Islamic loans. Besides the three we highlighted at the start (no riba, no haram assets, and mutual benefit is encouraged), we learned in this chapter about how contracts must be consecutive and separate in order to avoid riba.

We also learned that instalments are fixed to keep gharar in check, even when interest rates change, or when payments are late or early. In the end, Islamic banks have to put in place thorough due diligence procedures on customers to minimise loan defaults. Unlike conventional banks, Islamic banks cannot benefit from penalties arising from late payment.

Islamic financing principles based on debt, as we hope you have seen, are not difficult at all if you first have an understanding of how conventional loans work. Once you realise the surface similarities, the key differences between them become apparent.

In the next chapter, we learn about another popular Islamic financing method called *ijarah*, which works similarly to conventional leasing.

---

1   Note that conventional loans are mainly variable-rate loans.

2   Because of rounding, the last instalment amount will actually be smaller or larger than $2,865.72. The difference is usually not significant.

3   This formula uses present and future values to calculate the annual rate of the financing based on 10 monthly payments of $10,500 each and a purchase price today of $100,000. It is an easily available formula on financial calculators and spreadsheets.

4   The effective rate takes into account the compounding of interest at specified intervals. If the compounding interval is monthly, then interest is compounded monthly and payments are usually monthly as well. The term used is "monthly rest". Monthly rest is the most common compounding interval as it coincides with the most common payment interval.

5   The BLR is a minimum interest rate calculated by a financial institution based on a formula which takes into account the institution's cost of funds and other administrative costs.

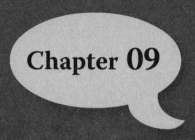

Chapter 09

FINANCING (BASED ON LEASING)

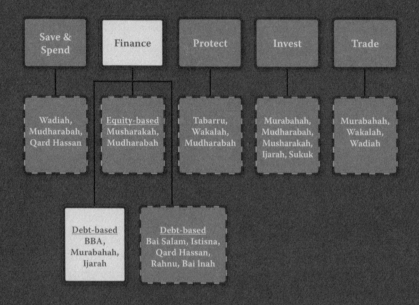

Save & Spend	Finance	Protect	Invest	Trade
Wadiah, Mudharabah, Qard Hassan	Equity-based Musharakah, Mudharabah	Tabarru, Wakalah, Mudharabah	Murabahah, Mudharabah, Musharakah, Ijarah, Sukuk	Murabahah, Wakalah, Wadiah

Debt-based
BBA, Murabahah, Ijarah

Debt-based
Bai Salam, Istisna, Qard Hassan, Rahnu, Bai Inah

LEASES HAVE EXISTED for thousands of years. In 1984, archaeologists found clay tablets from the ancient Sumerian city of Ur (in modern Iraq) that documented farm equipment leases from the year 2010 BCE. Two hundred and fifty years later, in 1760 BCE, the king of Babylonia in the famous Code of Hammurabi enacted the first leasing laws. The ancient civilisations of Egypt, Greece and Rome engaged in leasing transactions of real and personal property, while the Phoenicians actively promoted leasing by chartering ships to local merchants.

> **"Compared with renting, leasing is usually for a longer period and has more formal terms."**

A lease is a rental agreement in which the use of an asset is hired for a period of time. Compared with renting, leasing is usually for a longer period, such as two years, and has more formal terms.

Leasing today is popular all over the world in both conventional and Islamic finance. It is widely used among businesses of any size that need equipment and facilities, want to conserve cash and lines of credit, or wish to enjoy certain tax benefits.

How Is Leasing Different from Renting and Buying?

If you want to get a new or used car to drive around with, you have a choice of renting, leasing or buying it (see Figure 9.1). What is the difference?

If you need a car for a two-week driving vacation in Australia, you would very likely rent one. Renting allows you to use the car for a short period of time, and you usually have the option of extending the rental period by paying a pre-determined daily rate. But if you were studying overseas and need a car for work purposes outside the campus, you would do well to consider leasing it.

In comparison, a lease is like a long-term rental agreement where ownership of the asset stays with the lessor (the company that is leasing you the car), although it has more formal terms than renting. A lease obligates both the lessor and the lessee for a stated period of time, typically a year or more. An attractive feature of a lease is that the lessor cannot raise the rate or change other terms until the lease runs out, unless the lease allows such modifications. At the end of the lease term, you can renew the lease, return the car to the lessor, or even buy it. The terms are that flexible.

You could of course buy a car from the start, instead of leasing it, for your study and work stint abroad. But, there is the question of how you would pay for it. Besides, buying the car is normally for long-term, permanent use.

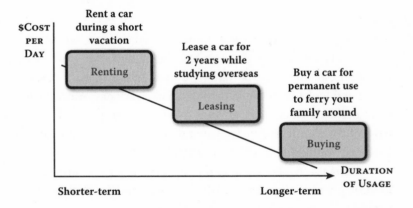

Figure 9.1 Comparing renting, leasing and buying

Between the financing terms of buying and leasing of a car, those of the latter are easier to execute as it involves less documentation and takes a shorter time to conclude a deal. Leasing does not require collateral, although enquiries are very often made into the creditworthiness of the lessee. The physical presence of a tangible asset, whose ownership remains with the lessor, makes certain formalities less necessary.

Let us take a closer look at leasing. (Fortunately, you would already know how to calculate the rental amount of a lease as it is determined in exactly the same way as in mortgage financing, which we discussed in Chapter 8.)

Conventional Leasing

There are two main types of conventional leases—operating leases and financial leases.

Operating Leases

An operating lease is an agreement between:

- a lessor who owns an asset and who wants to earn a return without losing ownership; and
- a lessee who needs to use the asset and who cannot afford to buy it or does not want to own it.

It is a very straightforward agreement as we can see in this example. Let us suppose that Isra has just begun a two-year MBA programme in the US. She finds a part-time job to help pay for tuition and looks for a car to drive to work every day. A car dealer offers her a new Ford Escort on a two-year lease term. She pays two months' instalment as deposit and drives the car off the lot the same day. The dealer agrees to arrange for insurance and take care of maintenance. At the end of two years, the car is to be returned to the dealer, and the leasing agreement would end for both parties. A summary is shown in Figure 9.2.

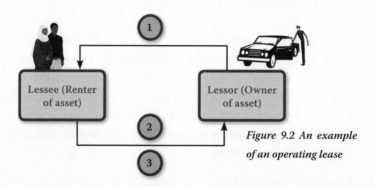

Figure 9.2 An example of an operating lease

❶ The dealer transfers possession of the car to Isra but retains ownership of the car throughout the lease period.

❷ Over the lease period, Isra makes monthly payments.

❸ At the end of two years, Isra returns the car to the dealer.

Financial Leases

A financial lease is the other major type of lease. The main difference between this and the operating lease is that the lessee has the option to purchase the asset at the end of the lease. There are other differences of course, but let us for now look at an example to see how a financial lease works. If Isra agrees instead to a financial lease, then the third step will be different (see Figure 9.3).

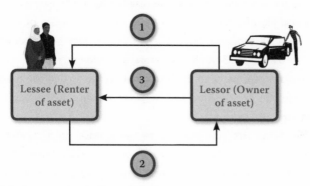

Figure 9.3 An example of a financial lease

❶ The dealer transfers possession of the car to Isra but retains ownership of the car throughout the lease period.

❷ Over the lease period, Isra makes monthly payments.

❸ At the end of two years, Isra decides to purchase the car. The dealer then transfers ownership of the car to Isra.

When Are Financial Leases Used?

A lease is considered a financial lease if any one or more of the following conditions is true:

I. The lease contains an option to purchase the property for less than fair market value.

2. The ownership of the asset is transferred to the lessee at the end of the lease term.
3. The lease term is 75%, or more, of the asset's estimated economic life.
4. The present value of the lease payments exceeds 90% of the fair market value of the property.

The first two conditions are self-explanatory. Both suggest that eventual ownership of the asset is a primary intention of the lease. The other two conditions require some explaining.

The economic life of an asset is the period of actual usefulness of the asset. Beyond this phase, it becomes cheaper to replace or scrap the asset than to continue maintaining it. For example, the physical life of a computer can be as long as 10 years or more, whereas its economic life is about three to four years because of obsolescence. Beyond four years, breakdowns can be costly as replacement parts are hard to come by. Continued use is also likely to be expensive as new software requires more memory and hard disk space to run.

Following this rule alone, a two-year lease on a computer with an economic life of four years would be accounted for as an operating lease, while a three-year lease would be accounted for as a financial lease.

The fourth condition roughly means that if you are paying over 90% of what the asset is worth, it should be considered a capital lease or purchase, because paying such a significant proportion is as good as buying the asset.

In the end, the lessor in a financial lease will have recovered all, or most of the cost, of the equipment from the rentals paid by the lessee. In an operating lease, the lessor will normally have a substantial investment or residual value on completion of the lease.

Why Leasing Is Popular

Leasing provides several advantages to lessees[1]:

- ◆ Leasing ready-to-use equipment can be more attractive if the asset requires lengthy preparation and setting up. Specialised computer and telecommunications equipment are popular assets used in leasing.

- ◆ Leasing avoids having to own the asset that will be required only for a season or temporary period.

- ◆ Leasing for short periods protects against obsolescence. But of course, lease payments are accordingly higher.

- ◆ Lease payments can provide up to 100 per cent financing, whereas there are usually downpayment requirements when buying.

- ◆ Leasing often comes with tax advantages and is employed by governments to encourage the use of certain assets. For example, if the government of a country is keen to promote computer literacy, it would provide generous tax deductions for computer leases.

An Overview of Islamic Leasing (Ijarah)

Islamic leasing and conventional leasing are similar in that it means to obtain a good or service on rent. The Islamic term for leasing is *ijarah*, and it is used in two ways.

1. First, it means to obtain the services of a person and paying him a wage in return. Such services may be provided regularly, as when a person is paid a monthly salary for legal work, or they may be one-off, such as paying $10 to a courier to deliver a package. This is not the type of ijarah that we are concerned with in this book.

2. The second type of ijarah, which we are discussing in this chapter, relates to the renting of an asset and acquiring the right to use and derive profit or benefit from it.

Ijarah was originally not a mode of financing. Over time, however, due to Islamic finance evolving around the long-existing conventional finance framework, ijarah became a financing product, a transformation that does not go against Shariah—so long as various rules of Islamic leasing are observed. For example:

◆ The lessor continues to own the asset during the lease period. Hence, the risks and obligations of *ownership* are borne by the lessor. On the other hand, the risks and obligations of *use* are borne by the lessee. For example, if Idris leases his home to Ilhan, Ilhan would be responsible for paying for utilities. If the price of the home falls 30 per cent during the lease period, Idris absorbs the loss completely—unless Ilhan used the home negligently that caused major damage and a drop in price.

◆ The rental amounts must be determined and fixed at the start of the contract for the whole duration of the lease. Different amounts can be charged at different phases of the lease, as long as the amount of rent for each phase is fixed at the start. For example, suppose Ilhan agrees to lease Idris' home for two years, the contract would be valid if it specified that Ilhan pays $2,000 a month in the first year, and $3,000 a month in the second year. In this case, the terms are certain at the start of the entire lease, and the contract would thus be Shariah-compliant.

◆ The lease begins only when the leased asset is delivered to the lessee, and not when payment is made or the lease contract is signed, as is usually the case in conventional leases.

The above list of Islamic lease features is an overview and is not complete. As we next look at how the various types of Islamic leases work, you will no doubt see strong similarities between them and conventional leases. For this reason, it is important that we clearly understand the significant differences, a subject we will return to later in the chapter.

TYPES OF ISLAMIC LEASES

Like conventional leases, Islamic leases have several variations although each is fundamentally based on either an operating or a financial lease.

Operating Leases

Like a conventional operating lease, an ijarah contract is an agreement between a lessor, who owns an asset, and a lessee who needs to use the asset and who cannot afford to buy it or does not want to own it. Let us look at a simple example to see how ijarah works.

Lease with Two Parties—Lessor and Lessee

Suppose Imram finds a car he wishes to lease for two years and he chooses an ijarah contract instead of a conventional lease. You will see that it is no different from a conventional operating lease at this point (see Figure 9.4).

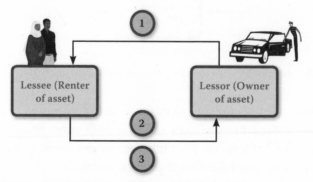

Figure 9.4 An example of an operating lease with two parties

❶ The dealer transfers possession of the car to Imram but retains ownership of the car throughout the lease period.

❷ Over the lease period, Imram makes monthly payments.

❸ At the end of two years, Imram returns the car to the dealer.

Lease with Three Parties—Lessor, Vendor and Lessee

In the example of Imram just discussed, the lessor in fact plays two roles—as owner of the asset, which he had financed himself, and subsequently as lessor. This is a relatively less common situation.

A far more common scenario involves three parties—an Islamic bank who plays the role of financial intermediary, a vendor of the asset to be sold and later leased, and the lessee. To illustrate this three-party lease arrangement, let us stick with Imran, who now wishes to lease a car for four years (see Figure 9.5).

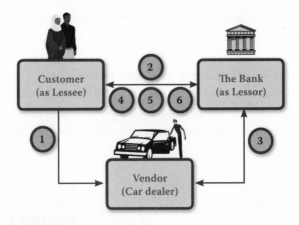

Figure 9.5 An example of an operating lease with three parties

❶ Imran finds a vendor and identifies a car that he wishes to lease.

❷ Imran approaches the bank and they both enter an agreement where the bank promises to buy the car and Imran promises to lease the car from the bank thereafter.

❸ The bank buys the car from the vendor. Car ownership is transferred to the bank.

❹ The bank transfers possession of the car to Imran for his use.
❺ Imran pays monthly lease payments over the next four years.
❻ At the end of the ijarah period of four years, Imran returns the car to the bank.

Lease with Customer Appointed as Agent

The bank may appoint the customer as an agent to mitigate its risk of ownership during the agency period (see Figure 9.6). This period would end just before the lease contract commences.

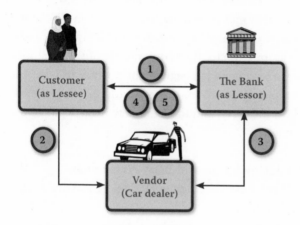

Figure 9.6 An example of an operating lease with customer as agent

❶ The bank appoints Imran as an agent in an operating lease agreement for a car.
❷ Imran identifies a vendor and selects a car on behalf of the bank (since Imran is acting as an agent of the bank).
❸ The bank pays the vendor, who in turn transfers ownership of the car to the bank.
❹ At this point, the agency contract comes to an end. The bank transfers possession to Imran, after which Imran pays the lease in instalments. Ownership remains with the bank.
❺ At the end of the ijarah period of four years, the car is returned to the bank.

In summary, an ijarah or Islamic operating lease contract provides for the sale of the right to use and enjoy the advantages of something belonging to another.

The lessor, such as a bank, retains ownership of the asset, together with all the rights and responsibilities that go with ownership. Once the asset is returned to the bank, it can lease the asset to another customer, or sell the asset. The bank, however, then faces the risk that the asset may not be in good shape, is outdated, or is a specialised piece of equipment for which there is a thin secondary market. As a result, the bank could be stuck with a hard-to-sell asset that may have to be sold at a heavily discounted price.

The bank would face less of such a problem if the ijarah period is the same as, or close to, the economic life of the asset, or the value of the lease payments is a significant portion of what the asset is worth. In such a situation, there is little or insignificant residual value left in the asset, and the bank may make a gift of the asset to the customer.

Comparing Ijarah and BBA-Murabahah

You may have noticed similarities between ijarah and BBA-murabahah:

- They are debt-based financing products where the bank gives the customer financing for which it charges a profit margin.
- The bank acquires ownership of an asset on behalf of the customer.
- Instalments are paid over time to cover the cost of the asset and to provide a profit margin for the bank.

In terms of differences, there are two main ones:

- In ijarah, the bank continues to be the owner throughout the ijarah period while the customer receives the benefits of using the asset. As such, the risks associated with ownership of the asset remain with the bank. In BBA-murabahah, on the other hand, the customer is the owner of the asset. This is not unique to Islamic finance. In a conventional lease, ownership stays with the bank, and in a conventional purchase, ownership is with the customer.

- The instalment amounts are fixed in the case of BBA-murabahah. When benchmark interest rates rise or fall, the instalment amount cannot be changed. In the case of ijarah, however, the instalment amounts can be adjusted depending on anticipated economic conditions, so long as the instalment amounts are specified and certain at the very start of the ijarah contract.

Financial Leases

A financial lease ends with a purchase option, which gives the customer the right to buy the asset at a pre-agreed price, at the end of the ijarah period. This is called Al-Ijarah-Thummal Al-Bai (AITAB) or Ijarah Muntahia Bittamleek (IMB)[2], and is similar to a hire-purchase contract in conventional finance.

AITAB consists of two separate contracts—a lease contract (*al ijarah*) and a sales contract (*al bai*). Upon completion of the rental period or early settlement, the lessor will then enter into the sales contract with the lessee to sell the asset at a pre-agreed selling price.

Once you know how an operating lease works, AITAB is clear-cut as it simply combines an operating lease contract with a sales contract. The steps outlined on the following page are identical to the steps described in Figure 9.7 with the only difference that step 6 refers to a sales contract.

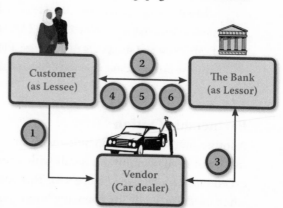

Figure 9.7 An example of a financial lease with three parties

In Figure 9.7 (see previous page):

❶ Imran finds a vendor and identifies a car that he wishes to lease.

❷ Imran approaches the bank, and they both enter an agreement where the bank promises to buy the car and Imran promises to lease the car from the bank thereafter.

❸ The bank buys the car from the vendor. Car ownership is transferred to the bank.

❹ The bank transfers possession of the car to Imran for his use.

❺ Imran pays monthly lease payments over the next four years.

❻ At the end of the ijarah period of four years, a separate sales contract (al-bai) is drawn up with Imran and ownership of the car is transferred to him.

IN THE MARKETPLACE

Dubai Islamic Bank in the United Arab Emirates (www.dib.ae) offers financial leases based on IMB. The lessee becomes the owner of the asset by purchasing it from the lessor during or at the end of the lease period at an agreed sale price. A minimum downpayment of 50% of the purchase price is required and the

financing period is up to 10 years. The bank's profit rate is fixed throughout the lease period.

Hong Leong Islamic Bank in Malaysia (www.hlisb.com.my) offers a financial lease based on AITAB for the hire-purchase of cars. New and used cars can be leased for up to 90% of their purchase price, and for a period of up to 108 months.

Partnership Option

Another method of ijarah ending with the transfer of ownership to the customer is combining ijarah with a joint-venture partnership called *musharakah* (see Figure 9.8). This option is not common and when used, is usually for financing home purchases.

Musharakah is discussed in greater detail in the next chapter. For now, here is a brief illustration of how an Islamic lease can be created using musharakah.

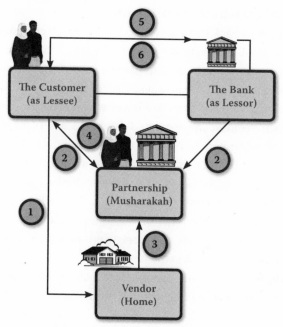

Figure 9.8 An example of a finance lease based on musharakah

❶ Izzah finds a vendor and identifies an apartment she wishes to purchase.

❷ The bank and Izzah enter into a partnership specifically formed to finance the purchase of the property identified by Izzah. They both contribute to the equity of the partnership in a certain ratio.

❸ The partnership buys the apartment from the vendor (ownership of the apartment is transferred to the partnership).

❹ The partnership leases the asset to Izzah for her use.

❺ Izzah pays monthly lease payments over the next four years. A portion of the rental is used to redeem part of the bank's ownership stake in the property. This results in a decrease in the bank's stake over time.

❻ At the end of the ijarah period of four years, the bank's stake in the property reduces to zero, and Izzah becomes the full owner of the property.

Sale-and-Leaseback Arrangement

A sale-and-leaseback (leaseback for short) is an arrangement where the owner of an asset sells the asset and leases it back for a period. Thus one continues to be able to use the asset, but no longer owns it. A leaseback is a suitable arrangement for the seller to raise money by offloading a valuable asset to a buyer who is interested in making a long-term secured investment. Leasebacks are common in the business world and are not usually requested by individuals.

When a leaseback takes place between a customer and a bank, the asset remains in the possession of the customer while ownership is transferred to the bank. The result is an immediate cash inflow to the customer (in the form of the sale price of the asset). The customer continues to use the asset while making periodic ijarah rentals to the bank, which is the new owner.

To further explain the ijarah leaseback arrangement, let us suppose that Ibrahim owns a printing business.

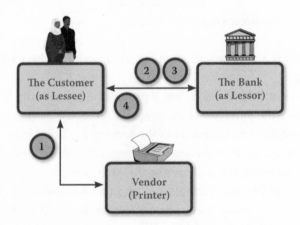

Figure 9.9 An example of a sale-and-leaseback arrangement

In Figure 9.9,

❶ Ibrahim purchases a printer from a vendor (or Ibrahim may already own the printer). The printer is worth $100,000 and Ibrahim needs working capital for his business.

❷ Ibrahim sells the printer to the bank on cash basis. The possession of asset remains with Ibrahim while ownership is transferred to the bank.

❸ Ibrahim and the bank enter into an ijarah leaseback contract. Ibrahim pays rentals over future time periods.

❹ The bank transfers ownership of the printer to Ibrahim at the end of the ijarah period either through a gift or a sale.

CLOSE-UP ON ISLAMIC LEASE FEATURES

We have seen how conventional and Islamic leases work, and that the differences between them do not appear to be many.[3] However, the few differences that exist are critical to observe because they determine whether a lease transaction is Shariah-compliant or not. For this reason, we feel it is important to have a more complete understanding of Islamic lease features.

The features can be generally categorised into those that are considered before the lease contract commences, and those that become important during the lease itself (see Figure 9.10).

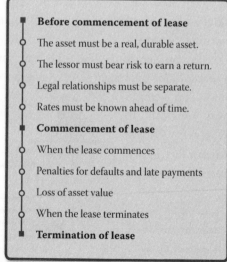

- **Before commencement of lease**
  - The asset must be a real, durable asset.
  - The lessor must bear risk to earn a return.
  - Legal relationships must be separate.
  - Rates must be known ahead of time.
- **Commencement of lease**
  - When the lease commences
  - Penalties for defaults and late payments
  - Loss of asset value
  - When the lease terminates
- **Termination of lease**

Figure 9.10 Considerations before and after commencement of lease

Before the Lease Commences

The Asset Must Be A Real, Durable Asset

Cars and homes are real assets. They can be touched and seen, and are long-lasting. Islamic leases must be based on such assets. On the other hand, food and money cannot be leased because they are short-lived; they are not real assets.

The involvement of real assets is a fundamental aspect not only of ijarah but of Islamic finance in general. The use of a real asset provides a linkage between the financial sector and the real sector, contributing to economic stability.

In conventional finance, on the other hand, financial assets can be multiplied many times in value without any direct linkage to real assets. Instruments such as futures and options can make the financial markets vulnerable to speculation.

The Lessor Must Bear Risk to Earn a Return

The lessor must bear ownership risk during the ijarah period in order for its profits to be deemed legitimate. In a conventional financial lease, ownership risk is transferred to the lessee as the transaction is accounted for as a purchase. This would not comply with Shariah because the lessor does not retain any ownership risk when earning its profits.

You can see in Figure 9.11 that the lessee acts as a trustee (*amanah*) for the leased asset. As we have seen for deposit products based on *wadiah yad amanah* in Chapter 7, no compensation can be paid to the

The Customer (as Lessee)	The Bank (as Lessor)
Trustee of asset	Must bear risk

Figure 9.11

Ensuring Shariah compliance for an Islamic lease

Lessor cannot receive compensation if the asset suffers an unexpected loss in value due to factors beyond the lessee's control, such as a fire or a flood.

lessor if the asset suffers an unexpected loss due to factors beyond the lessee's control.

A lessor can, of course, mitigate its risk by buying Islamic insurance (called *takaful*) to protect its bottom line in case the asset's value falls significantly as a result of negative unforeseen factors.

Legal Relationships Must Be Separate

In a financial lease arrangement where a sale takes place at the end of the lease, the legal relationships of the lease and sale must be separate as depicted in Figure 9.12.

If they are combined, the sale portion would look like a forward contract when one considers that the arrangement is made today. A forward agreement would cause major *gharar* (extreme uncertainty) as it is equivalent to "selling what one does not have".

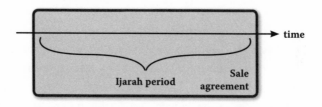

Figure 9.12 The lease and the sale should be separate events

If the ijarah and sale are separate, then the sales portion is activated only in the future when the ijarah is over.

- The ijarah is a lease contract with a unilateral promise to sell the asset to the customer at a pre-determined price.
- Once the lease expires and the lessee has made all payments, the sales contract kicks in and obligates the lessor to sell if the lessee chooses to buy.

By separating the legal relationships, the sale becomes a spot sale. By combining them, the sale becomes a forward contract.

Rates Must Be Known Ahead of Time

The regular lease amounts to be paid must be known at the time of contracting for the whole period of ijarah. This, however, could work against both the bank and customer as market rates and conditions may fluctuate during the ijarah period. There are a few ways to mitigate this risk:

1. First, the ijarah period can be divided into several shorter intervals with varying but pre-determined rates, thus creating a floating-rate ijarah.
2. Second, one may insert a rent adjustment clause in the ijarah contract, although this is not ideal—the rate adjustment is often pegged to a market interest rate, such as the inflation rate.

According to renowned Islamic scholar Dr Taqi Usmani:

> It is thus clear that the use of the rate of interest merely as a benchmark does not render the contract invalid as an interest-based transaction. It is, however, advisable at all times to avoid using interest even as a benchmark, so that an Islamic transaction is totally distinguished from an un-Islamic one, having no resemblance of interest whatsoever.[4]

During the Lease

When the Lease Commences

Rental is payable only when the leased asset is delivered to the lessee, and not from the day the asset is paid for. If the vendor has been paid but has delayed the delivery after receiving payment, the lessee should not be liable for the rent during the period of delay.

Penalties for Defaults and Late Payments

If a customer is late or defaults on a payment, the amount becomes a debt. The Islamic bank is not allowed to charge an additional amount for its own benefit. Rather, the customer would be expected to contribute a certain sum to charity. This sum of money is not considered *zakat*, and is thus not part of the obligatory contribution that every Muslim makes in his concern for the needy.

Loss of Asset Value

The lessee is responsible for any loss to the asset only by his negligence and for normal wear and tear. But he cannot be made liable for a loss caused by factors beyond his control, such as an outbreak of war or a financial crisis that would result in a huge drop in asset values.

When the Lease Terminates

An ijarah can be terminated under any one of the following situations:

- When the lease period is over.
- When the lessee breaches a term of the agreement. The lessor, who has the right to terminate the ijarah contract unilaterally, does so.
- When the lessor and lessee agree mutually to end the contract.

If the lessee does not breach any terms of the agreement, the lessor has no right to terminate the contract unilaterally.

CONCLUSION

Islamic leasing is especially important for public sector projects in Muslim countries where profit-sharing and joint ventures are difficult to practise. For example, large infrastructure projects on sovereign land, such as those that build and operate roads, bridges and airports, are based on leases.

Islamic leasing creates a great potential for securitisation, which refers to the combining of various large, lumpy income-producing assets into a pool, and then splitting that pool into shares or certificates. These are sold to investors who share the risk and reward of the performance of those assets. These ijarah certificates are called *sukuk,* and each certificate represents the holder's proportionate ownership in the leased asset.

Securitisation helps increase liquidity for Islamic banks and raises the participation of investors. These investors can use sukuk to increase their wealth by investing their savings in a security that is based on real assets and which complies with Shariah.

Leasing is an important form of financing for both Muslim and non-Muslim communities. Compared with conventional leasing, Islamic leasing follows Shariah principles. Among other things, Islamic leasing involves real assets, avoids *riba* (interest) and *haram* (forbidden) activities, is highly transparent in terms of contracting, and requires that the Islamic bank conducts thorough due diligence on a customer to minimise defaults.

Such Shariah practices have clear benefits for any economy. The linkage between the financial sector and the real sector is directly strengthened as speculative activity is minimised and economic stability is enhanced.

In the next chapter, we will discuss other forms of Islamic financing, which may be debt-based or equity-based.

---

1   For lessees that are companies, leases provide other advantages as well. When structured as an operating lease, the lease can be treated as "off-balance sheet" financing and does not show up on the books as debt. Leasing can be tax-advantageous when the lessee is unable to enjoy the tax benefits of owning.

2   AITAB and IMB are similar. AITAB, also called *ijara wa iqtina,* is a lease that ends with a sale, while IMB is a lease that ends with ownership transferred. AITAB is more popular in South-East Asia while IMB is more accepted in the Middle East. We will use AITAB generally to refer to both methods.

3   A study by Mateeha Fatima, who was a student at the Karachi Institute of Economics and Technology, (www.pafkiet.edu.pk) found that of 12 criteria used to examine the features of conventional and Islamic operating leases, 10 were found to be similar.

4   www.accountancy.com.pk/docs/islam_ijarah.pdf

Chapter 10

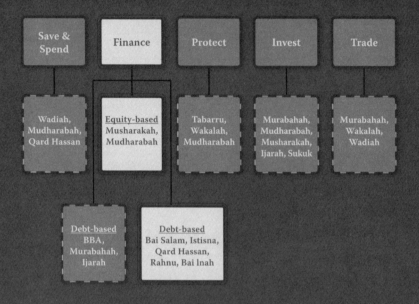

OTHER ISLAMIC FINANCING METHODS

WE HAVE COVERED the three methods on which most of Islamic financing in South-East Asia is based—BBA and *murabahah* (cost-plus financing methods) and *ijarah* (leasing). What we will look at in this chapter are brief descriptions of other Islamic financing methods, which can be broadly divided into two categories—those that are equity-based and those that are debt-based (see Table 10.1).

Table 10.1 Other Islamic financing methods

Category	Main purpose	Arabic name
Equity-based	Profit share	Mudharabah
Equity-based	Joint venture	Musharakah
Equity-based	Diminishing ownership	Diminishing musharakah
Debt-based	Deferred delivery	Bai salam
Debt-based	Manufacture-sale	Istisna
Debt-based	Benevolent loan	Qard hassan
Debt-based	Pawnbroking	Rahnu
Debt-based	Sale and buyback	Bai inah

EQUITY-BASED FINANCING METHODS

There are two main kinds of profit-loss sharing (or equity-based), financing contracts:

- *mudharabah*; and
- *musharakah.*

They are far less popular than debt-based financing methods because, as we will see, they are more challenging to implement. Nevertheless, while equity-based methods are less popular, they are ideal for community building.

Consider the plight of the entrepreneur who has a promising idea for a new venture but does not have sufficient capital. If he were to go for debt-based financing, the bank would very likely make him pay a higher profit mark-up. That is because his venture will be perceived as having a fairly high chance of failing within a year. High financing charges increase the danger of failure.

Equity-based methods of financing provide an important alternative where the entrepreneur and financier work together to receive a portion of profits from the venture. Compensation for the bank is determined directly by the fortunes of the business for which it has a hand in shaping.

Profit-Sharing (Mudharabah)

Profit-sharing or mudharabah was discussed in Chapter 7 on Islamic deposits where the customer is the capital provider to the bank. The concept is exactly the same in this chapter, except that in a financing situation, the bank (not the customer) is the capital provider. The customer plays the role of entrepreneur who seeks funds to operate a business.

If profits are generated, the profits are distributed according to a pre-agreed profit-sharing ratio (PSR). Losses, on the other hand, are entirely absorbed by the bank. A simple mudharabah financing structure is presented in Figure 10.1.

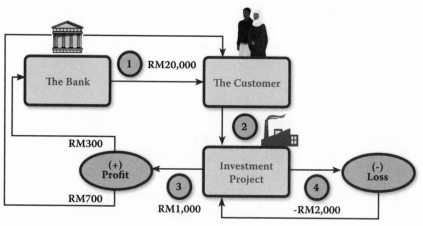

Figure 10.1 An example of a mudharabah financing structure

Let us suppose Jalilah has a business idea to recycle old computer parts for cash. The bank reviews her business plan and agrees to fund the project.

❶ Jalilah obtains financing of RM20,000 from the bank. The PSR is 30–70 (30% to the bank and 70% to Jalilah).

❷ Jalilah sets up the business and manages its operations.

❸ Suppose there is a net profit of RM1,000, then 30% or RM300 is the bank's share and 70% or RM700 is Jalilah's share.

❹ In the event of a loss of, say RM2,000, the bank (capital provider) is solely responsible for the loss.

IN THE MARKETPLACE

The Islamic International Arab Bank in the Kingdom of Jordan (www.iiabank.com.jo) offers a financing product based on the profit-sharing contract of mudharabah. It is used particularly for financing projects where the bank provides  the necessary capital to finance a specific project, whether partially or in full. On the other hand, the customer provides the necessary labour investment to run the project. Profits are shared through agreed upon percentages.

The customer can only face a loss if any negligence or infractions are revealed. In the case of an unsuccessful project, the customer loses his or her labour invested while the bank loses its capital investment.

Joint-Venturing (Musharakah)

A joint venture is a business enterprise undertaken by two or more entities (persons or companies) to share the expenses and profits of a particular business project. It is a form of partnership that is limited to a particular purpose. Among the main benefits of joint ventures is that partners save money and reduce their risks through capital and resource sharing.

Musharakah refers to an Islamic joint-venture partnership in which the bank and its customer agree to combine financial resources to undertake and manage a business venture, according to the terms of an agreement. Profits are shared according to a PSR while losses are shared in proportion to the amount of capital each contributed.

Figure 10.2 shows a basic musharakah structure where the customer Jamil and the bank put in equal capital of $50,000 each into a project. According to terms of the agreement, profits will be apportioned 60–40 in favour of Jamil as he will be the main party managing the project.

Losses, on the other hand, will be shared equally. Banks mostly leave the responsibility of management to the customer-partner, and retain the right of supervision and follow-up. Or they might even become active partners in a whole range of activities to ensure that the objectives of the company are met.

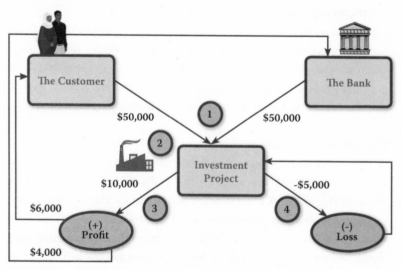

Figure 10.2 An example of a musharakah financing structure

❶ The bank and Jamil agree to each contribute $50,000 to a joint-venture project.

❷ Jamil is the main party to manage the project.

❸ Suppose profits amount to $10,000, these will be shared $6,000 or 60% to Jamil and $4,000 or 40% to the bank.

❹ If there is a loss of, say $5,000, the loss is shared 50–50, that is, $2,500 each. The loss directly brings down the value of the project's assets.

IN THE MARKETPLACE

The Kurdistan International Bank for Investment and Development in Iraq (www. kibid.com) offers a financing product based on the joint-venture contract of musharakah. Such contracts are commonly used for industrial, agriculture and infrastructure projects.

Comparing Mudharabah and Musharakah

Equity-based financing using mudharabah and musharakah involves the sharing of risk and returns. These two methods of financing are often compared in terms of their differences (see Table 10.2). To simplify the comparison, let us suppose that ABC Bank is the capital provider and Jason is the entrepreneur in a financing situation.

Diminishing Musharakah

A financing transaction based on diminishing musharakah is straightforward. At the start of the transaction, the bank owns most of the asset. As instalments are made by the customer, the customer's share increases while the bank's share declines or diminishes. The ownership of the bank ends when all payments are made and the customer completely owns the asset.

A Simple Diminishing Musharakah Example

Figure 10.3 on page 186 shows a basic diminishing musharakah financing structure between a bank and a customer called Jessica, who wants to purchase a store to run a printing business. We will follow this up with a more elaborate example later.

Table 10.2 Comparing mudharabah and musharakah

Feature	Mudharabah	Musharakah
Capital	This comes solely from ABC Bank.	Capital comes from ABC Bank and Jason in a specified proportion, such as 70–30.
Management of the business	Only Jason manages the business.	Both the bank and Jason take part in managing the business.
Profits	Profits are shared according to a PSR. The ratio is generally tilted in favour of the bank because it is the sole capital provider.	Profits are shared according to a PSR. The ratio is generally tilted in favour of the more active partner, who is normally the entrepreneur.
Losses	The bank absorbs all losses unless Jason is found to be negligent.	Losses are apportioned according to each partner's capital contribution or to a pre-agreed ratio.
Liability	The bank's liability is limited to the capital provided unless it has given authority to Jason to incur debt on its behalf.*	Each partner has unlimited liability.
Ownership of assets	The assets are owned solely by the bank.	Ownership is apportioned according to each partner's capital contribution. Each partner's assets can rise or fall in value due to market forces.
Liquidation of assets	Either party can withdraw from the business anytime it deems fit.**	Either party can withdraw from the business anytime it deems fit.**

* This is fair because the bank does not take part in the management of the business and cannot be held responsible for the risks created by Jason, the entrepreneur.
** This provides liquidity for the partners. However, a sudden withdrawal by a partner can cause instability and material damage. What is encouraged is constructive liquidation, where a valuation is done on the business and a partner may withdraw according to specified time periods.

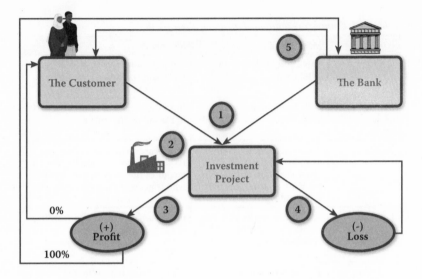

Figure 10.3 An example of a diminishing musharakah financing structure

❶ Jessica goes to the bank to seek a loan for her business. She and the bank agree to the business plan and to jointly contribute capital to the business based on diminishing musharakah.

❷ The store is purchased, and Jessica manages its operations while the bank oversees the accounting system. They share specific responsibilities as stated in the contract.

❸ Profits are shared on a PSR. Jessica has agreed to transfer her share of profits to the bank, thereby gradually diminishing the bank's ownership of the store.

❹ Losses are shared in proportion to their capital contributions. This brings down the value of the asset while keeping their respective shares in the store unchanged.

❺ Once the bank's ownership share has been redeemed, the ownership of the property is transferred to Jessica.

The financing of home loans is a naturally good fit for diminishing musharakah. Profits are sourced from generally-predictable rental payments of which a portion is set aside for reducing the bank's ownership share.

The diminishing musharakah structure has two main contracts:

- one for the musharakah agreement; and
- a separate sales and purchase agreement not linked to that of the musharakah, for the sale of the asset.

Another Diminishing Musharakah Example

Figure 10.4 shows a more detailed example of a diminishing musharakah structure that illustrates this point.

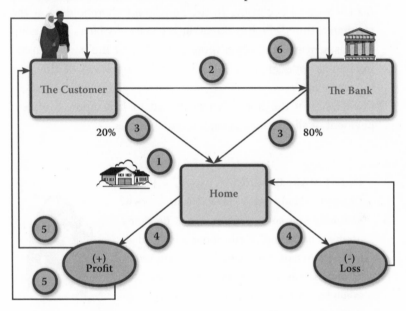

Figure 10.4 An example of a diminishing musharakah financing structure

❶ Jana identifies a home he wishes to purchase and obtains price and other relevant details.

❷ Jana approaches the bank with the details and financing is arranged using diminishing musharakah. Jana also agrees to take the house on lease and to make regular rental and capital payments to the bank.

❸ Jana contributes 20% and the bank, 80%, to own the home. The bank thus possesses 80% of the home initially.

❹ Jana pays a monthly instalment consisting of rental plus an additional sum to redeem a portion of the bank's share of the home. [Note: We drew this as profit appearing from the home just so it is consistent with the previous figure (Figure 10.3). For the same reason, we left the loss branch in the figure, even though a loss is not possible because contractual monthly instalments are expected.]

❺ The periodic rental amount is shared between Jana and the bank (as co-owners) according to the percentage shareholding at the particular time, which is 80–20 at the start. As Jana's ownership increases over time, when more and more of the bank's capital portion is redeemed by Jana, a larger proportion of the rent becomes Jana's.

❻ Ownership of the home is transferred to Jana upon complete payment of all rentals and capital redemptions.

IN THE MARKETPLACE

Dawood Islamic Bank in Pakistan (www. dawoodislamic.com) offers a financing product based on diminishing musharakah for the purchase, construction and renovation of homes. For the purchase of a home, for example, the bank's maximum financing is up to 85% and for a duration of up to 20 years.

Mudharabah and Musharakah Are Ideal for Partnerships

Moving our focus away from the consumer for a moment, let us look at how mudharabah and musharakah are ideal for partnership arrangements that support the mutual-benefit objective of Shariah.

With the bank playing the role of financial intermediary, a two-tier mudharabah framework can be created (see Figure 10.5).

The first tier is between the bank and depositors who place their money in the bank's investment account and agree to receive a PSR. The depositors are the capital providers (and are solely responsible for losses) while the bank is the manager of the funds.

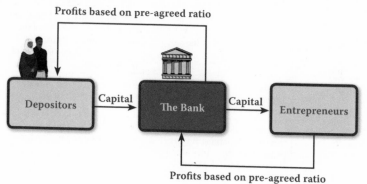

Figure 10.5 A two-tier mudharabah framework

The second tier is between the bank and entrepreneurs who seek financing from the bank for their business ventures. The bank agrees to receive a PSR. In this situation, the bank is the capital provider (and is solely responsible for losses) while the entrepreneurs are the managers of the funds.

Another variation is a mudharabah-musharakah framework where in the second tier, the entrepreneurs and the bank both provide capital and are jointly responsible for losses in proportion to their share capital. The second tier can also be based on diminishing musharakah where the bank's share is progressively reduced in favour of the entrepreneurs.

Comparing Diminishing Musharakah and BBA

You can see that both diminishing musharakah and BBA (from Chapter 8) can be used for financing home purchases.

What are the differences? Besides the fact that diminishing musharakah is based on equity and BBA is based on debt, there are other differences as listed in Table 10.3 overleaf. Some of their features are rather technical and would require more careful study beyond this book.

Table 10.3 *Comparing diminishing musharakah and BBA*

Feature	Diminishing Musharakah (DM)	BBA
Value of asset	The value of the home is continually adjusted over time to reflect market value.	The selling price is based on the purchase price plus the bank's profit margin. The selling price does not reflect market value.
Returns	The rental amount can be adjusted to reflect current market conditions.	Returns are based on a fixed selling price.
Penalties for defaults	The rental amount due to the bank depends on its proportionate equity share. Defaults cause the bank's share to remain constant (that is, not decrease), thereby entitling it to higher-than-expected rentals in subsequent periods.	Normally charged and contributed to charity.
Where used?	DM is globally recognised as Shariah-compliant.	BBA is mainly recognised in South-East Asia and generally not in the Middle East.
Transfer of ownership	Ownership is transferred at the end of the contract when the customer has redeemed 100% of the asset.	Ownership is transferred at the start of the contract after the bank and customer have entered into a sales and purchase contract.

We have thus far only skimmed the surface of mudharabah, musharakah and diminishing musharakah contracts. What is fundamental is that they are the basic methods by which financial resources are mobilised and combined with entrepreneurial and managerial skills for the purpose of mutual benefit and risk taking.

Equity-based methods are not easy for banks to implement because they have to perform an enhanced level of due diligence and put in place stringent risk-management controls while joint projects are ongoing. It is also difficult at the start of a project to determine who would be a good business partner and who is unsuitable. In the end, the bank has to utilise more resources, not only to perform due diligence but also to be more actively involved in the running of the joint-venture businesses.

OTHER DEBT-BASED METHODS

Now that we have covered the most important and popular debt-based contracts (BBA, murabahah and ijarah) and those that are equity-based (mudharabah and musharakah), let us briefly look at other debt-based methods. Some of these contracts are recent innovations while others contain some controversy:

1. Deferred delivery (*bai salam*);
2. Manufacture-sale (*istisna*);
3. Benevolent loan (*qard hassan*);
4. Pawnbroking (*rahnu*); and
5. Sale and buyback (*bai inah*).

Deferred Delivery (Bai Salam)

Bai salam is a contract where payment is made immediately while the goods are delivered at an agreed later date. It is equivalent to an advance payment. Bai salam was originally created to provide financing for farmers.

Basic Example

Suppose Jalil, a corn farmer, needs to plant his crop for the season but does not have enough funds to do so. He can approach the bank for bai salam financing. If the bank agrees, it will pay Jalil today for his crop while Jalil promises to deliver the corn to the bank in three months' time when the crop is harvested. In other words, this is a sale for the future delivery of corn. The bank expects to make a profit by selling the crop when it receives it in the future, for a price that is higher than what it is paying Jalil today. Figure 10.6 overleaf shows a basic bai salam structure.

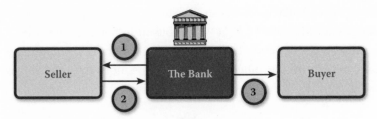

Figure 10.6 An example of a basic bai salam structure

❶ Jalil sells the corn crop to the bank on a forward basis. The bank pays Jalil $X.

❷ Three months later when the crop is harvested, it is delivered to the bank.

❸ The bank then sells the crop to a buyer in the market for $Y. The difference between $X and $Y is the bank's profit.

Bai salam is a contract where an asset is sold before it exists. It is in effect a forward agreement typically on the future delivery of commodities while payment is made today. There are, however, strict requirements for bai salam contracts to ensure Shariah compliance because a forward agreement is equivalent to "selling what one does not have", a practice that generates major *gharar* (extreme uncertainty). These requirements include the following:

- The bank must make full payment at the time of entering the contract. If funds are to be released in instalments, the bank should sign a separate bai salam contract for each instalment.
- The bank is not allowed to sell the commodity until it takes delivery of it.
- The commodity must be a standardised commodity that is freely available and tradeable in the market. The quality of the commodity must be fully specified, leaving no room for ambiguity. Examples include grain, fruits, vegetables and precious metals. Specific assets, such as land and specialised machinery, are not allowed.

♦ Other commodities that are not allowed are currencies because that would be making money on money, which amounts to *riba*.

IN THE MARKETPLACE

Islami Bank Bangladesh Limited (www. islamibankbd.com) offers a financing product based on bai salam. Alleviating poverty among the rural and agricultural communities in Bangladesh is one of the key objectives of the bank.

Parallel Example

In a basic bai salam structure, the bank has to deal with the risk of the commodity having fallen in price by the time it is delivered, thereby bringing losses to the bank. This risk can be mitigated in a modified structure called parallel bai salam, which is shown in Figure 10.7.

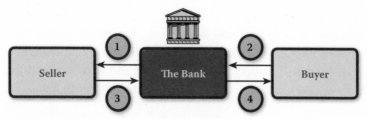

Figure 10.7 An example of a parallel bai salam structure

❶ Jalil sells the corn crop to the bank on a forward basis. The bank pays Jalil $X.

❷ At the same time, the bank sells the crop to the buyer also on a forward basis and receives $Y.

❸ Three months later when the crop is harvested, it is delivered to the bank.

❹ The bank in turn delivers the crop to the buyer.

As with the basic bai salam structure, the difference between $X and $Y is the bank's profit. Compared with the basic structure, parallel bai salam has benefits for all three parties:

- Jalil receives advance payment in exchange for the obligation to deliver the commodity at a future date. He also benefits from locking in a price for his commodity, thereby allowing him to manage his costs.
- The bank is able to broker the deal to earn a profit without committing funds.
- The buyer is able to lock in a price without incurring storage costs, thereby protecting him from price fluctuation.

Manufacture-Sale (Istisna)

Istisna is a contract that involves the sale of manufactured assets, such as buildings, airplanes and ships, where the bank pays the manufacturer in advance and the assets are delivered upon completion in the future. There is pre-agreement on the specifications of the assets, and the contract enables suppliers to be paid a pre-delivery advance.

Here is an example of istisna (a parallel version) where the bank plays a brokering role by assigning the job of manufacturing the asset to a third party, the home developer. The difference between what the buyer pays to the bank and what the bank pays the developer constitutes profit for the bank. Figure 10.8 illustrates these points.

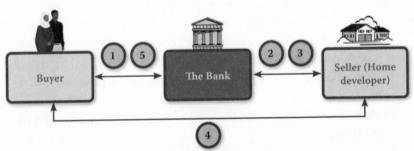

Figure 10.8 An example of an istisna structure

❶ Jemimah approaches the bank with clear details of her dream home and the developer that would build it.

❷ The bank and the developer enter an agreement where the developer builds the home and the bank makes progress payments.

❸ As the developer builds the home, it receives progress payments from the bank.

❹ When the home is completed, ownership is transferred to Jemimah.

❺ Jemimah pays in instalments over an agreed period of time.

IN THE MARKETPLACE

Sharjah Islamic Bank in the United Arab Emirates (www.sib.ae) offers an istisna financing product for the construction of buildings, residential towers, villas, aircraft, ships and other real assets. Financing is provided for freehold property for a maximum duration of 10 years, including up to two years for construction.

Important Contract Conditions and Features

One unique feature of istisna is that no payment or instalment is made at the time of contracting. It is in fact a pure forward contract where the financial obligations of both parties are settled in the future. The buyer (of the home) pays in full, or in instalments, over an agreed time period, usually when the asset has been delivered in the future.

The terms of istisna can be quite flexible. For example, the bank could choose to pay the developer in one lump sum and the customer could pay the bank in one lump sum as well. In another variation, the customer may at the start merely specify the asset she wishes to have created, without giving details of any particular manufacturer. The bank, rather than the customer, would then choose the manufacturer. A valid istisna contract must meet certain conditions:

- ◆ The price must be fixed between buyer and seller.
- ◆ The specifications of the asset to be manufactured must be fully defined between buyer and seller.
- ◆ Either party may cancel the contract by giving notice to the other party. However, once the manufacturer has started work, the contract cannot be cancelled unilaterally.

Risks with Istisna Contracts

Istisna has several construction-related risks. For instance, the customer could default on his payments, or the manufacturer could do a poor and shoddy job. To protect itself against customer defaults, the bank could use the land as security for the loan and hire a third-party surveyor to monitor the progress of the project. Or it could make the customer an agent to oversee the completion of the job. This typically happens when the customer, and not the bank, has specialised knowledge of the asset being manufactured.

Comparisons with Other Contracts

There is one fundamental difference between istisna and BBA. While they are both sales and purchase agreements, with istisna, delivery is deferred till the asset is manufactured, and with BBA, the asset is delivered at the start of the contract.

Istisna and bai salam too are similar in that both are forward agreements. However, they have two fundamental differences as shown in Table 10.4.

Table 10.4 Comparing istisna and bai salam

Feature	Istisna	Bai Salam
Type of asset	Usually an asset that requires manufacturing	Usually for agricultural products
Payment	Can be paid by instalment	Payment is made on the spot because of the need to use financing to manufacture the asset

Are Derivatives Allowed?

Islamic financial instruments must be free of riba, major gharar and *maysir* (gambling). In addition, there are basic conditions to the sale of real assets, such as land, cars and buildings—an asset must currently already exist in its physical sellable form, and the seller should have legal ownership of the asset in its final form. These conditions cause conventional derivatives to be non-Shariah compliant. For example, a farmer who wants to manage his risk by selling his future crop at a specified price today would be violating Shariah.

However, you would have noticed with bai salam and istisna that deferred sales are allowed, as long as certain conditions are observed. In bai salam, two parties agree to carry out a sale and purchase of an asset at a fixed future date, and at a price fully paid for today. This is similar to a conventional forward contract except that the buyer pays the entire amount in full at the start of the contract. Shariah recognises the need to help businesses with working capital financing, and hence allows such pre-payment when the asset does not currently exist.

Istisna is also similar to a conventional forward agreement where a buyer contracts with a manufacturer to create a product to his specifications. The price for the product is agreed upon and fixed but unlike bai salam, payment is not made in advance.

Istijrar, on the other hand, is an Islamic derivative instrument that originated in Pakistan quite recently. It is like an exotic options contract where either the buyer or the seller has the right to buy or sell. Istijrar is complex as it combines options, average prices and murabahah.

Benevolent Loan (Qard Hassan)

This is the simplest of financing schemes where a borrower takes a loan of, say, $100, and repays the lender on maturity exactly the same amount of $100, nothing more or less. Early loan schemes before modern Islamic banking were based on this concept.

To protect the lender against default by the borrower, the lender is allowed to:

- ◆ ask for an asset as collateral. The loan amount allowed is typically no greater than a certain percentage, such as 70 per cent, of the market value of the asset.
- ◆ charge the borrower administrative expenses incurred in providing the loan.

Figure 10.9 shows a simple qard hassan structure.

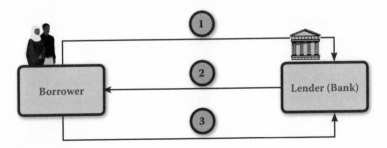

Figure 10.9 An example of a qard hassan structure

❶ A customer approaches the bank for a loan.
❷ The bank agrees on condition that collateral is provided whose market value is greater than the loan by a specified percentage.
❸ The customer repays the loan with expenses in part, or in full, in the future.

Qard hassan began as a form of social service among the rich to help the poor and those in need of financial assistance. The word qard is Arabic for "to cut". In a financing situation, it means to "cut" a certain part of a lender's wealth and give it as a loan to a borrower. Hassan means "kindness to others".

Qard hassan is thus a type of loan given to a needy person for a specified period without requiring the payment of interest or profit. The receiver of a qard hassan loan is only required to repay the original amount of the loan. It is thus not surprising that qard hassan has these broad benevolent objectives. To:

- enhance brotherhood among Muslims;
- establish a caring society;
- help needy people;
- establish better relationship among the poor and the rich;
- mobilise wealth among people in society;
- perform a good deed that is encouraged and appreciated by Allah (swt);
- strengthen the national economy; and
- wipe out unemployment.

Adapted from Khalifah Institute website (www.islamic-world.net)

IN THE MARKETPLACE

Dubai Islamic Bank in the United Arab Emirates (www.dib.ae) offers qard hassan loans to assist customers who are facing financial difficulties. Such funds held for qard hassan purposes are meant for promoting benevolence among Muslims. Profit generation is not a motive.

Pawnbroking (Rahnu)

Pawnbroking or *rahnu* works hand in hand with qard hassan. In rahnu financing, a valuable asset is used as collateral to obtain a loan. The collateral may be used as payment if the loan is not repaid within the specified period.

Islamic pawnbroking combines three concepts to work:

1. Qard hassan—The bank provides a benevolent loan to the borrower.
2. Rahnu—The borrower places a valuable asset as collateral for the loan.
3. *Wadiah*—The bank provides safe custody of the valuable asset and charges the customer for this service.

Rahnu provides quick and easy access to short-term microfinancing for lower income groups. Loans are typically small, averaging a few hundred to a few thousand dollars.

IN THE MARKETPLACE

Bank Rakyat in Malaysia (www.bankrakyat. com.my) offers a financing product based on rahnu using 18–24k gold jewellery as the pawned item (collateral). The loan duration is six months at a time.

Sale and Buyback (Bai Inah)

Some financing methods that are widely used in certain countries are banned in others, generally on the basis that those products allow riba through the back door. Bai inah is one such controversial contract.

Bai inah is a contract that involves the sale and buyback of an asset by a seller. Let us suppose that Judi wants to borrow money from the bank. She sells an asset, say a laptop, to the bank for $2,000. The bank pays Judi $2,000. Judi then agrees to buy the laptop back from the bank at a higher price that includes the bank's profit margin. She pays the bank in instalments over the next two years.

Bai inah also works in reverse where the bank first sells an asset to the customer at a marked-up price that includes the bank's profit margin. Payment by the customer will be made by instalments during a specified period. The bank then buys back the asset from the customer at cost price and pays the customer on the spot. Figure 10.10 illustrates this.

❶ The customer approaches the bank for financing.
❷ The bank approves the request and identifies the asset for the bai inah contract.

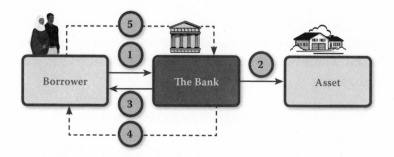

Figure 10.10 An example of a bai inah structure

❸ The bank and the customer sign a first sales and purchase contract where the bank sells an asset at a marked-up price (cost price + the bank's profit margin) on instalment to the customer. Ownership of the asset is transferred to the customer.

❹ The bank and the customer sign a second sales and purchase contract where the bank buys back the asset at cost price. The bank pays the customer on the spot.

❺ The customer begins his instalment payments to the bank.

IN THE MARKETPLACE

Bank Rakyat in Malaysia (www.bankrakyat.com.my) offers a commercial financing product based on bai inah for companies seeking working capital. Financing of up to 80% of the working capital requirement is provided. The maximum loan duration is 10 years.

Some Islamic scholars have classified bai inah as a back-door legal excuse to legitimise riba, which is a very strong stand against bai inah. They insist that bai inah is ethically flimsy as the sale and purchase of the asset is a fake sale and just a means of masking riba. The conflict boils down to differences in opinion. There are numerous interpretations within Islam on what is acceptable, given that the schools of thought on Shariah law are not homogenous.

Bai inah is permissible in Malaysia but subject to strict compliance with certain conditions. Bai inah is used in money market transactions, bond issuance, debt securitisation and credit card facilities.

Court Rulings in Malaysia on Bai Inah and BBA

In September 2008, the central bank of Malaysia, Bank Negara Malaysia (BNM), issued a circular that strongly advised Islamic banks to review their heavy reliance on BBA. This was after a number of High Court judgements had declared BBA-based, home-financing contracts to be contrary to the Islamic Banking Act 1983 of Malaysia.

The circular was seen as an effort to get the industry to think beyond BBA, which prompted some banks to introduce home financing based on diminishing musharakah.

Then in April 2009, the Court of Appeal not only overturned the judgements on BBA but also on bai inah. According to Datuk Zukri Samat, the president of the Association of Islamic Banking Institutions Malaysia (AIBIM), the ruling of the court gives clarity as well as strengthens public confidence in these products.

BBA and bai inah, however, remain controversial and are banned in the Middle East. So despite the Malaysia Court of Appeal ruling in favour of BBA and bai inah, some Malaysian Islamic banks who have Middle East scholars on their Shariah boards have still banned such products.

CONCLUSION

We covered Islamic financing over the last three chapters. What we learned in Chapters 7, 8 and 9—BBA, murabahah and ijarah —form the majority of Islamic financing contracts. These three contracts are debt-based.

The other debt-based products which we covered in the second half of this chapter are less popular, generally because they are for very specific purposes and do not cater to the consumer population at large. Bai salam, for example, caters mainly to agricultural financing, and rahnu is for very short-term financing featuring collateral.

Some debt-based contracts such as BBA are prone to controversy because their cash flows can resemble those of conventional interest-based loans. Additionally, their profit margins may be determined according to conventional benchmarks like the market rate of interest. This understandably raises feelings of discomfort. However, we need to bear in mind that the Islamic finance system works in conjunction, and in competition, with the conventional system. It is thus natural for a person seeking financing to compare what each system offers, and for both systems to have comparable cost schedules.

That is why very strict contracting principles must be observed to ensure that Shariah principles are not breached in debt-based financing. Contracts must be based on real assets. Contracts must be separate and cannot be combined. Profit rates must be known for the duration of the contract right at the start of the contract.

If one were to ask what might be the most ideal basis for Islamic financing, the answer would likely be equity-based financing. Contracts like mudharabah and musharakah run parallel to the fundamental Islamic teachings of risk-sharing, entrepreneurship, transparency and mutual benefit. In a musharakah contract, for example, the bank and the customer jointly invest and share both risk and returns. Such an arrangement forces both sides to be transparent for the sake of a win-win outcome.

In the next chapter, we discuss insurance, a very essential financial instrument that individuals and businesses all over the world use for managing financial and other risks.

Chapter 11 — INSURANCE

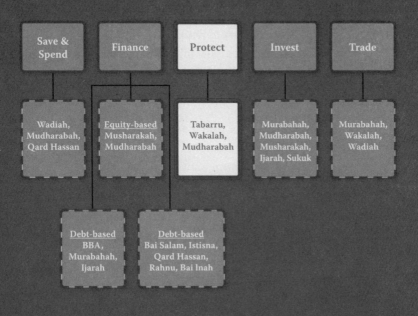

YOU PROBABLY OWN some form of insurance—whether it is to obtain financial protection for your life, your car or your business.

In fact, many aspects of life and business will cease without insurance:

- Without car insurance, you would be afraid to drive your car and risk getting involved in a costly accident.
- Without mortgage insurance, a bank may not want to give you a loan to buy a home.
- Without life insurace, you will have a constant fear that your children would be left penniless if you suddenly passed away.

In this chapter, we discuss how conventional insurance works, and why it violates Shariah principles. Then we introduce *takaful*, the Islamic version of insurance. Takaful models are largely based on *wakalah* (agency) and *mudharabah* (profit-sharing) methods. We will end the chapter with an assessment of some takaful issues.

How Conventional Insurance Works

Insurance protects against the risk of potential loss. It can be thought of as a guaranteed small loss to prevent a large, possibly devastating loss. An insurer is the company selling the insurance while the insured is the person buying the insurance. Risks that are insurable typically share these six characteristics:

1. **The Law of Large Numbers.** According to this principle, there must be a large number of homogeneous exposure units so that losses are predictable. The vast majority of insurance policies are thus provided for individual members of very large groups. Automobile insurance, for example, covers about 300 million vehicles in the US.

2. **Accidental Loss.** The event that triggers a claim should be accidental and beyond the control of the insured individual. The loss should be due to pure risk rather than speculative risk. With pure risk, the outcome can only be a loss or no loss; there is no possibility for gain. Pure risk arises from events

over which one has little or no control. Getting disabled from an accident and your home catching fire are examples of pure risk.

In contrast, speculative risk means that uncertainty about an event could result in either a gain or a loss. Such risk could come about from running a business or investing in stocks, for example, where making profits and incurring losses are both possible outcomes.

> **"Many aspects of life and business will cease without insurance."**

3. **Circumstances of Loss Should Be Identifiable.** The time, the place and the cause of an event that give rise to the loss should all be known. A suitable example to explain this point is the death of an insured person on a life insurance policy. The circumstances involving time, place and cause of this insured person's death should be clear enough that a reasonable individual could objectively verify all three pieces of information.

4. **Large but Not Catastrophic Loss.** The size of the loss must be meaningful and not miniscule, like a one-dollar loss. Insurance premiums need to cover the expected costs of setting-up and administering the policy and losses. Because of these fixed costs, miniscule losses are not worth covering. At the same time, losses should not be catastrophic to the insurer. In earthquake insurance, the ability of an underwriter to issue a new policy of immense size would depend on the number, and sum total, of the policies that it has already underwritten.

5. **Affordable Premium.** If the likelihood of an insured event is so high, or the cost of the event so large, that the resulting premium is substantial relative to the amount of protection offered, it is not likely that anyone will buy the insurance, even if on offer. For example, if you had a farm with a $100,000

crop to harvest a month later, and rain would destroy it, the cost of rain insurance would be so high that you will not want to buy it.

6. **Calculable Loss.** The probability of loss, and the cost from the loss, can generally be estimated.

How a Conventional Insurer Earns a Profit

The business model can be reduced to a simple equation:

Profit = premiums + investment income − (claims + expenses)

Insurers earn returns in two main ways. Through underwriting, which is the process by which insurers select the types of risk to insure and decide the amount in premiums to charge for accepting those risks, and by investing the premiums they collect from insured parties.

The most complicated aspect of the insurance business is the underwriting of policies. Using a wide assortment of data, insurers predict the likelihood that a claim will be made against their policies, and they then price products accordingly.

Of course, from the insurer's perspective, some policies are winners (that is, the insurer pays out less in claims and expenses than it receives in premiums and investment income) and some are losers (that is, the insurer pays out more in claims and expenses than it receives in premiums and investment income).

Some Issues with Conventional Insurance

Insurance Can Encourage Moral Hazard

Moral hazard is the lack of any incentive to guard against a risk when you are protected against it. For example, if you had life insurance and you know your family will be taken care of if you pass away, you might be tempted to take on riskier behaviour than you would without insurance.

To reduce their own financial exposure, insurance companies use contractual clauses to release their obligation to pay if policyholders injure themselves, or cause their own deaths, through risky behaviour, such as race-car driving and skydiving.

Insurance Policy Contracts Can Be Complex

Insurance policies can be complex, and many policyholders themselves do not understand the fees and coverages included in their policy contracts. As a result of possible complexity, people may unknowingly buy policies on unfavourable terms.

Stock versus Mutual Companies

Conventional insurance companies are generally organised as either shareholder-owned companies or mutual insurers. The objective of a shareholder-owned insurer is to produce profits for its shareholders.

Mutual insurers, on the other hand, are owned by their policyholders. The objective of such an insurer is to minimise the cost of insurance to its policyholders. To fulfil its objective, the mutual insurer would pay dividends to these policyholders, based on company performance.

In the absence of takaful in a community, Muslims generally seek protection with mutual insurance.

ISLAMIC OBJECTIONS AGAINST CONVENTIONAL INSURANCE

Muslims wishing to comply with Shariah cannot buy conventional insurance products because these products contain elements that are *haram*, or forbidden, to Islamic principles. Such principles include gambling (*maysir*), extreme uncertainty (major *gharar*), interest (*riba*) and investment in haram activities.

Gambling (Maysir)

Let us consider a conventional insurer that is organised as a shareholder company. When the insurer takes out actuarial and statistical tables to calculate the probability of risks occurring in the future, Shariah scholars find that it is no different from gambling or maysir.

If underwriting estimates are calculated accurately and premiums are appropriately priced, then the insurer makes a profit for its shareholders—at the expense of policyholders. If, on the other hand, the insurer underestimates the premiums and makes a loss, policyholders will have benefited from having paid less.

What is haram in this situation is that it is a zero-sum game, like in gambling, where if one wins, the other loses. This is unfair for both shareholders and policyholders.

Extreme Uncertainty (Major Gharar)

Shariah scholars declare that extreme uncertainty (major gharar), which is prohibited, exists in conventional insurance.

At the time a policy is written, the insurer does not know when or whether he will have to pay a claim, or the size of it. Likewise, the insured pays a premium but does not know whether any financial benefit will be derived in the future. This is unfair for both the insurer and the insured, and goes against the co-operative objective of Shariah.

Interest (Riba)

Interest or riba can occur in two main ways—one involving riba generated from premiums paid and the other, where premiums are used to invest in interest-based instruments.

When an insurance policy promises a pre-determined amount that is greater than that placed as premiums, riba is generated. The problem of riba can be avoided if the contract provides for a share of profit rather than fixed interest.

When premiums are invested in businesses such as conventional interest-based bonds, for example, riba occurs with the fixed interest. Investments must not produce riba and must always be Shariah compliant.

Investment in Haram Activities

Conventional insurers are known to invest in companies that are involved in activities considered haram.

For example, major US, Canadian and British life and health insurance companies have billions of dollars invested in tobacco companies, according to the *New England Journal of Medicine*.[1] Even non-Muslim critics have pointed out that insurers continue to put their profits above people's health because tobacco is considered the leading cause of lung cancer.

TAKAFUL—THE ISLAMIC INSURANCE ALTERNATIVE

Islamic insurance, or *takaful*, is permissible when it is co-operative in nature. This is the basis of takaful. It is not a sales-and-purchase agreement where one party offers and sells protection, and the other party accepts and buys the service at a certain price. It is, instead, an arrangement by a group of people who have the desire to protect each other from defined risks and mishaps, by contributing to a pool of money out of their own resources.

Such a practice of mutual help and shared responsibility was laid down by the principle of *Aqilah* (persons of relationship), which was customary in some tribes at the time of Prophet Muhammad (pbuh). Whenever a misfortune occurred, each member of the tribe provided contributions to relieve the affected parties. This principle of Aqilah is the foundation of takaful.

The takaful operator (the company that operates the insurance scheme on behalf of its policyholders) divides the contributions into two parts. An amount for *tabarru* (donations) is set aside for meeting policyholder losses and mishaps. The second part is set aside for investment.

After all obligatory takaful benefits are distributed, the remaining surplus is paid back to the policyholders or donated to charity. There is no win-or-lose element in this arrangement where one side benefits and the other side does not. The group comes together to co-operate for mutual protection and benefit.

The history of takaful as a business is very recent. The first such company was set up in Sudan in 1979. Then, in 1985, the grand council of Islamic scholars (Academy of the Organization of Islamic Conference) reached an agreement on Islamic insurance and formally forbade conventional insurance. Following the agreement, they encouraged Islamic institutions to establish insurance contracts based on voluntary contribution, mutual co-operation and adherence to Shariah principles.

Major Stakeholders in a Venture

There are two major stakeholders in a takaful venture—the policyholders (also called participants or members) who need insurance, and the operator who provides the Islamic insurance expertise (see Figure 11.1).

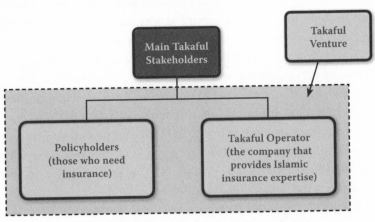

Figure 11.1 Main stakeholders in a takaful operation

This is quite similar in concept to how a unit trust is set up—investors pool their money together and hire a professional fund manager to manage their funds.

With the presence of the operator, the takaful venture takes on a more commercial and entrepreneurial direction. The operator, typically owned by a group of shareholders, seeks a reasonable return on their investment.

Table 11.1 summarises some self-explanatory differences between takaful and conventional insurance.

Table 11.1 Some key differences between conventional insurance and takaful

Feature	Conventional Insurance	Takaful
Who are the owners?	Shareholders own the insurance company. The objective is to maximise profits.	Policyholders own the company. The operator receives compensation (through profit-sharing or fees). The objective is to minimise the cost of insurance.
Sources of law and regulations	Man-made	A Shariah board consisting of Islamic scholars help ensure that operations, products and investments are Shariah-compliant.
Risk of loss	Assumed by shareholders	Assumed by policyholders
Investments	No general restrictions	Investments must be Shariah-compliant.
Underwriting surplus	Management decides at various times how this should be distributed between shareholders and policyholders. As a result, there is a conflict of interest.	How exactly the surplus is distributed and in what proportions is specified in the takaful contract.
Winding up of company	Reserves and surpluses belong to shareholders	Reserves and surpluses are returned to policyholders or donated to charity.

How Takaful Products Are Structured

Takaful products are structured along the lines of a few main models (see Figure 11.2 overleaf):

- non-profit basis (tabarru);
- operator earns an agency fee (wakalah);
- operator shares profits with policyholders (mudharabah); and
- hybrid of profit-sharing and agency.

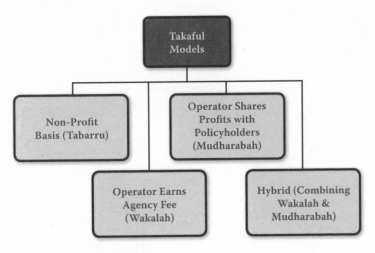

Figure 11.2 Main takaful models

Non-Profit Basis (Tabarru)

Takaful can be run on tabarru or a non-profit basis. Under this model, the initial contribution to organise the venture may come from a promoter, such as the government, as an interest-free loan (*qard hassan*). Policyholders make donations to the takaful fund, which is then used to provide financial protection to any policyholder. The policyholders are the operators of the fund, and hence also the shareholders of the takaful company. This model is used in Sudan.

Tabarru-based takaful ventures do not become large-scale businesses. They are typically found in social enterprise programmes that are operated on a non-profit basis.

Operator Earns Agency Fee (Wakalah)

Using the wakalah model, the operator manages the takaful fund as an agent of the policyholders and is paid an upfront fee for its services. Any surplus from the fund belongs to the policyholders. The operator's fee is determined in advance and does not vary whether the surpluses are large or small. Wakalah is a very straightforward model. From Figure 11.3, you can see exactly the sort of expertise the operator brings to the table—from investing and handling claims to managing policyholder funds and directing overall operations.

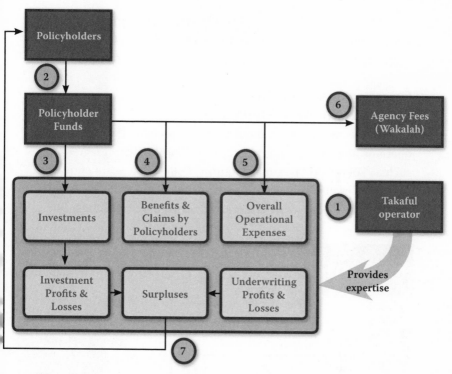

Figure 11.3 An example of a wakalah-based takaful structure

❶ A takaful operator is selected to provide expertise in running an Islamic insurance venture. The operator has its own shareholder funds.

❷ Policyholders make contributions into the policyholder fund.

❸ The takaful operator invests the policyholder funds.

❹ Takaful benefits are paid to beneficiaries when claims are made.

❺ Operational expenses are charged to the policyholder fund, since those expenses are incurred by the operator on behalf of policyholders.

❻ The takaful operator receives a known remuneration that is paid from the policyholder funds. The amount may be an absolute amount or a percentage of gross contributions received.

❼ At various time intervals, surpluses are computed (sum of investment and underwriting profits). Policyholders receive their proportionate share of each surplus, and they have to make additional payments if there is a deficit. The operator often funds the deficit in the form of interest-free loans (qard hassan).

Operator Shares Profits with Policyholders (Mudharabah)

This is the mudharabah model, and as seen in Figure 11.4, the operator and policyholders enter into a profit-sharing agreement, such as 70–30, on investment returns. Policyholders are entitled to a share of profits only when the company is profitable. The takaful operator does not receive any fees for managing the business.

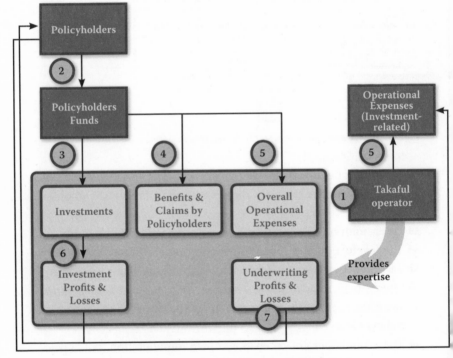

Figure 11.4 An example of a mudharabah-based takaful structure

The first four steps are the same as for wakalah. Steps 5 to 7 are specific to mudharabah:

❶ A takaful operator is selected to provide expertise in running an Islamic insurance venture. The operator has its own shareholder funds.

❷ Policyholders make contributions into the policyholder fund.

❸ The takaful operator invests the policyholder funds.

❹ Takaful benefits are paid to beneficiaries when claims are made.

❺ Operational expenses (investment-related) are charged to the takaful operator's shareholder funds. Operational expenses (overall expenses other than investment-related expenses) are charged to the policyholder funds.

❻ Profits generated from investing the policyholder funds are shared between the policyholders and the operator according to a pre-agreed sharing ratio (PSR). Losses, however, are charged only to the policyholder fund (since the policyholders are the capital provider).

❼ At various time intervals, underwriting surpluses are computed (difference between contributions received and claims paid). Policyholders receive their proportionate share of each surplus, and they have to make additional payments if there is a deficit. The operator often funds the deficit in the form of interest-free loans (qard hassan).

Hybrid of Profit-Sharing and Agency

Mudharabah, with its profit-sharing element, provides a suitable incentive for the operator to manage the investment portfolio. When investment returns are strong, the operator benefits directly.

Wakalah, on the other hand, does not provide such an incentive because, whether investment returns are good or poor, the operator fee does not change. It does, though, provide a suitable incentive for the operator to properly run and operate the takaful business.

Operating the takaful business is a separate function from managing the investment portfolio. Combining mudharabah and wakalah is perhaps the best of both worlds because the operator really does perform two sets of functions—fund management and operations—for which he should be rewarded and incentivised accordingly. The operator receives a fixed proportional share of policyholder contributions, plus a pre-agreed share of investment profits.

The hybrid model is used by Hong Leong Tokio Marine Takaful in Malaysia (www.hltmt.com.my) and increasingly by Middle East operators. In fact, the Accounting and Auditing Organization for Islamic Financial Institutions (AAOIFI) recommends the hybrid model because it exploits the strengths of wakalah and mudharabah.

SOME PRODUCT ISSUES AND CONTROVERSIES

Like most Islamic finance products, takaful products have the twin challenge of having to comply with Shariah and being market-competitive with their conventional counterparts.

Sharing of Underwriting Surpluses

Should underwriting surpluses be shared with the operator? In the mudharabah model described above, it was shown that underwriting surpluses are for policyholders only and are not shared with the operator. Those who are opposed to sharing contend that there is a conflict of interest.

Let us look at an example, starting with Peter as an insurance operator who has just collected $1,000 in contributions from John. After paying claims and expenses that amount to, say, $800, Peter would have an underwriting surplus of $200. Now suppose Peter had charged $1,200 instead and the total cost of insurance also comes up to $800, he would now have a surplus of $400.

You can see where this is going. The operator can earn more just by charging more, without any increased benefit for policyholders. Because the contributions are made to a mutual pool for policyholders, surpluses should go back to the policyholders and not be a source of returns for the operator.

In some takaful companies using the mudharabah model, however, underwriting surpluses are shared with the operator. The practice with these companies is to make the contribution rates comparable to those required by conventional insurance companies, in order to make the takaful product competitive.

Without access to underwriting surpluses, the operator may charge a higher contribution rate and cause the product to weaken in its competitiveness. Receiving a share of the underwriting surplus is one way in which the operator can compensate itself for charging rates that are compatible with conventional rates.

Some wakalah models in use are structured to share underwriting surpluses in addition to receiving an agency fee. Supporters say that surplus sharing reduces the moral hazard problem associated with wakalah where the operator, who knows what he is getting regardless of operating results, would not be incentivised to do his best job. Surplus sharing is thus an incentive for the takaful operator to perform its job effectively, and for it to price its products in a competitive manner.

Differences in Takaful Models

The ultimate responsibility for Shariah compliance lies with the Shariah supervisory board of each company. Since these boards are not unanimous in their decisions, takaful models are implemented slightly differently depending on the market, the country and the company. Nevertheless, takaful models are more similar than different in their adherence to Shariah principles.

Challenges Highlighted by IFSB

Retakaful (Islamic reinsurance) is a critical component of the takaful industry to spread and balance the risks held by operators. It is a risk-management tool used by operators to transfer part of the risk under a takaful fund to another takaful operator or retakaful operator.

Without retakaful growing alongside takaful, the industry would be unable to develop to its potential. According to the report *Islamic Financial Services Industry Development: Ten-Year Framework and Strategies*[2] by the Islamic Financial Services Board (IFSB), there is still a general lack of highly-rated retakaful companies. As a result, there have been Shariah rulings permitting the use of conventional reinsurance. This means that the takaful industry as a whole is a hybrid of Islamic and conventional institutions.

Fortunately, retakaful does not in principle differ from takaful operations as both share the same Shariah principles.[3] The main difference is that takaful operators are the policyholders of retakaful, while individual policyholders are the policyholders of takaful. This reduces the technical challenges of setting up retakaful companies.

However, the single most important challenge faced by the takaful industry is the lack of an overall supportive legal and regulatory framework. Besides Bahrain, Malaysia and Sudan, other countries regulate takaful within the regulatory framework of conventional insurance and thus treat takaful like conventional insurance. As a result, takaful services providers face difficulty in competing with conventional insurance providers.

Conclusion

Among the major challenges to the growth of takaful is the diversity of opinion and practice. Takaful allows various interpretations to co-exist, and continued standardisation of the operating models would help the industry grow to a larger scale. Standardisation will reduce costs, enhance clarity amongst customers and free up resources at financial institutions offering Shariah-compliant products. However, some differences in interpretation will remain.

Another challenge is the general lack of Shariah-compliant investment assets that are tradable in the market. Despite the healthy growth of global *sukuk* (Islamic bonds) issuance, which grew from US$1 billion in 2001 to US$35 billion in 2007, supply is still inadequate. Long-term sukuks are usually oversubscribed and not traded frequently. As a result, takaful companies have had to seek instruments from different markets to diversify their risk, including sometimes-volatile equity and real estate markets.

Islamic banking has grown over the past 30 to 40 years, while takaful is still in its early stages. The success of Islamic banking will benefit takaful. In urban areas, *bancatakaful*—the distribution of takaful products via banks—could play a significant role in raising insurance awareness among Muslim populations. Banks have good reputations, and takaful products can be distributed through their branches just as bancassurance (the distribution of conventional insurance through banks) has become a major distribution channel.

The future of takaful looks bright. There is low insurance penetration and pent-up demand for insurance among Muslims. Furthermore, Muslim-majority countries, especially those in the Middle East and South-East Asia, have strong economic fundamentals and growth prospects.

In the next chapter, we will discuss important investment principles that comply with Shariah. We will see that the investment choices for Islamic investors can be found in many parts of the world, not just in certain countries.

---

1   As reported in "Life, Health Insurers Invest Big in Tobacco," by Agence France Presse (AFP) on 4 June 2009.

2   www.ifsb.org/docs/10_yr_framework.pdf

3   Based on an opinion of Fathi Lashin, a member of the Shariah Supervisory Board of the Dubai Islamic Bank, as reported in www.accountancy.com.pk/articles.asp?id=157

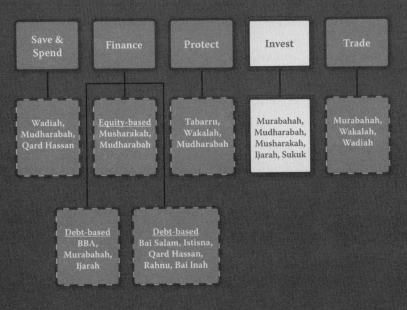

Chapter 12   INVESTING

Save & Spend	Finance	Protect	Invest	Trade
Wadiah, Mudharabah, Qard Hassan	Equity-based Musharakah, Mudharabah	Tabarru, Wakalah, Mudharabah	Murabahah, Mudharabah, Musharakah, Ijarah, Sukuk	Murabahah, Wakalah, Wadiah

Debt-based
BBA,
Murabahah,
Ijarah

Debt-based
Bai Salam, Istisna,
Qard Hassan,
Rahnu, Bai Inah

IF YOU WERE to leave your money in a savings account, chances are that inflation would erode the value of your money. Over a period of time, your money would be worth less, and you would be financially worse off in the future.

Growing the value of your money, and avoiding the negative effects of inflation, are consequently the main reasons for investing. Whether your ultimate objective is to have enough financial resources for retirement or to fund your children's education, an appropriate investment strategy can be far more effective than leaving your money 'idle' in a bank.

Of course, leaving your money in the bank is 'safe' and virtually free of risk. We learned, for example, in Chapter 7 that if you were to start a savings account based on *wadiah yad dhamanah* (safekeeping), the bank is obligated to return 100 per cent of it to you.

> **"Investing over time almost always brings returns and grows your money."**

Investing over time almost always brings returns and grows your money. But there are risks. You might buy a number of good stocks only to run right into an economic recession that crashes the prices of securities in general. Or you could put your total savings of $100,000 into a technology company that 10 years later earns you $1 million in returns.

The successful investor has a keen understanding of how to manage risk. The world's greatest investor, Warren Buffet, manages risk by avoiding big mistakes. He once said, "You only have to do a very few things right in your life so long as you don't do too many things wrong."

In this chapter, we have allocated a fair bit of space to discussing basic investment concepts and managing risk. This foundation is very crucial to achieving investment success, but more importantly, to avoiding financial disasters. These concepts apply whether you are dealing with conventional or Islamic investing. We will also look at how Islamic investing differs from, and how Islamic securities compare with, conventional ones in terms of performance.

What Is Your Objective for Investing?

For Muslims, an additional major objective (besides funding one's retirement and children's education) would be to have sufficient money for the Hajj, which is the pilgrimage to Mecca that the Holy Koran obligates every physically- and financially-able Muslim to perform at least once in his life.

Let us take the case of Leena, who is 30 years old and married with a two-year-old son. She wants to have $100,000 in the bank in 15 years' time for the Hajj as well as to fund her son's university education.

How much money would Leena need to save every month to reach her goal? Table 12.1 shows the monthly amount that she should set aside, based on four different rates of return possibilities.

Table 12.1 Monthly savings needed to accumulate $100,000

Rate of Return	Monthly Savings Needed: 15 Years to Retirement	Monthly Savings Needed: 20 Years to Retirement
0.0%	$556	$417
2.5%	$458	$322
6.0%	$344	$216
12.0%	$200	$101

If Leena keeps her savings in a shoebox at home earning 0 per cent returns, she would need to set aside $556 every month. Now if she were to invest and is able to achieve 6 per cent returns, her monthly burden would go down to $344. At higher and higher rates of return, her burden starts to look lighter and lighter.

If she were to invest for 20 instead of 15 years, the amount she needs every month would be even less. That is the whole idea behind investing—to reach our financial objectives at a pace that best suits us.

Islamic and conventional investing are quite different, although they are built on the same fundamental concepts of risk and return. If you are quite new to investing or have never invested before, how do you start? Let us take a quick tour of essential investing concepts by looking at the most common conventional investment instruments and how investment risk can be managed with diversification.

STOCKS, BONDS AND UNIT TRUSTS

When a company needs funds to begin a new business project, it raises money usually by issuing stocks and bonds. Stocks and bonds are thus the two most basic investment products for any investor.

Stocks and Bonds

Stocks have historically outperformed most other investments, including bonds, over the long run. But stocks are considered more risky than bonds because their returns are more uncertain. Let us suppose you bought $10,000 worth of stock in XYZ Company and sold it five years later. As illustrated in Table 12.2, your returns would not be certain because companies:

 - pay dividends only if they make a profit; and
 - are not legally obliged to pay dividends even if they make profits, and may choose to reinvest these profits.

Table 12.2 *Unpredictable cash flows from a stock investment*

Year	1	2	3	4	5
Price	- $10,000				?
Dividends	?	?	?	?	?

Therefore, you may get dividends some years and none in others. Another reason why your returns would be uncertain is that company earnings are seldom stable—they can be high in some years and low in others. This causes expectations of the company and its stock price to fluctuate from year to year. In the end, your stocks may sell for $15,000, $8,000, or anything in between.

Bond returns, on the other hand, are more stable.[1] If you bought $10,000 of bonds in XYZ Company that will mature in five years' time and pay 5 per cent annual interest, that means the company will pay you $500 interest every year for five years, and then return your entire capital to you on maturity. This is illustrated in Table 12.3.

It is noteworthy that compared with dividends, which are discretionary, interest payments are contractual. From the same example, the company *has* to pay you interest of $500 a year for five years (that is why bonds are also called fixed-income securities).

With a bond investment, therefore, you will know exactly the amount of money you will receive in the future. For this reason, bonds are generally safer than stocks.

Table 12.3 Predictable cash flows from a bond investment

Year	1	2	3	4	5
Price	- $10,000				$10,000
Interest	$500	$500	$500	$500	$500

Conventional bond investments, however, are not permitted by Shariah because they produce *riba* (interest), but as we will see later, there are Islamic funds that behave like income-producing bond funds yet avoid riba, and are Shariah-compliant.

Unit Trusts

If you do not have the time or expertise to invest directly in stocks and bonds, unit trusts[2] can do that for you.

When you buy a unit trust, you have in effect hired a team of full-time investment professionals to analyse, select, and buy and sell stocks and bonds on your behalf. (Note that we will focus our subsequent discussion on funds rather than direct investments into individual stocks and bonds.)

Unit trusts are very flexible in their investments. For example:

◆ **Global Equity Funds** invest in promising companies anywhere in the world.

- **Regional Equity Funds** invest in the stocks of a geographic region, such as Asia and Europe.

- **Single-Country Equity Funds** invest in the stocks of an individual foreign country, such as China, Singapore or the US. Such funds are considered riskier than regional and global funds because of their narrower focus and less diversified nature.

- **Sector Funds** invest in a specific industry, such as technology and healthcare. Investing in a narrow segment has high risk because if fortunes in that sector fall, the whole portfolio is vulnerable.

- **Fixed-Income Funds** (or Bond Funds) are unit trusts consisting of bonds. These funds invest in bonds issued by companies and governments. Like equity funds, there are fixed-income funds that invest globally, regionally and in individual countries.

- **Other types of funds.** There are dozens of other types of funds to suit almost any investing objective. The largest funds industry in the world is in the US where an investor may choose from over 8,000 funds.

With thousands of stocks, bonds and funds available, just how do you go about choosing something suitable? How do you make sure you are not going to be the next 75-year-old retiree to lose his or her life savings in another minibond-type mess? We recommend a simple and effective strategy called the 3-Basket System.[3]

Managing Risk—The 3-Basket System

This easy-to-use system works for most investment sums large or small. It is a practical portfolio strategy to manage risk. Let us now see how this system works.

How It Works

Let us suppose Latifah wants to invest for retirement. Her situation is described in Table 12.4. She is 45 years old, works as an engineer and wants to retire 15 years from now. She is a balanced investor, which means that she is comfortable with about an equal allocation between equity and bonds in her portfolio, such as 60 per cent in equity and 40 per cent in bonds.

Table 12.4 Latifah's profile

Investor	Latifah
Age	45 years
Retirement age	60 years
Years to retirement	15 years
Type of investor	Balanced
Suggested portfolio	60% equity and 40% bond
Available for investment	$130,000
Monthly income	$5,000

Table 12.5a shows the state of her three baskets at the start (empty at this point):

Table 12.5a The Three Main Baskets

	Basket 1 (for Emergencies)	Basket 2 (Main Basket)	Basket 3 (Supplementary)
Amount invested	--	--	--

Basket 1 is for emergencies. Basket 2 contains her main retirement portfolio. Basket 3 holds her supplementary retirement securities, where she can have riskier investments for the purpose of learning, adventure and potentially higher returns.

Latifah has $130,000. As she earns $5,000 a month, she should first leave six months of her salary or $30,000 in her savings account for emergencies. Before she invests even a single dollar, her emergency basket should be filled, in case she unexpectedly finds herself in an unpleasant situation, such as her losing her job or being in an accident. These funds will mean she does not have to sell her investments in a hurry—just in case the market is down when the emergency occurs.

She now has $100,000 that she can use for investments. Figure 12.1 shows an easy way to begin—by allocating $60,000 in a global equity fund and $40,000 in a global bond fund.

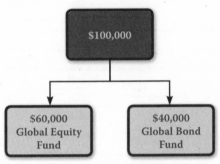

Figure 12.1 An easy way to invest Latifah's $100,000

For those who are new to investing or are starting out with a modest sum such as $2,000, a global equity and bond fund portfolio is a perfect way to begin. You can rely on the fund manager to invest around the world for you according to the fund's objectives. How much exactly is invested in each major economic region of the world (such as the US, Europe and Asia) is not in your control.

If you have a larger sum to invest like what Latifah has, and you want more control over how much is invested in each major economic region, you can consider the suggested allocation in Table 12.5b.

Table 12.5b Investing by region

Region	Suggested Allocation	Amount
US	30%	$18,000
Europe	30%	$18,000
Asia	40%	$24,000
TOTAL	100%	$60,000

These three regions represent about 80 per cent of world economic output. Now say Latifah has a view that Asia is going to outperform other regions, she could have an allocation that emphasises Asia (see Table 12.5c).

Table 12.5c Investing by region with focus on Asia

Region	Suggested Allocation	Amount
US	25%	$15,000
Europe	25%	$15,000
Asia	50%	$30,000
TOTAL	100%	$60,000

Table 12.5d shows what her baskets look like now (Basket 3 is still empty at this point):

Table 12.5d After filling Baskets 1 and 2

	Basket 1 (for Emergencies)	Basket 2 (Main Basket)	Basket 3 (Supplementary)
Amount invested	$30,000	$100,000	--

A few months later, Latifah receives a $50,000 bonus from her job. She wants to take a spa holiday in Nepal and shop in Hong Kong. But first, she wants to invest $25,000. Just when she was about to put her money into more unit trusts, her friend Lufti called her about an investment in water treatment plants in the Middle East that use new technology to desalinate sea water. Lufti is an adventurer who loves buying securities all over the world.

This sounds risky, but Latifah loves new technology. Can she invest without wrecking her retirement plan? Yes she can, so long as she contains the risks of doing so. There is a simple rule of thumb we can follow:

- Allocate no more than 20 per cent of your retirement money to riskier, non-diversified investments. We can put this investment into Basket 3.

Latifah's investments now look like this (see Table 12.5e):

Table 12.5e *After filling all three baskets*

	Basket 1 (for Emergencies)	Basket 2 (Main Basket)	Basket 3 (Supplementary)
Amount invested	$30,000	$100,000	$25,000

At this point, Basket 1 contains her emergency funds equal to six months of her salary. Basket 2 holds her main retirement funds that are apportioned according to her risk profile. Basket 3 is filled with her adventurous investments, which equals 20 per cent of her total investments for retirement ($25,000 / [$100,000 + 25,000] = 20%).

Risk is controlled because if anything goes wrong with the water treatment investment, such as it loses 30 per cent in value, while her main retirement portfolio generates 6 per cent, the net effect on her retirement portfolio is just -1.2 per cent (see Table 12.5f):

Table 12.5f *How the three baskets help to control risk*

	Basket 2 (Main Basket)	Basket 3 (Supplementary)	Total (Retirement only)
Amount invested	$100,000	$25,000	$125,000
Current value	$106,000	$17,500	$123,500
Return	6%	-30%	-1.2%

The 3-Basket method of investing is simple and easy to implement. Most of all, the focus is on controlling risk and making sure you have money to deal with emergencies, to put aside for retirement, and to enjoy riskier investments for learning, adventure and potentially higher returns.

Introducing Islamic Investing

For an Islamic investment to be *halal* (permissible) for a Muslim, it has to comply with Shariah principles. There are two main criteria that determine the halal standing of an investment:

- The first is the no-*riba* (no-interest) rule. One cannot buy investments such as bonds which generate interest.
- The second is that money is to be invested only in halal causes. This is similar in some ways to socially responsible investing (SRI).

In order to separate the halal investments from those that are *haram* (forbidden), a series of screening processes is performed.

Screening Using Islamic Indexes

One of the best ways to determine whether an investment is considered permissible is to see if it is found in Islamic indexes. Such indexes put thousands of securities through their own individual screens to sieve out those that pass or fail their various criteria.

The first major Islamic index initiative is the group belonging to the Dow Jones Islamic Market Indexes (DJIM Indexes). The indexes were introduced in 1999 to benchmark Islamic-compliant equities. An index such as the DJIM Technology Index would provide an indication of how Shariah-compliant technology stocks are performing as a group. Today there are more than 70 DJIM Indexes. Dow Jones uses a two-step screening process to find permissible investments:

1. First, companies from undesirable industries are screened out. These industries include alcohol, tobacco, pork-related products, conventional financial services (such as banking and insurance), weapons and defence, and entertainment (such as casinos and pornography).
2. Second, after removing companies with undesirable primary business activities, the remaining stocks are put through a set of riba-type financial filters to remove those with unacceptable levels of debt or interest income.

The DJIM Financial Ratio Filtering Process

The financial ratio filters are based on criteria set up by the DJIM Index Shariah Supervisory Board. Companies that fail any one of the following criteria are screened out:

1. Total debt divided by trailing 12-month average market capitalisation must be less than 33%.

2. The sum of a company's cash and interest-bearing securities divided by trailing 12-month average market capitalisation must be less than 33%.

3. Accounts receivable divided by trailing 12-month average market capitalisation must be less than 33% (Note: under Shariah investment principles, accounts receivable are viewed as loans to distributors).

The market capitalisation of a company is what you would have to pay if you were to buy all of its shares. So if XYZ Company has 10 million shares issued, and each one is priced at $10, its market capitalisation is $100 million. Each of the abovementioned ratios is meant to screen out companies whose debt-related accounts are more than $33.333 million.

Companies with zero debt are rare. For this reason, if a company has a halal business but keeps its surplus money in an interest-bearing account, it does not render the entire business of the company haram. Some Muslim investors may find these ratios, albeit acceptable, too liberal and may prescribe something more exacting like 20%. Companies that pass the two screens can then be included as selectable components for the various DJIM Indexes.

There are other Islamic indexes besides DJIM Indexes, such as those by the FTSE Group, MSCI Barra and Standard & Poor's (S&P). Not all Islamic indexes are created the same way. For instance, S&P Islamic indexes screen out companies that engage in the trading of gold and silver as cash on a deferred basis, while the MSCI Islamic indexes sieve out companies involved in the music industry, hotels, and the film and television industry.

Purifying Earnings

If you consider the Islamic fund in which you have invested to be insufficiently strict about its financial ratio screening, you can take the initiative to purify investment earnings on your own.

For example, if XYZ Company earns interest income from cash it holds in the bank, you will find the interest income reported on its balance sheet. Then when a dividend is declared, or some other distribution is made to you, you can give away the impure portion of your dividends to charity. In so doing, you purify your earnings, and what remains is legitimate.

Such a donation is not the same as *zakat* (concern for the needy). When a Muslim pays zakat, it represents a requirement and a demonstration of his faith. On the other hand, donating impure income provides no benefit because it was tainted in the first place. In fact, such donations should be given away anonymously so that the donor does not receive any unjustifiable gratitude.

Purification of Unit Trust Gains

Islamic funds can simplify this process of purification by calculating the parts that constitute impure income. The fund would then report the amount from which you can perform your own cleansing, or it may itself handle the purification and distribute only cleansed income to investors. The DWS Noor Islamic Funds[4], for example, adopts the following approach to purify their own earnings:

> *In order to purify the income received from prohibited activities, an amount equivalent to 5% of all cash dividends received within each Sub-Fund will be donated to a charity.*

Sacrificing Returns on Religious Grounds?

For both Muslim and non-Muslim investors, one obvious question is whether Islamic funds provide inferior returns to conventional funds. After all, Islamic funds have a smaller universe of securities to choose from, and even have returns deducted for purification.

Let us start by viewing Islamic funds as part of the overall SRI landscape. The question we need to ask is, "How do you know if trusting your hard-earned money to a socially-responsible fund manager will actually do something positive for your net worth?" The reality is that there are no guarantees that your money will even come back to you, let alone add to your net worth.

Critics of SRI say that screening costs money, and the resulting smaller investment universe negatively affects both investment returns and diversification opportunities.

SRI advocates argue that screening helps eliminate companies that have risks not generally recognised by traditional financial analysis. For example, WorldCom and Enron were removed from the DJIM Indexes when their debt levels exceeded 33 per cent. These shares lost their entire values when they later collapsed.

What does the evidence show?

- The FTSE KLD 400 Social Index (KLD400), created in 1990, is modelled on the S&P 500, an unscreened index. It has outperformed that index on an annualised basis since its inception.

- Professor of Finance Meir Statman of Santa Clara University, US, reviewed 31 socially-screened mutual funds and found that they outperformed their unscreened peers, but not by a statistically significant margin. The bottom line appears to be that SRI funds do not behave all that differently from regular funds, and that investing in a SRI fund does not negatively affect your returns compared with choosing a conventional index fund.

- Amana Growth Fund, a US Islamic fund established in 1986, has consistently beaten its conventional peers through the years (see Table 12.6). We will examine this fund in greater detail later.

There are thus reasons to be confident that investing in a socially-responsible manner does not equate to giving money away.

As investors ourselves, we can safely say that Islamic investing and SRI as a whole are viable investment strategies.

Table 12.6 *Average annual total returns (quarter ended 30 June 2009)*

Name of Fund	1 Year	5 Years	10 Years
Amana Growth Fund	-18.82%	5.99%	4.81%
S&P 500 Index	-26.21%	-2.24%	-2.22%
Russell 2000 Index[5]	-25.01%	-1.67%	2.44%

Source: www.amanafunds.com

ISLAMIC FUND STRUCTURES

Suppose a fund contains only securities that are components of a DJIM Index—this fact alone is not sufficient to qualify it to be a Shariah-compliant fund. The fund must have a structure that is compliant.

In addition, the fund must have a Shariah council to oversee its investments and operations. The council ensures that the fund observes Islamic contracting principles of transparency and mutual benefit. It also ascertains that the fund is not involved in haram operational activities, such as raising money from casinos or obtaining riba-oriented loans to pay for fixed assets.

Let us look briefly at some of the most common Islamic fund structures—debt funds, equity funds and lease funds.

Debt Funds　　　　　**Equity Funds**　　　　　**Lease Funds**

Debt Funds

Islamic debt funds and conventional bond funds have three fundamental differences:

1. Islamic debt funds do not contain securities that involve riba.
2. Islamic debt funds consist of cash flow-generating real assets

like property, machinery and land. For example, money from investors can be used to finance *murabahah* (cost-plus sale, a financing method we learned in Chapter 8) projects in return for riba-free fixed income. Conventional debt funds, on the other hand, can be backed purely by the promise to pay, and this can be done without any real underlying assets involved.

3. Investors receive returns from the fund through a Shariah-compliant contract such as a *mudharabah* contract (based on pre-agreed profit-sharing ratios). For example, an investor may place $1,000 with the fund manager and share returns based on, say, a 60–40 ratio in favour of the manager. In this way, the income to be received by investors becomes predictable and similar to what conventional debt funds provide, even if the funds themselves are fundamentally different in terms of their structure and underlying asset.

Equity Funds

Islamic equity funds such as the Amana Growth Fund put up their own screens to select stocks to pass its criteria. The screening process is similar to that used by Islamic indexes. Selected companies belong to permissible industries; businesses not permitted include those dealing in alcohol, casinos, pornography and gambling.

Islamic equity funds would not make any investments that pay interest, such as conventional bonds, or invest in companies whose debt levels exceed specified limits. These criteria limit investment selection and income-earning opportunities more than is customary for conventional funds.

Lease (Ijarah) Funds

In an *ijarah* fund, the subscription amounts are used to purchase assets like real estate, motor vehicles or other equipment for the purpose of leasing them out to their ultimate users.

The ownership of these assets remains with the fund, and the rentals are charged to the users. These rentals are the source of income for the fund, which are then distributed on a pro-rated basis to the subscribers. Each subscriber is given a certificate to evidence his participation and pro-rated share of the income.

These certificates are called *sukuk*, an Arabic name for a financial certificate that is considered an Islamic equivalent of a conventional bond. Since these sukuk represent the pro-rated ownership of the tangible assets of the fund, they are fully negotiable and can be bought and sold in the secondary market. An investor who buys sukuk replaces the seller in the pro-rated ownership of the relevant assets, and all the rights and obligations of the original subscriber are transferred to the buyer.

Islamic ETFs

An exchange-traded fund (ETF) is a fund that typically tracks an index and trades like a stock on an exchange. ETFs experience price changes throughout the day as they are bought and sold. Indexes such as the Straits Times Index (STI), the S&P 500 and the FTSE 100 each contain a basket of stocks that together are representative of the overall stock market in Singapore, the US and the UK, respectively. The STI, for example, contains 30 stocks such as SingTel, Keppel Corp and DBS.

The first Islamic ETF was set up in 2006 based on the DJIM Turkey Index (see Table 12.7). Since then, there has been strong expansion across the globe.

Table 12.7 *Examples of Islamic ETFs (continued overleaf)*

Name of Fund	Country	Year	Comment
DJIM Turkey ETF	Turkey	2006	World's first Islamic ETF
DJIM Titans 100 ETF	Switzerland	2007	Europe's first Islamic ETF
MSCI World, USA and Emerging Markets ETFs based on FTSE Islamic indexes	UK	2007	UK's first Islamic ETFs

Table 12.7 (cont'd from previous page) Examples of Islamic ETFs

Name of Fund	Country	Year	Comment
DJIM Malaysia Titans 25 ETF	Malaysia	2008	Malaysia's first Islamic ETF
Daiwa FTSE Shariah Japan 100 ETF	Singapore	2008	Singapore's first Islamic ETF

EXAMINING THE AMANA GROWTH FUND

The Amana Growth Fund, a US Islamic fund, has been a strong performer since its inception in 1986. It is a stellar example of an Islamic investment performing no worse, and usually better, than its conventional peers—even after screening and purification.

The primary objective of the fund is long-term capital growth, consistent with Islamic principles. Figure 12.2 shows its top holdings as of 30 June 2009.

Top Ten Holding:	
Apple	2.6%
Oracle	2.0%
Amazon.com	1.9%
PepsiCo	1.9%
Novartis AG ADR	1.8%
Hewlett-Packard	1.8%
Potash Corp of Saskatchewan	1.7%
Johnson & Johnson	1.7%
Qualcomm	1.6%
Anglo American PLC ADR	1.6%
Total:	18.6%

Figure 12.2 Top 10 holdings as of 30 June 2009

Figure 12.3 (opposite top) shows that an investment of US$10,000 in the fund 10 years ago (in June 1999) would be worth US$17,150 today (in March 2009). In comparison, its benchmark, the Russell 2000 Index, would be worth US$11,121 or 35 per cent less.

GROWTH OF $10,000:

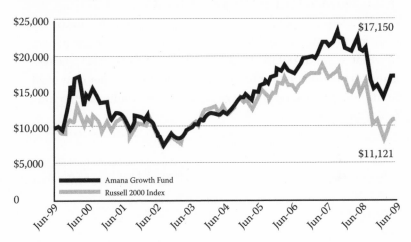

Figure 12.3 Growth of $10,000 over 10 Years (June 1999 to June 2009)
This chart illustrates the performance of a hypothetical $10,000 invested at the
beginning of the period and redeemed at the end of the period, and assumes
reinvestment of all dividends and capital gains.

Figure 12.4 shows the fund's sector allocation, which reflects the
bearish sentiment caused by the subprime crisis at the time with
17.7 per cent in cash, the second highest allocation. The highest
was in technology at 29.2 per cent.

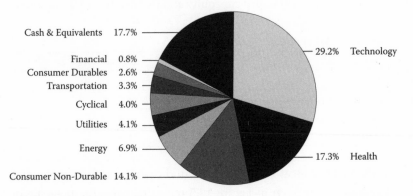

Figure 12.4   Sector Allocation
Industry weightings are shown as a percentage of net assets.

THE ISLAMIC FUND INDUSTRY

Eurekahedge, an independent consultancy and research house
dedicated to alternative investments, maintains a database of over
670 Islamic funds out of about 750 existing in the world.[6] Malaysia
is the top jurisdiction for funds, accounting for 24.7 per cent of all
funds. Most funds, however, are set up in the Middle East region
(see Table 12.8):

Table 12.8 Where funds are set up

Country of domicile	Percentage of funds
Malaysia	24.7%
Saudi Arabia	18.5%
Kuwait	9.2%
Cayman Islands	7.9%
Bahrain	6.1%
Indonesia	3.9%
Luxembourg	3.7%
Channel Islands	2.7%
Pakistan	2.7%
United Arab Emirates	1.8%
Others	13.4%

Equity funds represent over 52 per cent of total funds while a
distant second goes to private equity and real estate (see Table 12.9):

Table 12.9 Types of Islamic funds

Type of Fund	Percentage of funds
Equity	52%
Private equity/Real estate	18%
Leasing funds	4%
Others	26%

Due to the local focus of most fund managers, fund sizes tend
to be small. As seen in Figure 12.5 opposite, the large majority of
funds have US$20 million or less in assets.

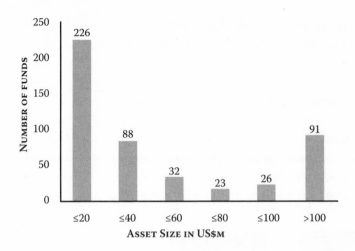

Figure 12.5 Asset sizes of Islamic funds

Among the major jurisdictions for Islamic funds, Saudi Arabia has the largest average fund size while Indonesia has the smallest[7] (see Table 12.10).

Table 12.10 Average fund size of selected jurisdictions

Type of Fund	Percentage of funds
Saudi Arabia	US$170 million
Kuwait	US$170 million
Malaysia	US$44 million
Indonesia	US$10 million

Islamic Alternative Investments

An alternative investment is any investment product other than what is traditional, such as stocks, bonds, cash and retail unit trusts. This broad definition makes it impossible to list all alternative strategies, but some of the most common are real estate, private equity, commodities and hedge funds (see Figure 12.6 overleaf).

Compared with traditional investments, alternative investments generally have the following characteristics:

◆ price movements that are lowly correlated to traditional investment returns and as a result provide diversification opportunities for investors.

◆ higher risk-return profiles.

Alternative investments are an important aspect of investing because they widen the offerings of financial markets, and provide greater opportunity for diversification, liquidity and wealth creation. We will now look briefly at private equity and hedge funds.

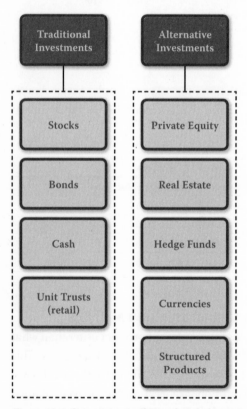

Figure 12.6 Comparing traditional and alternative investments

Private Equity Funds

Private equity consists of equity securities that are not publicly traded on a stock exchange. There is a wide range of styles of private equity, including leveraged buyouts, venture capital and distressed investments. The most common structure for private equity is a limited partnership where a general partner (with unlimited liability) invites investors (with limited liability) to provide capital for the venture. This is shown in Figure 12.7.

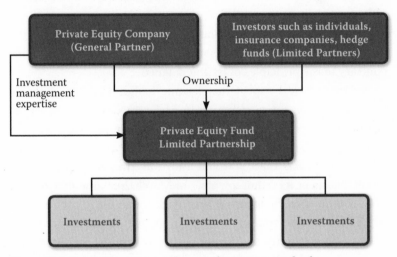

Figure 12.7 Ownership structure of a typical private equity fund

Investments can range from large assets in telecommunications, energy and infrastructure to smaller assets in restaurants, car dealerships and real estate.

Private equity funds are particularly attractive for Islamic investors because they provide higher returns, diversification and a broad range of investment opportunities.

A more important consideration is that private equity funds uphold the important Shariah principles of shared risk and mutual benefit by investing directly into real assets. This helps to foster new growth within communities through profit-sharing.

Hedge Funds

A hedge fund is an unregulated investment fund open to a limited range of investors who are deemed to be sophisticated and to have deeper pockets than do retail investors. Hedge funds undertake a wide range of alternative investments and high-risk trading activities, such as short selling, arbitrage and leverage (borrowing). The net asset value of a hedge fund can run into many billions of dollars, and this will usually be multiplied by leverage.

The 2008 subprime crisis was blamed in large part on the activity of hedge funds. These funds are controversial even in conventional finance, no less in Islamic finance. Some say, for example, that the idea of short selling, or selling something that you do not own, runs contrary to the principles of Islamic finance.

We nevertheless expect that Islamic hedge funds will become more popular in the near future. In Malaysia, despite criticism by Islamic scholars that Islamic hedge funds open the back door to gambling in Islam, its market watchdog, the Securities Commission, said in April 2009 that "it would award licences to Islamic hedge funds that meet its requirements".[8] In March 2009, the first Islamic fund of long/short hedge funds was marketed in the Middle East.[9]

As the Islamic marketplace grows in sophistication, investors will "expect more than the traditional returns offered by real estate and commodity funds. Hedge funds could be the answer."[10]

CONCLUSION

If you are new to investing, learning about the subject in general is vital before you even think about Islamic investing. One of the most effective ways to investment success and avoiding financial disaster is how successfully you manage risk. Whether you are an aggressive or conservative investor, we recommend you consider using the 3-Basket system that we devised and use ourselves.

Many people new to investing would start with investing in funds. If you prefer to buy stocks directly, examine the component stocks of Islamic indexes like those of the DJIM and S&P. Stocks are selected after going through screens of criteria to weed out those that are haram. You may also select stocks that are favoured by fund managers, such as the higher-ranking holdings of Islamic funds. We saw, for example, the kind of companies and sectors selected for investment by top-performing Amana Growth Fund.

Islamic alternative investments are an important addition to the Islamic investment landscape. At this stage, some private equity funds are generally accepted and others, such as hedge funds, will remain controversial like their conventional versions in the near future.

In the next chapter, we bring in the perspective of a business owner who buys and sells internationally, and how trade finance smooths his day-to-day operations.

---

1   We assume that these are five-year bonds that we will be holding till they mature.

2   Unit trusts are synonymous with mutual funds. They are also often referred to as just 'funds'.

3   Adapted from *Make Your Money Work For You* (2nd edition), by Keon Chee and Ben Fok. Marshall Cavendish Business, Singapore, 2008.

4   "DWS Noor Islamic Funds PLC—Singapore Prospectus," 5 May 2009, page 43 para 4.3.

5   The Russell 2000 Index measures the performance of small US companies based on market capitalisation.

6   The tables and figures in this section are based on data from Eurekahedge, taken from their Islamic Fund database as at September 2009 and the report "Key Trends in Islamic Funds 2008".

7   To be exact, Jersey, the US and British Virgin Islands have higher average fund sizes, but have very few funds. What we are examining here are the major jurisdictions listed in Table 12.8.

8   www.reuters.com/article/rbssBanks/idUSKLR42162520090416

9   www.reuters.com/article/rbssFinancialServicesAndRealEstateNews/idUSL968954120090309

10   "Access to Islamic Hedge Funds," Hedge Funds Review, November 2008.

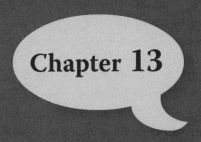

Chapter 13 TRADE FINANCING

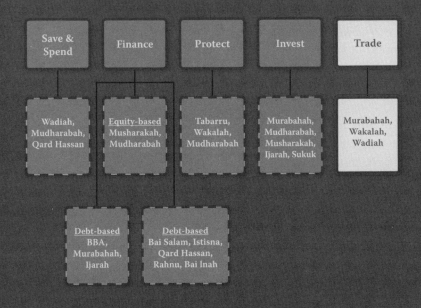

Save & Spend	Finance	Protect	Invest	Trade
Wadiah, Mudharabah, Qard Hassan	Equity-based Musharakah, Mudharabah	Tabarru, Wakalah, Mudharabah	Murabahah, Mudharabah, Musharakah, Ijarah, Sukuk	Murabahah, Wakalah, Wadiah

Debt-based
BBA, Murabahah, Ijarah

Debt-based
Bai Salam, Istisna, Qard Hassan, Rahnu, Bai Inah

STARTING A BUSINESS is the dream of many people. From the student who opens an online shop for costume jewellery of her own designs to the executive who wants to list his bakery business on the stock exchange, all would-be entrepreneurs have the common desire of wanting to be in control, make a dream idea come true or just have more time flexibility.

And for most businesses—small, medium or large—the need to buy and sell abroad is a basic activity. After all, most of the world's buyers and sellers of goods and services live outside of our country's borders. If you are selling only domestically, you are reaching just a small share of potential customers.

For the seller who exports overseas, there are many benefits, including reaching more buyers, broadening the company's customer base and protecting its bottom line from slower growth in the domestic economy. The buyer who imports from overseas experiences similar benefits too, on the opposite side—more sources of supply and the opportunity to work with the most price-competitive suppliers.

International trade, however, is not as simple as buying and selling goods at the corner grocery store. Although the concept of buying and selling is the same, challenges appear when we have to deal with shipping goods outside of our countries. For example, we may be buying from a country that is politically unstable, or whose foreign currency exchange is highly volatile. Trade finance is a large area of study in itself.

In this chapter, we will explain some of the most basic trade finance methods that apply to both conventional and Islamic finance. The key differences, as you will see, are the underlying contracts that are used. We have discussed these Islamic contracts in previous chapters such as *wakalah* (agency), *murabahah* (cost-plus sale) and *wadiah* (safekeeping).

WHAT IS TRADE FINANCE?

Buying and selling internationally, while benefitting both importer and exporter, has its fair share of risks, as seen in Figures 13.1 and 13.2.

For you, the seller, shipping goods overseas before you are paid exposes you to the risk that the buyer will not pay up after delivery has been made.

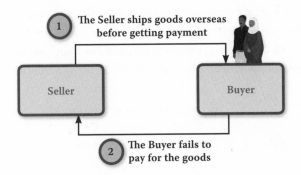

Figure 13.1 A risky situation for the seller

On the other hand, the buyer faces a similar risk if he were to pay without first receiving the goods.

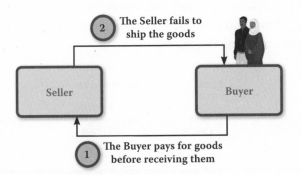

Figure 13.2 A risky situation for the buyer

This is where trade finance comes in. Trade finance fundamentally facilitates the ways in which the risks associated with doing business internationally are managed between buyers and sellers.

How International Payments Are Made

There are four main types of payment for international transactions, each presenting a different level of risk. From the perspective of a seller (see Figure 13.3) who expects to receive payment for goods sold, he faces a spectrum of risks from no risk (he receives payment in advance before the goods are shipped) to high risk (he ships the goods before payment is received using an open account).

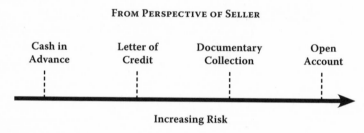

Figure 13.3 Payment types and risks from perspective of seller

On the other hand, as seen in Figure 13.4, the buyer is challenged by an identical risk spectrum but on the opposite side—from no risk (he receives the goods before making payment) to high risk (he pays before receiving the goods).

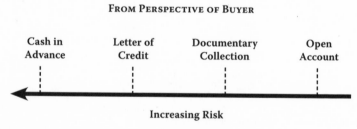

Figure 13.4 Payment types and risks from perspective of buyer

We will now discuss each of these four main methods, from your perspective as seller, and elaborate on the risks you will face when you export goods overseas.

Cash in Advance

With this method, the seller avoids credit risk altogether because payment is received before the ownership of the goods is transferred. Wire transfers and credit cards are commonly-used options. Cash in advance is not uncommon; it is often used when the buyer is new or is from a politically-risky country. Those who buy through the Internet, or who desire a much sought-after product, normally have to provide cash in advance.

Letters of Credit (LC)

One of the most secure instruments available for international buying and selling is the Letter of Credit (LC). An LC is a commitment by a bank on behalf of the buyer to pay the seller, when the terms and conditions stated in the LC have been met.

Who pays for the LC is a matter for negotiation between seller and buyer. Let us understand the practice with LCs by referring to Figure 13.5.

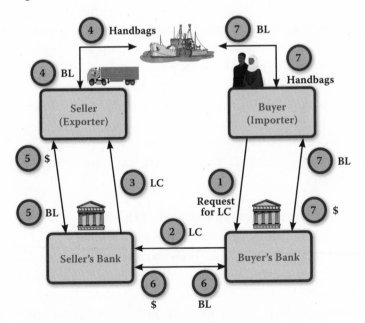

Figure 13.5 An example of buying and selling with Letter of Credit

Suppose you are a trader located in Thailand, selling and exporting branded handbags to many countries. A buyer from Ireland, who has never done business with you before, wants to purchase a shipment costing $100,000. Both the Irish buyer and you, the seller, enter into a sales contract. Note that the contracts for the sale and the LC are separate.

As a seller, you would be unwilling to ship your handbags without payment, while the Irish buyer would be reluctant to release funds before the goods arrive. Here is how an LC helps:

❶ The Irish buyer approaches her bank to request for an LC.
❷ The buyer's bank provides an LC to the seller's bank, promising payment upon presentation of certain documents.
❸ The seller's bank forwards the LC to the seller.
❹ The seller forwards the goods to a carrier in exchange for a document called a bill of lading (BL). The carrier dispatches the goods to an Irish seaport. (A BL is used to acknowledge the receipt of a shipment of goods. A carrier issues this document to a shipper. Additionally, a BL indicates the particular vessel on which the goods have been placed, the destination, and the terms for transporting the goods to the destination.)
❺ The seller provides the BL to his bank in exchange for payment.
❻ The seller's bank submits the BL to the buyer's bank for payment. At this point, payment is made.
❼ The buyer's bank submits the BL to the buyer for payment.
❽ The buyer submits the BL to the carrier and takes delivery of the handbags.

An LC mitigates risk for both sides in the following manner:
1. As the seller, an LC is useful to you when a foreign buyer is new to you or credit information about the buyer is sketchy, but you are satisfied with the creditworthiness of the buyer's foreign bank.
2. The buyer is at the same time protected because no payment is made until the terms and conditions stated in the LC are met.

Islamic Letters of Credit

Islamic LCs are typically issued under murabahah (cost-plus sale) and wakalah (agency) contracts.

In a murabahah LC, the Islamic bank acts as the financier for the buyer. As you recall from Chapter 8, in a murabahah transaction, the bank purchases the goods on your behalf, and then sells the goods to you on a cost-plus-profit margin basis. The only difference in this case is that we are introducing an LC into a murabahah contract.

Let us look at a simplified example of a murabahah LC. This time, we assume you are the buyer and that you wish to purchase a container of cashew nuts from India.

❶ You inform your bank (buyer's bank) of your purchase requirements.

❷ The buyer's bank produces an LC to pay the seller's bank in India for the cashews. The bank takes ownership of the cashews.

❸ When the cashews arrive as evidenced by a BL, the bank sells the cashews to you at a marked-up price comprising its cost and profit margin.

❹ The bank in India pays the cashew seller.

The diagram of a murabahah LC is similar to that of a conventional LC. Where fundamental differences exist are in the contracts as described in Table 13.1.

Table 13.1 Comparing conventional and murabahah Letters of Credit

	Conventional LC	Murabahah LC
Sales contract	A conventional bank is not part of the sales contract and deals only with documents, not goods.	The Islamic bank takes title of the goods before selling them to the buyer.
How the bank earns	The cost of the LC is based on an interest rate that is multiplied against the value of the LC.	The Islamic bank charges a profit margin based on murabahah terms.

In the case of a wakalah LC:

❶ The buyer appoints the Islamic bank as an agent to act on its behalf.

❷ The buyer is required to place a safekeeping deposit (based on wadiah) equal to the full amount of the price of the goods to be imported.

❸ The bank establishes the LC and makes payment to the seller's bank with the client's wadiah deposit.

❹ The BL is released to the buyer who then takes delivery of the goods.

❺ The bank charges the buyer agency fees for its services.

Letters of Credit are an important trade finance instrument to facilitate international trade. Their Islamic versions are commonly available at most Islamic banks offering trade finance. Bank Muamalat in Malaysia, for instance, offers an extensive list of Islamic trade finance products. Each of the listed products on its website comes with a simple explanation (www.muamalat.com.my). Its Letter of Credit offering can be issued under three contracts—wakalah, *mudharabah* (profit-sharing) and *musharakah* (joint venture).

Documentary Collections (DC)

A documentary collection (DC) is like an international COD (cash on delivery), where the buyer pays for goods on delivery. Banks act as intermediaries to collect payment from the buyer in exchange for the transfer of documents that enables the holder to take possession of the goods. The procedure is easier than that of an LC and less risky for the buyer. Also, the bank charges are lower. An important difference is that the bank does not guarantee payment like in an LC, but rather only acts as a collector of funds in exchange for documents.

Let us use the same example of the shipment of handbags, and once again suppose the buyer and you, the seller, agree on the terms of the sale of handbags in a sales contract. Refer to Figure 13.6. As with the LC, the contracts for the sales and the DC are separate.

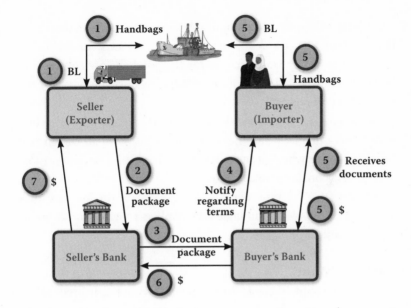

Figure 13.6 An example of a Documentary Collection

❶ The seller initiates the shipment of goods to the buyer and obtains a BL from the carrier.

❷ The seller prepares for his bank a document package consisting of the BL and a collection order. This order specifies the terms and conditions under which the bank is to hand over documents to the buyer to receive payment.

❸ The seller's bank sends the document package to the buyer's bank with instructions to present the documents to the buyer to collect payment.

❹ The buyer's bank notifies the buyer about the terms and conditions of the collection order, and that the documents will be released upon payment.

❺ The buyer makes payment, receives the documents, presents the BL to the carrier and then takes possession of the shipment.

❻ The buyer's bank pays the seller's bank.

❼ The seller's bank then pays the seller.

Although DCs are less complicated and less expensive than LCs, they present higher risk for the seller than do LCs. Under a DC, the buyer is not obligated to pay for the goods before shipment is received, and the seller has little recourse against the buyer in the event of non-payment.

Documentary collections should be used carefully under certain conditions, such as when the buyer and seller have an established relationship, or when an open account sale is considered too risky, and an LC is unacceptable to the buyer.

Islamic DCs are typically based on wakalah.[1] In the case of a seller, for example, he nominates the bank as an agent to act on his behalf to collect payment.

Open Account

An open account is a sale where the goods are delivered before payment is made. This option is clearly the most desirable for the buyer, but it is also the highest-risk option for the seller. Because of competition in export markets, foreign buyers often press sellers for open account terms. Sellers who are reluctant to extend credit may lose sales to their competitors. Fortunately, it is possible to mitigate the risk of non-payment associated with open accounts by using various techniques described below.

Export Working Capital Financing (EWCF)

Exporting sellers who lack sufficient funds to extend open accounts in the global market can use EWCF to cover the entire cash cycle, from the purchase of raw materials to the collection of the sales proceeds. Facilities with EWCF, which are offered by commercial banks, are secured by personal guarantees, assets or receivables.

Islamic working capital financing contracts are typically based on murabahah. For example, an Islamic bank may take the following steps:

1. The bank either purchases, or appoints the client as its agent to purchase, the goods on its behalf.
2. Upon delivery of the goods, the bank pays the seller.

3. The bank subsequently sells the goods to the client on cost-plus basis.
4. The buyer undertakes to settle the selling price.

Export Credit Insurance (ECI)

This technique provides protection to exporters from the risk of payment default by their buyers and from political losses such as war. It allows sellers to increase sales by offering more liberal open-account terms to new and existing customers. The ECI approach also provides security for banks when they supply working capital, and are financing exports.

Islamic ECI is not new although its use has been increasing only recently. The Islamic Corporation for Insurance of Investments and Export Credits (ICIEC), a member of the Islamic Development Bank (IDB), was established in 1994 to provide ECI for its Islamic member countries.

Export Factoring and Forfaiting

Factoring is the sale of usually short-term accounts receivable that are due within the next 180 days or so. If you are owed $10,000 for goods that you shipped to Europe 30 days ago, and you need the money urgently, you can sell the receivables at a discount of, say, $9,000, to a factoring house or factor. You, the seller, would then transfer title of the short-term foreign accounts receivable to the factor. The factor assumes the responsibility of collecting on the receivables. Factoring usually takes place with consumer goods.

Forfaiting is like factoring except that we are dealing with longer-dated receivables of between 180 days and a few years. The forfaiter, the purchaser of the receivables, becomes the entity to whom the buyers are obliged to pay their debt.

By purchasing these receivables—which are usually guaranteed by the buyer's bank—the forfaiter provides cash to the seller and frees the seller from the risk of not receiving payment from buyers. While giving the seller a cash flow, forfaiting allows the buyer to import goods for which he cannot immediately pay in full. These purchased receivables become a type of debt that can be bought and sold in debt markets in the form of bills of exchange and promissory notes.

Factoring and forfaiting are based on the discounting of a principal sum of money. There are no underlying assets exchanged in the transaction and neither is title to the assets assumed by the financier. This amounts to *riba* (interest) and is prohibited under Shariah.

Islamic alternatives can be structured using the various financing modes such as murabahah, mudharabah and musharakah. We have however seen very few examples of Islamic factoring and forfaiting products.[2]

Managing Foreign Exchange Risk

Foreign exchange (FX) is a risk factor that is often overlooked by small and medium-sized enterprises (SMEs). Although most SME exporters prefer to sell in their local currency, foreign buyers often demand to pay in their local currencies. If you are an Indonesian seller exporting to a Singapore buyer, the FX risk you face is the potential financial loss from a devaluation of the Singapore Dollar against the Indonesian Rupiah.

This exposure can be avoided by insisting on selling only in Rupiah. However, this may result in losing out to competitors who are willing to accommodate foreign buyers by selling in their local currencies. This approach could also result in the non-payment by a foreign buyer who may find it impossible to meet Rupiah-denominated payment obligations due to the devaluation of his local currency against the Rupiah.

The primary objective of FX risk management is to minimise potential currency losses, not to make a profit from FX rate movements, which are unpredictable and frequent. A variety of options are available for reducing short-term FX exposure. Note that not all of these techniques may be available in the buyer's country, they may be too expensive to be useful and Islamic versions are hard to come by.

Non-Hedging Techniques

The exporting seller can avoid FX exposure by using a simple non-hedging technique—price the sale in a foreign currency and then demand cash in advance. The current spot market rate will determine the local currency value of the foreign proceeds. A spot transaction is where the exporting seller and the importing buyer agree to pay using today's exchange rate and settle within two business days.

Another non-hedging technique is to net out foreign currency receipts with foreign currency expenditures. For example, a Malaysian seller who exports in Singapore dollars to a buyer in Singapore may want to purchase supplies in Singapore dollars from a different Singapore trading partner. If the company's export and import transactions with Singapore are comparable in value, FX risk is minimised. The risk is further reduced if those dollar-denominated export and import transactions are conducted on a regular basis.

Forward Hedges

The most direct method of hedging FX risk is a forward contract. It enables the exporter to sell a set amount of foreign currency at a pre-agreed exchange rate with a delivery date typically from three days to one year into the future.

For example, let us suppose US goods are sold to a Japanese company for ¥125 million on 30-day terms, and that the forward rate for "30-day yen" is ¥125 to the dollar. The US exporter can eliminate FX exposure by contracting to deliver ¥125 million to his bank in 30 days, in exchange for payment of $1 million dollars. Such a forward contract will ensure that the US exporter can convert the ¥125 million into $1 million, regardless of what happens to the dollar-yen exchange rate over the next 30 days.

However, if the Japanese buyer fails to pay on time, the US exporter will be obligated to deliver ¥125 million in 30 days. Accordingly, when using forward contracts to hedge FX risk, exporters are advised to pick forward delivery dates conservatively. If the foreign currency is collected sooner, the exporter can hold on to it until the delivery date, or can "swap" the old FX contract for a new one with a new delivery date at a minimal cost. Note that there are no fees or charges for forward contracts since the lender hopes to make a "spread" by buying at one price and selling to someone else at a higher price.

It appears that Islamic scholars generally agree that, in principle, forwards and futures may be compatible with Shariah principles. What makes them objectionable is when they are abused by speculators, or are used to exploit counterparties.[3] Hence if FX forwards are used genuinely and specifically to manage FX risk arising from trade, their use could be justified.

CONCLUSION

At the heart of trade finance is the basic need for exporters and importers to exchange capital and goods across borders. Without instruments such as LCs and the participation of banks, financiers, carriers and many other partiers, it would be impossible for entrepreneurs to trade, and for countries to exchange capital, goods and services across the world.

International trade represents a significant share of GDP (gross domestic product) of a country and directly affects the development of nations. It was with this important understanding that the International Islamic Trade Finance Corporation (ITFC) was set up in 2007. The ITFC is the trade arm of the IDB and its mandate is to develop and expand intra-trade between member countries of the Organization of the Islamic Conference (OIC). By providing Shariah-compliant trade financing, OIC member countries and the rest of Muslim world can expect to establish new trade links among themselves as well as with non-Muslim countries.

---

1   www.muamalat.com.my

2   An example is offered by the Haji Saeed Ahmed Lootah Group
     in Dubai (www.fcsdubai.com)

3   www.kantakji.com

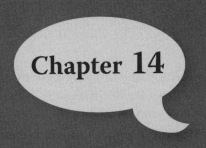

Chapter 14

PROSPECTS: ORDINARY OR EXTRAORDINARY?

ISLAMIC FINANCE principles are not only ethical, they are also sensible. Transparency, risk sharing, interest-free financing, asset-based transactions and the avoidance of undesirable activities—these are hallmark features.

Non-Muslims find them appealing as well. The OCBC Al-Amin Bank in Malaysia, for instance, has non-Muslims making up half of the bank's Islamic banking customers.[1] Also, to quote the Vatican's official newspaper *L'Osservatore Romano*, the "ethical principles on which Islamic finance is based may bring banks closer to their clients and to the true spirit which should mark every financial service."[2]

> "The ethical principles on which Islamic finance is based may bring banks closer ... to the true spirit which should mark every financial service."
> – *L'Osservatore Romano*

Conventional finance has similar principles that encourage transparency, risk sharing, asset-based transactions and the avoidance of undesirable activities. It strongly supports the principle that resources are best allocated through the free choice of consumers, and each person owns his or her own labour and therefore is allowed to sell the use of it.

Where there are marked differences is the forbidding of interest and the strong adherence of Islamic finance to an unchanging, codified set of laws called Shariah. Every instrument, every product and every contract has to undergo the scrutiny of Shariah councils who determine whether Shariah-compliance is being satisfied.

Conventional finance, on the other hand, is based on man-made law. There is normally a strict "separation of church and state"—a principle that religion should not interfere with economic decision-making. This is a major difference with Islamic finance, which is tightly governed by religious laws and principles.

Is Islamic finance inherently less risky than conventional finance to the point that crises in the system can never occur? What are the long-term prospects of Islamic finance? Can it work together with the conventional system for common good? We address these and other issues in this last chapter.

IS ISLAMIC FINANCE LESS RISKY THAN CONVENTIONAL FINANCE?

If both systems are equally competitive in terms of returns and performance, but Islamic finance is deemed less risky, it would make sense for many conventional finance users to switch preferences. Given the severe negative effects of past financial crises in the conventional system, adopting Islamic finance to some extent makes economic sense. But is Islamic finance really less risky than conventional finance?

Yes, It Is

The US subprime mortgage crisis caused several large international banks to collapse and brought many others to the brink of it. Yet to our knowledge, no Islamic banks have failed as a result of the mortgage crisis.

- One explanation is that Islamic finance requires the use of real assets and prohibits highly speculative financial derivatives. Such derivatives were a major cause of the mortgage crisis. The focus on asset-based financing puts natural limits on the level of debt, preventing excessive leverage.

- A second explanation is that Islamic finance encourages the sharing of risk, such as between banks and consumers. When investments in a *mudharabah* (profit-sharing) deposit account, for example, do poorly, the depositors (capital provider) absorb the full loss. But at the same time, Islamic banks are fully aware that if depositors do not receive ample returns on their investments, they would take their business elsewhere. This encourages Islamic banks to be conservative in order to minimise losses yet ensure that a reasonable and competitive return is generated.

Heavy risk taking is curtailed as a result of these principles of asset-based financing and profit-sharing.

No, It Is Not

Can we conclude that Islamic banks are less risky per se? While that might be a tempting conclusion, they can be prone to serious risks as well. For example:

- Islamic banks are more exposed to the property and infrastructure sectors. Given the size and nature of such assets, and the tendency for asset bubbles and crowd sentiment to build up quickly, it is a risk that could mimic even the subprime crisis (although probably not as strongly because the expansion of debt is restricted to asset-based financing).

- There are risks unique to Islamic finance such as Shariah-compliance risk. If products are later found to be not Shariah-compliant, the institutions face both reputation damage and the costly unwinding of such structures, with likely losses for investors.

- By providing financing based on risk sharing (rather than just lending money), Islamic institutions open themselves to risks that conventional banks do not normally have. Risk sharing means that a bank's equity is directly affected.

The last point holds up, according to an IMF (International Monetary Fund) study on the risk profile of Islamic banks and conventional commercial banks (see Figure 14.1). The study found that over the 11-year period from 1993 to 2004[3]:

1. small Islamic banks were financially stronger than small and large commercial banks[4];
2. large commercial banks were financially stronger than large Islamic banks; and
3. small Islamic banks were financially stronger than large Islamic banks.

An important observation of the study was that smaller Islamic banks provided more debt-based financing than equity-based financing, and for larger Islamic banks, it was the opposite—they provided more equity-based financing.

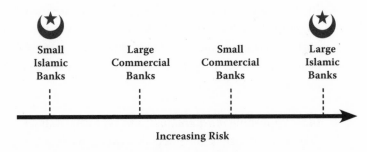

Figure 14.1 *The risk extent of banks by size and type*

A reasonable explanation is that larger Islamic banks take on more risk-sharing projects which bring about extra due diligence and surveillance costs because of the uniqueness of each project. Smaller Islamic banks that focus on debt-based financing provide loans which tend to be more or less standard in structure.

How Islamic Banks Already Mitigate Risk

Some market commentators have declared that Islamic finance has not only withstood the financial crisis, it has grown stronger. There are also others who have proclaimed the collapse of any Islamic financial institution to be simply unthinkable.

We feel it may still be premature to make these proclamations. Modern Islamic finance is just a youthful 50 years of age, and it will have to survive and thrive from many future challenges to earn its stripes. Furthermore, while the vehicle (Islamic finance) is like an impregnable armoured tank, it still depends on the man behind the wheels (the financial sector and its participants).[5]

If you recall, for example:

- In a *murabahah* (cost-plus sale) debt-financing contract (Chapter 8), the bank can use an agency contract to assign certain responsibilities to the customer during the initial procurement of an asset. The bank can also purchase insurance to limit the risks of asset ownership and use special purpose vehicles (SPVs) to hold assets.

- In an Al-Ijarah-Thummal Al-Bai (AITAB) lease-financing contract (Chapter 9), ownership of an asset is transferred to the customer at the end of the lease, either as a gift or through a sale. This mitigates the risks of ownership for the bank.

- In a diminishing *musharakah* (joint venture) contract, (Chapter 10), risk is mitigated as ownership of the asset is gradually transferred to the customer.

- Banks commonly take collateral from customers in order to have recourse on customers if they default.

The vehicle itself, which is Islamic finance, has provided its users with a set of rules and principles that if followed strictly, would result in a system that is just, fair and equitable to all parties, Muslims and non-Muslims alike.

PEERING INTO THE FUTURE

There are expectations that Islamic finance will grow to significant size and provide a viable alternative for people all over the world. For this to happen, two questions come to mind:

1. Can Islamic finance continue to grow by leaps and bounds in the short-term to reach a sizeable critical mass?
2. What could Islamic finance do to make such growth sustainable in the long term?

Growth in the Shorter Term

The first question is easy to answer, and most would agree to the answer 'yes'. Islamic finance is working from a low base. For example, while Islamic assets under management (AUM) comprise 1 per cent of global AUM, Muslims make up over 20 per cent of world population. There is also low insurance penetration among Muslim countries. Moreover, Middle East money, the Western world's desire to raise an alternative "socially-responsible" system and Asian economic growth will continue to provide a virtuous backdrop.

Growth in the Longer Term

There are a few points to consider about its long-term competitiveness.

1. First, the benefits of Islamic finance have to go beyond social responsibility and the reduction of wealth gaps and poverty. Economic benefits have to be clear. Investing in Islamic funds has to produce good, reasonable returns that are compatible with, if not better than, the offers of conventional investing. *Takaful* (Islamic insurance) has to be competitively priced, and its features have to be rich and adapted to consumer needs. The cost of financing must also be competitive when compared with conventional alternatives.
2. Second, Islamic finance has to address many criticisms from within its own community about manufacturing products using conventional parts.

The BBA contract, for example, is disputed by many Middle East scholars as one that is Shariah-compliant only in form, but in substance, it is similar to its conventional *riba*-based (interest-based) counterpart. Islamic bonds (*sukuk*), financing based on deferred sales (*istisna*) and exotic options (*istijrar*) are products that have also attracted criticism.

The role of Shariah councils, which is a vital instrument to ensure Shariah compliance of products and services, has also been questioned within the Muslim community. One criticism is about corporate governance—since council members are sought after, they receive potentially large payments. This creates conflicts of interest because scholars who are known to be supportive of certain structures can be expected to be part of certain councils while those who are against these structures will probably be ignored. Well-regarded Islamic scholar Dr Mahmoud El-Gamal, a professor of Rice University in the US, charges such scholars with promoting "rent seeking Shariah arbitrage" and earning large sums for doing so.

3. Third, would it serve Islamic finance better to work separately or co-operatively with conventional finance especially in the important areas of regulations, product development and financial reporting?

Some favour a path that is separate because the Islamic system, being governed by Shariah principles, is very distinct. These proponents believe that Islamic products should be built entirely with Islamic parts.

Those who favour working together say that Islamic finance can thrive alongside the conventional system by focusing on the similarities of both systems rather than emphasising their differences.[6] In an interview entitled "Can Equilibrium Be Reached?" by *Islamic Finance Asia* (Feb–Mar 2009 issue), Yavar Moini, executive director of global capital markets at Morgan Stanley based in Dubai, said, "It is, however, important to strike a balance between innovation and adaptation because the Islamic finance industry is too nascent in its life cycle and cannot yet hope to offer the breadth and depth of products and markets in relation to its conventional counterpart."

Countries that have existing conventional systems would find this strategy effective. For example, the Monetary Authority of Singapore (MAS) has created a single regulatory framework to apply to both conventional and Islamic banking, as it recognises the strong similarities between the two while acknowledging the differences: "MAS' approach is to look through the form of the Islamic products to assess the economic substance and risks involved, and use that assessment as the basis for regulation."[7]

FOR THE BENEFIT OF ALL

Islamic and conventional finance can co-exist peaceably for the benefit of all. So can there be greater collaboration and understanding between Muslims and non-Muslims at the grassroots level? The Holy Koran encourages positive feelings for non-Muslims. Islam does not wage war on non-Muslims just because they are non-Muslims:

> *Allah forbids you not, with regard to those who fight you not for (your) Faith nor drive you out of your homes, from dealing kindly and justly with them: for Allah loveth those who are just. Allah only forbids you, with regard to those who fight you for (your) Faith, and drive you out of your homes, and support (others) in driving you out, from turning to them (for friendship and protection). It is such as turn to them (in these circumstances) that do wrong. (60:8-9)*

Islam also encourages Muslims and non-Muslims to co-operate in noble causes, as demonstrated by the involvement of Prophet Mohammad (pbuh) in Hilf Al-Fudhul, which was a pact made by several Arab tribes to defend a man who was abused cruelly by a member of another Arab tribe. The Prophet participated in this pact before he was appointed a prophet. When he recalled this incident during his prophethood, he said:

If I were to be invited to enter into such a pact again, I would do so.[8]

Here are some modern day examples of grassroots collaboration:

- In the US, the Catholic Church has since 1965 encouraged its followers to engage in dialogue with people of other faiths. Muslim-Catholic dialogues began formally in 1985. National and regional meetings have been co-sponsored by the US Conference of Catholic Bishops, the Islamic Society of North America and several other Muslim organisations. In 2003, a joint statement was thus concluded: "Friends and Not Adversaries: A Catholic-Muslim Spiritual Journey."

- In the UK, the Christian Muslim Forum was formed in 2006 as a charitable company to offer practical ways of bringing Christians and Muslims together through common initiatives. Dr Ataullah Siddiqui, who heads the Muslim part of the Forum, said, "We want to work together not simply for the benefit of two communities but jointly for the wider society."

- At Cairo's Al-Azhar University in June 2009, Barack Obama delivered a speech near the start of his US presidency to underscore US respect for Islam. During the speech, he called for an end to "suspicion and discord" so that a new chapter of co-operation can start, based "upon mutual interest and mutual respect".

We do hope that in time, these collaborations are motivated more by the desire to build a world that embraces and celebrates diversity rather than to merely avoid conflict, terrorism and fear.

FINAL WORDS

These are exciting times for Islamic finance for both Muslims and non-Muslims.

For Muslims, Islamic finance has entered mainstream consciousness. It is built on principles that reflect their faith. Most Islamic contracts are universally and generally accepted as being Shariah-compliant. Growth rates should be strong in the near future.

For non-Muslims, Islamic finance provides an increasingly viable alternative for various—although not all—areas of finance. Whether Christian, Buddhist or Hindu, non-Muslims find the underlying principles of Islamic finance appealing and economically feasible.

We leave you with a beautiful piece of calligraphy featuring the Arabic greeting *Assalamu Alaikum*, which is used by Muslims as well as Arab Christians and Jews. It means "Peace Be Upon You".

"Assalamu Alaikum" was painted by Haji Noor Deen, a renowned Chinese Muslim master of Arabic calligraphy. Born in 1963 in Shandong province, China, he is one of 20 million Muslims in China. You can view his other works at www.hajinoordeen.com.[9] The Chinese words that run vertically on the left read "Year of the fifth Heavenly Stem and first Earthly Branch, collection by Mi Guangjiang". They mean "painted in the year 2008 by Mi Guangjiang". Mi Guangjiang is Haji Noor Deen's given Chinese name.

1   "More non-Muslims trying Islamic banking: OCBC," Business Times, 1 December 2008.

2   As reported in "The Relevance of Islamic Finance Principles to the Global Financial Crisis," Harvard Law School Paper, 27 March 2009.

3   "Study Shows Larger Islamic Banks Need Prudential Eye," IMF Survey Magazine, June 2008. Note that the study focused only on full-fledged Islamic banks and did not cover Islamic windows (Islamic branches operated by some commercial banks).

4   Large banks are those with total assets of more than US$1 billion.

5   Likewise, the conventional system is governed by many rigorous and ethical principles. The problem, as has often been the case, is "the man behind the wheels."

6   *Islamic Finance: Law, Economics and Practice* by Mahmoud El-Gamal. Cambridge University Press, 2006.

7   "Guidelines on the Application of Banking Regulations to Islamic Banking," Monetary Authority of Singapore, May 2009.

8   Excerpted from "Ramadan Builds Righteous Muslims," Friday sermon at Islamic Religious Council of Singapore, 5 October 2007.

9. According to his website (www.hajinoordeen.com): "The Chinese and Arabic calligraphic traditions have often been compared as two of the world's finest manifestations of the written word, but never likened; indeed, they are at once opposites and complements. When combined the result is an artistic piece that is a work of incredibly unique beauty, and a testimony to man's synthesizing genius."

GLOSSARY OF
TERMS USED

The explanations of the terms in this section will be useful to readers who wish to find in one location the key terms used in the book. The terms have been categorised as follows:

The organisation of the terms approximates the pathway that a person new to Islam and finance would take on his or her educational journey.

At the end of the glossary, you will find a short "Introduction to the Arabic Language". It explains the importance of Arabic as the sacred language of the Holy Koran, and one that every Muslim uses in prayer although not necessarily in daily life.

TERMS RELATED TO ISLAM

The terms in this category are mainly discussed in Chapters 1, 2 and 3.

Allah (swt)

The name for God in the Arabic language and the common name for God in Islam. According to the Holy Koran, Allah is the Creator of the Universe, known as "God the Father" to Christians and "Yahweh" to Jews. The set of initials "swt" stands for *subhanahu wa ta'ala*, and means "Glorified and Exalted is He". It is considered more pleasing to Allah to praise Him as such when He is mentioned.

Islam

The religious faith of Muslims, based on the words and religious system defined in the Holy Koran and founded by the Prophet Muhammad (pbuh). The most fundamental principle of Islam is absolute submission to Allah (swt).

Prophet Muhammad (pbuh)

Muhammad, born circa 570 in the Arabian city of Mecca, is the founder of Islam and is regarded by Muslims as a messenger and prophet of Allah (swt), the last law-bearer in a series of Islamic prophets. Muslims show their devotion to the Prophet by putting the set of initials "pbuh" after his name; "pbuh" stands for 'peace be upon him.'

Muslim

A person who submits to the faith of Islam.

Shariah

Islamic finance is based on Shariah or the body of Islamic law. Shariah means "the right path to the water source". Shariah is filled with moral purpose and lessons on the truth and is hence more than just a set of legal rules. At its core, Shariah represents the idea that all human beings and all human governments are subject to justice under the law. It is a term that summarises a way of life prescribed by Allah (swt) for His servants and it extends to everything from business contracts and marriage to punishment and worshipping. Islamic law is now the most widely used religious law, and one of the three most common legal systems in the world alongside common law and civil law.[1]

Haram

Haram is an Arabic word and it refers to anything that is forbidden. Worshipping a god other than Allah (swt) is perhaps the most serious aspect of haram. Haram also includes behaviours like adultery and lust, foods like alcohol and pork, ill-gotten wealth obtained through interest, cheating or any means that causes harm to another human being.

Halal

Halal is the opposite of haram, and it refers to anything that is Shariah-compliant, that is, permissible, under Islam. This includes aspects of human behaviour, speech, clothing and diet.

Holy Koran

The sacred book of Islam. Muslims believe the Holy Koran to be the book of divine guidance and direction for mankind, and they consider the original Arabic text to be the final revelation of Allah (swt). The Holy Koran itself expresses that it is the book of guidance. It emphasises the moral significance of events and rarely offers detailed accounts of historical events.

Hadith

The Hadith is the second primary source of Islamic law besides the Holy Koran. The Hadith are the reports of the sayings and deeds of Prophet Muhammad (pbuh). The Prophet's sayings and deeds outside the revelations of Allah(swt) are called his Sunnah (which means "example").

Other Sources of Islamic Law

Besides the Holy Koran and the Hadith, there are other sources of Islamic law that have less absolute effect. These consist of Ijma (rulings on Islamic matters that are made by qualified Islamic legal scholars based on consensus) and Qiyas (analogies drawn from the Holy Koran and Sunnah to make new rulings).

Aqidah

These are beliefs over which Muslims have conviction. There are six main aspects including belief in Allah (swt), belief in the prophets and messengers sent by Allah (swt) and belief in the Holy Koran and the Hadith.

Akhlaq

Akhlaq is the practice of virtue and morality. To attain perfection and happiness, man must purge bad traits before he can integrate moral virtues.

Ibadah

Ibadah refers to man-to-God activities. It means submission to Allah (swt) as one's Master and one as His slave to heed in obedience. One's life is ibadah if it is in harmony with the laws of Allah (swt).

The Five Pillars

The Five Pillars describe the good works that each Muslim is expected to carry out in order to achieve ibadah. These Five Pillars revolve around faith, prayer, concern for the needy, self-purification and the pilgrimage to Mecca.

Zakat

Zakat expresses concern for the needy, and is one of the Five Pillars of Islam. It is the giving of a small percentage of one's income to charity. Muslims believe that their possessions are purified by setting aside a portion for those in need, and, like the pruning of a plant, this cutting back encourages new growth. Each Muslim calculates his own zakat individually, which typically amounts to 2.5 per cent of one's earnings. It is the duty of an Islamic state not just to collect zakat but to distribute it fairly as well.

The Hajj

This is the pilgrimage to Mecca. It is an obligation only for those who are physically and financially able to perform it. It was at Mecca that Abraham built the first house of worship (the Kaabah), towards which all Muslims stand in unity in their daily prayers.

Muamalat Ammah

Muamalat Ammah governs man-to-man activities including marriage and family life, commercial transactions and punishment. Muamalat refers to those activities surrounding commercial transactions.

Jinayat

Jinayat refers to punishment. There are five categories of human action, broadly defined as obligatory, recommended, permitted, discouraged and forbidden. Punishment is incurred for neglecting obligatory actions (such as for not believing in Allah (swt)) and for engaging in forbidden actions (such as gambling).

Tawhid

Tawhid is the concept of monotheism or one God in Islam. It holds that Allah (swt) is one and unique.

Archangel Gabriel

Muslims believe archangel Gabriel to have been the angel who revealed the Holy Koran to Prophet Muhammad (pbuh). Gabriel's primary task is to bring messages from God to His messengers. In Christianity, Gabriel is said to be the angel that informed Mary of how she would conceive Jesus.

Mecca

Prophet Muhammad (pbuh) was born in Mecca, and thus Islam has been inextricably associated with Mecca ever since. It is the holiest meeting site of the Islamic religion and the capital of Saudi Arabia's Makkah Province.

Sunni and Shiite

After the death of the Prophet Muhammad (pbuh), two major positions developed about the nature of authority over the Muslim community. One group, which came to be called Sunni (meaning tradition), accepted the succession of the Prophet by the caliphs, who were followers elected by the Prophet himself. About 85 per cent of the world's Muslims are Sunni.

Shiites, on the other hand, believed that any head of the community had to be a direct descendant of Prophet Muhammad (pbuh). About 15 per cent of Muslims are Shiites with a small minority who are members of other Islamic sects. Shiites form the majority in Iran, Azerbaijan, Bahrain, Lebanon and Iraq. The historical divide between the Sunnis and the Shiites was caused more by political dispute over successors than by doctrinal differences, although differences gradually assumed theological overtones.

Riba

Riba means interest and covers any return of money on money— whether the interest is fixed or floating, simple or compounded, and at whatever the rate. Riba is strictly prohibited. The presence of riba in any contract would void the contract. Besides its religious restriction, riba is considered unfair and exploitative. A borrower who pays interest means that his money is being taken without getting anything in return. Not only does this make the borrower worse off, it does not bring about mutual co-operation and goodwill between lender and borrower.

Gharar

Gharar means uncertainty. It is considered to be of lesser significance to riba in that while the prohibition of riba is absolute, some degree of gharar is acceptable. Minor gharar, which exists in most transactions, is permitted. Only excessive gharar must be avoided where uncontrollable risk leads to speculation and gambling. Gharar also implies deceit and this can be seen in business transactions that cause injustice of any form to any of the parties. For example, if the seller of a home intentionally conceals a termite problem, the buyer would be exposed to unfair risk or gharar.

Maysir

Maysir means gambling and is prohibited. Gambling includes games of chance such as betting money in a slot machine or borrowing money to speculate on currency movements. Maysir is often used as grounds for rejecting conventional insurance and derivatives. What makes gambling highly objectionable is when it takes place, say, in a casino where the odds of winning are strongly stacked against the player. Islam does not tolerate this unjust seizure of another person's wealth, something that cripples the poor and widens the wealth gap between rich and poor.

TERMS RELATED TO FINANCE

Dow Jones Industrial Average (DJIA) *[See Chapter 12]*
The DJIA is a price-weighted average of 30 major stocks (including General Electric, Disney, Wal-Mart and Microsoft) traded on two US stock exchanges—the New York Stock Exchange and the Nasdaq. Created in 1896, the DJIA (also called the Dow) is the oldest and most watched index in the world. When the US media say "the market is up today", they are generally referring to the Dow.

Domini 400 SocialSM Index (DS400) *[See Chapter 12]*
The DS400 is a common stock index of US equities. Launched in May 1990, the DS400 is the first benchmark index constructed using environmental, social and governance (ESG) factors. It is a widely recognised benchmark for measuring the impact of social and environmental screening on investment portfolios.

The Great Depression of 1929 *[See Chapter 1]*
The Great Depression was a worldwide economic downturn which started in the US with the Dow crashing on October 29, 1929, known as Black Tuesday. It was the largest and most severe economic depression in the 20th century. Cities all around the world were hit hard, and construction was virtually halted in many countries. Farming and rural areas suffered as crop prices fell by over 50 per cent.

9/11 *[See Chapter 1]*
9/11 or the September 11 attacks were a series of suicide attacks by Al-Qaeda on the US on September 11, 2001. On that day, Al-Qaeda terrorists hijacked four commercial passenger jet airliners, and on the same day crashed all of them. Two were intentionally crashed into the Twin Towers of the World Trade Center in New York City. Both buildings collapsed within two hours. The hijackers crashed the third airliner into the Pentagon in Arlington, Virginia, and the fourth into a field near Shanksville in rural Pennsylvannia. The death toll was 2,974 victims and 19 hijackers.

The 2008 Subprime Mortgage Crisis *[See Chapter 1]*

The subprime crisis was triggered by a dramatic rise in home ownership in the US. Low interest rates, a recovering US economy and the inflow of foreign funds created easy credit conditions for a number of years prior to the crisis, fuelling a housing market boom and encouraging debt-financed consumption. As interest rates rose and mortgages were adjusted, mortgage delinquencies rose while housing demand fell. All this brought major negative consequences for banks and financial markets around the world.

Microfinance *[See Chapter 1]*

Microfinance refers to the provision of financial services to low-income customers. It can range from providing credit, loans, insurance and a range of banking services normally beyond the reach of such customers. Those who promote microfinance believe that it can help poor people out of poverty. In 2006, Bangladeshi economist and banker Professor Muhammad Yunus and Grameen Bank were jointly awarded the Nobel Peace Prize for their work in microfinance.

Socially Responsible Investing (SRI) *[See Chapters 1 and 12]*

SRI is an investment strategy that seeks to maximise both financial returns and social good. Corporate practices favoured by SRI practitioners include environmental protection, human rights and the avoidance of businesses involved in armaments, pornography, alcohol, tobacco and gambling.

Usury *[See Chapter 3]*

Usury originally meant the charging of interest on loans. Today, the word means the charging of unreasonable or relatively high rates of interest.

Special Purpose Vehicles (SPV) *[See Chapter 12]*

An SPV is a separate subsidiary company set up to contain investments. Such a company protects its assets secure even if the parent company goes bankrupt. SPVs are typically used to finance large projects without putting the entire firm at risk.

International Financial Reporting Standards (IFRS)
[See Chapter 5]

IFRS are accounting standards adopted by the International Accounting Standards Board (IASB). IFRS are generally accepted by international organisations such as the EC and the OECD.

Stocks and Bonds *[See Chapter 12]*

Stocks are issued by a company as a way to obtain financing from investors. The holder of a stock is thus an owner in the company, and has a claim on the company's earnings and assets. Bonds are also issued by a corporation to obtain financing. The difference is that bond-issuing companies are contractually obligated to provide income at regular intervals and the return of capital by a specified time.

Unit Trusts *[See Chapter 12]*

A collective investment scheme that invests in securities on behalf of investors or unit holders. The success of a unit trust depends on the expertise of the fund management company. The term "unit trust" is synonymous with "mutual fund" as it is used in the US.

Exchange-Traded Fund (ETF) *[See Chapter 12]*

An ETF is a fund that typically tracks an index and trades like a stock on an exchange. ETFs experience price changes throughout the day as they are bought and sold. By owning an ETF, an investor gets the diversification of an index fund. Another advantage is that the expense ratios of ETFs are mostly lower than those of the average unit trust.

Alternative Investments *[See Chapter 12]*

An alternative investment is an investment product other than a traditional investment such as a stock, bond, cash and retail unit trust. Alternative investments are held mainly by sophisticated investors, such as institutional investors and high-networth individuals, as these investments are normally complex, have limited regulations and are less liquid. Alternative investments include hedge funds, private equity, real estate, commodities and structured products.

Derivatives *[See Chapter 6]*

A derivative is a financial product whose value is derived from an underlying asset. This can be a stock, an apartment or even a tonne of flour. An example of a derivative is a call option on a stock. If you buy such an option, it is nothing more than your buying the right to own within a specified time the underlying asset at a stated price.

Forward Contract *[See Chapter 6]*

A transaction in which delivery of an asset is made in the future while the price is determined on the initial trade date. Most forward contracts do not have standards and are not traded on exchanges. A wheat farmer would use a forward contract to lock in a price for his grain for his upcoming harvest.

Futures Contract *[See Chapter 6]*

A futures contract is like a forward contract in that delivery of an asset is made in the future based on a price established today. The difference is that futures contracts are traded on an exchange and thus have standardised terms to facilitate trading.

Swaps *[See Chapter 6]*

A swap is a derivative in which two counterparties agree to exchange one stream of cash flows for another stream. There are many types of swaps. In an interest-rate swap, counterparty A may swap her fixed-interest payments with the variable-interest payments of counterparty B. Most swaps are traded over-the-counter and are tailor-made for the counterparties.

Insurance *[See Chapters 6 and 11]*

Insurance provides an individual or entity with financial protection against losses. Insurance is offered by insurance companies, which pool client risks to make payments more affordable, in exchange for a premium.

Reinsurance *[See Chapters 6 and 11]*

The process of an insurance company seeking insurance from other institutions in order to reduce overall risks associated with its underwritten policies. Reinsurance is insurance for insurers.

Initial Public Offering (IPO) *[See Chapter 6]*

An IPO is a company's first stock offering to the public. The primary market is the market in which investors have the first opportunity to buy the newly-issued stock. Once the IPO is completed, the stock begins trading in the secondary market on a formal exchange. Examples of such an exchange include the Singapore Exchange (SGX) and the New York Stock Exchange (NYSE).

Over-the-Counter (OTC) *[See Chapter 6]*

A security that is traded OTC means that it is not listed or available on a stock exchange, but is traded directly between buyers and sellers.

Mortgage *[See Chapter 8]*

When a homeowner mortgages her property, it means that she has transferred her ownership in the property to the bank as a security for a loan. The ownership will be returned to the owner when the terms of the mortgage have been satisfied.

Flat Rates versus Effective Rates *[See Chapter 8]*

Loans based on flat interest rates are often used in developing countries. One reason for their popularity is their ease of use. For example, a loan of $1,000 can be structured with 10 monthly repayments of $100, plus interest of 1 per cent or $10 a month, resulting in a total monthly payment of $110. Flat rates are easy to calculate and track as they require no compounding calculations. Loans are also quoted using the effective interest rate, which describes the interest rate for a whole year (annualised) with compounding included. Effective rates are always higher than flat rates for the same loan duration. For example, a 5-year loan with a flat rate of 3 per cent would have an effective rate of 5.84 per cent.

Leasing *[See Chapter 9]*

A lease is a rental agreement in which the use of an asset, such as a car, is hired for a period of time. Compared with renting, leasing is usually for a longer period, such as two years, and it has more formal terms. There are two main types of leases. In an operating lease, the lessor who leases the asset remains the owner of the asset before and after the lease period. In a financial lease, the lessee has the option to purchase the asset at the end of the lease.

Sales and Leaseback (or Leaseback) *[See Chapter 9]*

A leaseback is an arrangement where the owner of an asset sells the asset and leases it back for a period. Thus one continues to be able to use the asset, but no longer owns it. A leaseback is a suitable arrangement for the seller to raise money by offloading a valuable asset to a buyer who is interested in making a long-term secured investment.

Letters of Credit (LC) *[See Chapter 13]*

An LC is a commitment by a bank on behalf of the buyer to pay the seller when the terms and conditions stated in the LC have been met. LCs are used in international trade.

Documentary Collections (DC) *[See Chapter 13]*

A DC is like an international COD (cash on delivery) where the buyer pays for goods on delivery. Banks act as intermediaries to collect payment from the buyer in exchange for the transfer of documents that enables the holder to take possession of the goods. The procedure is easier than an LC and less risky for the buyer, and the bank charges are lower.

TERMS RELATED TO ISLAMIC FINANCE

Islamic Finance *[See Chapter 1]*

Islamic finance refers to the system of finance that is consistent with Islamic law or Shariah. The overriding principle around which all of Islamic finance revolves is the belief in divine guidance. Man needs such guidance because he does not have the power to reach the truth on his own. It is the firm belief of every Muslim that the commands given by Allah (swt) are to be followed in letter and spirit. Additionally, Islamic finance has four distinctive features—interest is prohibited, haram activities are prohibited, risk sharing between business partners is encouraged, and financing should be extended only when real assets are involved.

Islamic Assets Under Management *[See Chapters 1 and 12]*
Assets Under Management (AUM) refers to the market value of assets that an investment company manages on behalf of investors. AUM goes up and down as the value of underlying investment assets rise and fall, and by the amount of investor money inflows and outflows. Islamic AUM refers to those assets that are managed by investment managers that adhere to Shariah principles.

Islamic Financial Contracts *[See Chapter 4]*
An Islamic commercial contract is a formal, binding contract drawn up by parties involved in a commercial transaction. The names of Islamic financial contracts are English transliterations of Arabic words. For an English speaker, the terms can be daunting at first. To make the terms easier to learn, we have categorised contracts by the type of financial transaction in which they are usually used:

1. Saving and Spending
When you open a deposit or checking account at a commercial bank, you have three main choices.

- A **Wadiah** savings account *[See Chapter 7]* provides safekeeping for deposits. There are two types of wadiah accounts, of which the more popular type is a **Wadiah Yad Dhamanah** account. In this account, the bank is allowed to utilise the money for projects and investments, and is not obligated to offer the depositor a return on investments. However, the bank will guarantee paying back of the deposit. It is also allowed to provide returns in the form of a gift, as long as those gifts are not officially promised or guaranteed.

- A **Mudharabah** savings account *[See Chapter 7]* is a profit-sharing account. When such an account is first opened, the depositor and the bank agree to a profit-sharing ratio. The bank takes the deposit, invests it and shares the profits with the depositor accordingly. The capital provider (that is, the depositor) is solely responsible for losses.

❖ A **Qard Hassan** savings account *[See Chapter 7]* provides no returns at all. This is equivalent to an interest-free loan in conventional finance.

2. Financing Based on Debt

Three types of debt-based contracts form the very large majority of financing contracts.

❖ A **Bai Bithaman Ajil** (BBA) contract *[See Chapter 8]* is commonly used in long-term mortgage loans on which the homeowner pays instalments for typically 10, 20 or more years. In a BBA contract, the bank buys the asset that the customer has identified. The bank then sells the asset to the customer with profit on a deferred payment basis.

❖ A **Murabahah** contract *[See Chapter 8]* is similar to a BBA contract but for shorter-term needs. Payment can be by lump sum or by instalment (as in BBA).

❖ An **Ijara** contract *[See Chapter 9]* is used for leasing assets for which ownership of the asset stays with the bank or financier. Leasing is like renting except that the duration of using the asset is longer-term and the asset is usually large in value, such as a car, a house or heavy machinery. An Ijara contract can be structured as a hire purchase to give the customer the right to own the asset at a pre-agreed price at the end of the Ijarah period. Two common versions are **Al-Ijarah-Thummal Al-Bai** (**AITAB**, also called **Ijara Wa Iqtina**) and **Ijarah Muntahia Bittamleek** (**IMB**).

3. Financing Based on Equity

Equity-based financing methods have general agreement among Islamic scholars about how they work, but are less popular because these methods are less familiar to consumers when it comes to financing.

❖ In a **Mudharabah** financing contract *[See Chapter 10]*, the bank provides capital to the customer for a project based on a profit-sharing ratio. Note that unlike a Mudharabah savings account where the bank puts the money to productive use, a Mudharabah financing contract is the exact opposite where the customer is the entrepreneur who puts the money financed to productive use. This sort of financing requires the bank to do more due diligence on the nature of the borrower's project.

 ♦ In a **Musharakah** financing contract *[See Chapter 10]*, the bank and the customer become joint-venture partners. Both parties provide capital and decide on a profit-sharing agreement. As in Mudharabah financing, Musharakah financing requires the bank to be very careful about who is a good business partner. Losses are shared in proportion to the amount of capital that each partner puts in.

4. Other Financing Contracts

There are other financing contracts that are less popular or are used for specific purposes. There are also some that remain controversial.

 ♦ A **Bai Salam** *[See Chapter 10]* is a contract in which payment is made immediately while the goods are delivered at an agreed later date. It is equivalent to an advance payment. Bai Salam was originally created to provide financing for farmers.

 ♦ An **Istisna** contract *[See Chapter 10]* involves the sale of manufactured assets such as buildings, airplanes and ships where the bank pays the manufacturer in advance and the assets are delivered upon completion in the future. The specifications of the assets are pre-agreed. This contract enables suppliers to be paid a pre-delivery advance.

 ♦ A **Qard Hassan** loan *[See Chapter 10]* is a benevolent "interest-free" loan. It is the simplest of financing schemes where a borrower takes a loan of say $100 and repays the lender on maturity exactly the same amount of $100 without an increment.

- A **Rahnu** contract *[See Chapter 10]* is a pawnbroking contract in which a valuable asset is used as collateral to obtain a loan. The collateral may be used as payment if the loan is not repaid within the pre-agreed period.

- A **Bai Inah** contract *[See Chapter 10]* is a contract that involves the sale and buyback of an asset by a seller. In such a contract, a customer sells an asset to the bank for, say, $100. The bank pays the customer $100. The customer buys the asset back from the bank at a higher price of $100 + $X with the bank's profit margin being $X. The customer then pays the bank in instalments. Bai Inah is considered controversial by some as it brings about riba "through the back door".

5. Other Financial Transactions

Other Islamic finance transactions that deal with insurance, investments and trade finance are all mostly structured using previously mentioned contracts. Takaful, the Islamic version of insurance, largely uses Mudharabah and Wakalah. Investment securities typically use Musharakah, Mudharabah and Ijara contracts.

TERMS RELATED TO
ISLAMIC FINANCIAL INSTITUTIONS

Islamic Development Bank (IDB) *[See Chapters 1 and 5]*

Founded in December 1973 to support the economic development of member countries and Muslim communities in non-Member countries. IDB (www.isdb.org) accepts deposits and provides financing through Shariah-compliant means.

Mit Ghamr *[See Chapters 1 and 5]*

A town in Egypt in which was set up the first modern Islamic bank in 1963. The bank was a savings bank based on profit-sharing principles. In 1972, the Mit Ghamr Bank became part of Nasser Social Bank (www.nsb.gov.eg) which still exists today.

Tabung Haji *[See Chapter 1]*

Tabung Haji (www.tabunghaji.gov.my) was set up in 1963 to facilitate savings for the pilgrimage to Mecca through investment in Shariah-compliant assets.

**Accounting and Auditing Organization
for Islamic Financial Institutions (AAOIFI)** *[See Chapter 5]*

The AAOIFI (www.aaoifi.com) was established in 1990 to issue international standards on accounting, auditing and corporate governance. It is supported by over 160 institutional members from around 40 countries. It has its corporate office in Kingdom of Bahrain.

Islamic Financial Services Board (IFSB) *[See Chapter 5]*

The IFSB (www.ifsb.org) was set up in 2002 to put forth standards for supervision and regulation. Its members include over 40 regulatory and supervisory authorities. It has its corporate office in Kuala Lumpur, Malaysia.

International Islamic Financial Market (IIFM) *[See Chapter 5]*

IIFM (www.iifm.net) was founded collectively by the central banks and monetary agencies of Bahrain, Brunei, Indonesia, Malaysia and Sudan, and the Islamic Development Bank to develop and promote the Islamic capital and money markets.

Islamic Window *[See Chapter 5]*

A unit within a conventional bank through which Shariah-compliant instruments are formulated and distributed. Islamic windows are more common in South-East Asia and Western countries than in the Middle East, where the tendency has been to establish full-fledged Islamic banks.

Islamic Research and Training Institute (IRTI) *[See Chapter 5]*

The IRTI (www.irti.org), established in 1981, is part of the IDB group. It undertakes research and provides training and information services to the member countries of the Islamic Development Bank and Muslim communities in non-member countries.

International Centre for Education in Islamic Finance (INCEIF)
[See Chapter 5]
INCEIF (www.inceif.org) in Malaysia offers professional and academic qualifications up to PhD level in Islamic Finance.

International Islamic University Malaysia (IIUM) *[See Chapter 5]*
IIUM (www.iiu.edu.my) is a private university which opened in 1983 in Malaysia. It operates under the direction of a Board of Governors with representatives from eight sponsoring governments and the Organisation of Islamic Conference (OIC).

Bahrain Institute of Banking and Finance (BIBF) *[See Chapter 5]*
Founded in 1981, the BIBF (www.bibf.com.bh) was recognised as the "Best Islamic Finance Training Institute 2008" by *Islamic Business and Finance* magazine.

Islamic International Rating Agency (IIRA) *[See Chapter 5]*
Established in 2005, the IIRA (www.iirating.com) is the sole rating agency established to provide capital markets and the banking sector in predominantly Islamic countries with a rating scale that covers the full array of capital instruments, specialty Islamic financial products and risk evaluation. Its objective is also to enhance the level of analytical expertise in those markets. IIRA functions similarly to conventional rating agencies like S&P and Moody's in providing independent benchmarks with which to make Shariah-complaint investment and financial decisions.

International Islamic Trade Finance Corporation (ITFC)
[See Chapter 13]
The ITFC (www.itfc-idb.org) is an autonomous entity within the Islamic Development Bank. It was formed in 2007 to promote international trade among members of the Organisation of the Islamic Conference (OIC).

TERMS RELATED TO OTHER INSTITUTIONS AND GROUPS

Middle East *[See Chapter 1]*

The Middle East (or formerly the Near East as opposed to the Far East) is a region that spans southwestern Asia, southeastern Europe and northeastern Africa. It has no clear boundaries although these countries are generally included in the definition—Algeria, Bahrain, Cyprus, Egypt, Iran, Iraq, Israel, Jordan, Kuwait, Lebanon, Libya, Oman, Palestine, Qatar, Saudi Arabia, Syria, Turkey, United Arab Emirates and Yemen.

United Nations Development Project (UNDP) *[See Chapter 1]*

The United Nations (UN) was founded in 1945 after World War II to maintain international peace and security, develop friendly relations among nations and promote social progress, better living standards and human rights. UNDP (www.undp.org) is the UN's global development network. In 2008, it established the Millennium Development Goals to half global poverty by 2015.

Organization of the Petroleum Exporting Countries (OPEC) *[See Chapter 1]*

OPEC (www.opec.org) is an inter-governmental organisation made up of 13 oil producing nations. It was created at the Baghdad Conference in September, 1960. OPEC members co-ordinate their oil production policies in order to help stabilise the oil market and help oil producers achieve a reasonable rate of return on their investments; it also aims to ensure that oil consumers continue to receive stable supplies of oil.

Organization of Arab Petroleum Exporting Countries (OAPEC) *[See Chapter 1]*

OAPEC (www.oapecorg.org) consists of the Arab members of OPEC, Egypt and Syria.

Gulf Cooperation Council (GCC) *[See Chapter 2]*
Created in May 1981, the GCC is a trade bloc involving six Arab states of the
Persian Gulf, namely: Bahrain, Kuwait, Oman, Qatar, Saudi Arabia and the
United Arab Emirates. Iran and Iraq are currently excluded although both
nations have a coastline on the Persian Gulf.

Bank of St. George *[See Chapter 6]*
The world's first modern bank, founded in Italy in 1406. As a modern bank,
it dealt with money, accepted deposits and gave out loans. The bank lent
considerable sums of money to many rulers throughout Europe during the
15th and 16th centuries. In comparison, the first modern experiment with
Islamic banking called **Mit Ghamr** bank took place in Egypt only in 1963.

International Swaps and Derivatives Association (ISDA) *[See
Chapter 6]*
The ISDA (www.isda.org) is a trade organisation of participants in the
market for OTC derivatives. Headquartered in New York and chartered in
1985, its members are from about 60 countries and include most of the
world's major institutions that deal in OTC derivatives.

INTRODUCTION TO THE ARABIC LANGUAGE

Arabic is the language of the Holy Koran. Muslims consider Arabic to be
the language chosen by Allah (swt) to speak to mankind.

Arabic has many dialects. The Holy Koran is written in Classical Arabic
(CA). Because the Holy Koran is written in CA, the language is considered
by Muslims to be sacred. It is the only language in which Muslims recite
their prayers, regardless of what language they use in everyday life.

CA is one of the Semitic languages, which are part of the Afro-Asiatic
language group that includes Arabic, Hebrew, Amharic, and Aramaic. These
languages share many similarities in grammar and pronunciation.

An adapted form of Arabic is called Modern Standard Arabic (MSA).
MSA is the literary standard across the Middle East and North Africa,
and one of the official six languages of the United Nations. Most printed
matter in the Arab World—including most books, newspapers, magazines
and official documents—is written in MSA. MSA is also used on television

and in conversation between Arabic speakers from different countries (for example, at international conferences and events).

While Arabic is associated with Islam, most of the world's Muslims do not in fact speak Arabic as their native language. But most of them can read the words of religious texts. Arabic is also spoken by some Christians and Jews.[2]

The Arabic that we use in this book are transliterations. An Arabic transliteration means to change an Arabic word into the corresponding characters of another language, such as English, so that it can be pronounced and understood in English.[3]

The spelling of Arabic terms is not consistent. The holy book of Islam may be spelt "Koran", "Quran" or "Qur'an", and each is generally acceptable as are all attempts at a phonetic transliteration into English. Some consider "Quran" to be the closest to Arabic while "Koran" is phonetically closer to English.

There are a few style standards for Arabic words. For example, for nearly 25 years, the Associated Press Stylebook used "Koran" and "Mohammed" as the correct ways to spell two commonly-used Arabic words. Then in 2000, it opted instead for "Quran" and "Muhammad". The Associated Press has tried to come up with a spelling that is understandable to US readers and as close as possible to the actual pronunciation.[4] As seen in their recent change, spellings and styles do change over time.

Our approach is to be clear and consistent for all readers and at the same time try to be sensitive to traditional usages. In the end, it is not possible to have a single universal style because of the diversity of the Arab-speaking world and Islamic practices around the world.

---

1   "Islamic Law: Its Relation to Other Legal Systems" by Badr, Gamal Moursi in *The American Journal of Comparative Law*, Spring 1978.

2   To be specific, Arabic is spoken by Arab Christians and Mizrahi Jews. The Mizrahi Jews represent the oldest Jewish communities in the world and most of them live in Israel today.

3   Another example of transliteration into English is Hanyu Pinyin, based on Chinese Mandarin.

4   "Quran or Koran?" American Journalism Review, December 2006/ January 2007.

INDEX

* The terms "Shariah" and "Shariah-
  compliant" are used extensively
  throughout the book, and in a
  multitude of applications. For
  space reasons, only their respective
  meanings and significance are
  listed in this index.

SELECTED REFERENCES

Verses quoted from the Koran are based on a translation by Yusuf Ali and found at www.quranexplorer.com.

Islamic Finance: Law, Economics, and Practice by Mahmoud A. El-Gamal. Cambridge University Press, 2006.

Islamic Banking And Finance in South-east Asia: Its Development And Future by Angelo M. Venardos. World Scientific, Oct 2006.

Islamic Banking: A Practical Perspective by Kamal Khir, Lokesh Gupta and Bala Shanmugam. Pearson Malaysia (Petaling Jaya, Selangor) 2008.

"Fighting against Poverty in Islamic Societies" by Dr Muhammed Obaidullah. islamicvoice.com, Dec 2007.

"Yunus makes nation proud" in the *Daily Star* (Bangladeshi English daily newspaper), 14 October 2006.

An Introduction to Islamic Finance by Mufti Muhammad Taqi Usmani. Idara Isha'at-e-Diniyat (P) Ltd, 1999.

The Islamic Development Bank—A Case Study of Islamic Co-operation by Dr S.A. Meenai. Taylor and Francis. 1989.

World Christian Encyclopedia: A Comparative Survey of Churches and Religions—AD 30 to 2200 by David Barrett. Oxford University Press, 2001.

Islam: The Straight Path by John Esposito. Oxford University Press, 3rd Edition, 2004.

Islamic Economics—A School of Thought and a System: A Comparative Study by Ibrahim al-Tahawi. Majma' Al-Buhuth al-Islamiyah, 1974.

Muslim Economic Thinking: A Survey of Contemporary Literature by Muhammad Nejatullah Siddiqi. Islamic Foundation, 2007.

The Modern Universal Paradigm by Rodney Shakespeare. Universitas Trisakti, Lembaga Penerbit Fakultas Ekonomi, 2007.

Muslim Economic Thinking: A Survey of Contemporary Literature by Muhammad Nejatullah Siddiqi. International Centre for Research in Islamic Economics, Islamic Foundation, 1981.

The Economic System of Islam—A Discussion of its Goal and Nature by M. Umer Chapra. Islamic Cultural Centre (London) and University of Karachi, 1970.

"Introducing Islamic Banks into Conventional Banking Systems" by Juan Solé. IMF Working Paper No. 07/175, 2007.

Islamic Commercial Law: An Analysis of Futures and Options by Mohammad Hashim Kamali, Islamic Texts Society, 2001.

Penubuhan Bank Islam (The History and Background of Bank Islam). 1982.

"Key Trends in Islamic Funds 2008." www.eurekahedge.com

"The Relevance of Islamic Finance Principles to the Global Financial Crisis." Harvard Law School Paper, 27 March 2009.

"Study Shows Larger Islamic Banks Need Prudential Eye." IMF Survey Magazine, June 2008. "Guidelines on the Application of Banking Regulations to Islamic Banking." Monetary Authority of Singapore, May 2009.

"Ramadan Builds Righteous Muslims." Friday sermon at Islamic Religious Council of Singapore, 5 October 2007.